ADDITIONAL PRAISE FOR
THE NUREMBERG LEGACY

"In this pertinent, thorough overview, Ehrenfreund revisits the initial trial and considers its legacy, both as it affected his decision to become a trial lawyer, and the important precedents it has set in terms of prosecuting and checking future crimes against humanity. . . . The author makes a tremendous case for adhering to the Nuremberg legacy of fair treatment for even the most odious offenders."

—Kirkus Reviews

"*The Nuremberg Legacy* offers a compelling and original contribution to our understanding of the first international criminal tribunal in history. Through each passing decade and with each succeeding generation, we must take greater care to uphold its memory. And Judge Norbert Ehrenfreund reminds us why we should never forget."

—*Professor William Aceves, California Western School of Law, San Diego*

"This book describes the horror of the Nazi genocide, and my life as one of the *Untermenschen* Hitler sought to exterminate, but what is different about this work is that Judge Ehrenfreund tells what that experience means for modern times."

—*Lou Dunst, Holocaust survivor, Auschwitz and Mauthausen (Ebensee) concentration camps*

THE
NUREMBERG
LEGACY

How the Nazi
War Crimes Trials
Changed the Course of History

NORBERT EHRENFREUND

palgrave
macmillan

THE NUREMBERG LEGACY

Copyright © Norbert Ehrenfreund, 2007.

Excerpts from letters from Judge Francis Biddle to his wife Katherine in 1945 and 1946, reproduced by permission of the Special Collections Research Center, Syracuse University Library.

First published in 2007 by
PALGRAVE MACMILLAN™
175 Fifth Avenue, New York, N.Y. 10010 and
Houndmills, Basingstoke, Hampshire, England RG21 6XS.
Companies and representatives throughout the world.

PALGRAVE MACMILLAN is the global academic imprint of the Palgrave Macmillan division of St. Martin's Press, LLC and of Palgrave Macmillan Ltd. Macmillan® is a registered trademark in the United States, United Kingdom and other countries. Palgrave is a registered trademark in the European Union and other countries.

ISBN–13: 978–1–4039–7965–0
ISBN–10: 1–4039–7965–0

Library of Congress Cataloging-in-Publication Data

Ehrenfreund, Norbert.
  The Nuremberg legacy : how the Nazi war crimes trials changed the course of history / Norbert Ehrenfreund.
    p. cm.
  Includes bibliographical references and index.
  ISBN 1–4039–7965–0 (alk. paper)
  1. Nuremberg Trial of Major German War Criminals, Nuremberg, Germany, 1945–1946—Influence. I. Title.
  KZ1176.5.E37 2007
  341.6'90268—dc22
                                                              2007006581

A catalogue record of the book is available from the British Library.

Design by Letra Libre

First edition: October 2007

10 9 8 7 6 5 4 3 2 1

Printed in the United States of America.

To
My Children
Laurel and Zachary

Will there ever be an end to discussion of the Nuremberg trials? Although only limited new or startling facts or opinions may appear in the future, each new intellectual mood or development may return to judge the Tribunal. As long as the monstrous outrages of Dachau, Buchenwald, and Bergen-Belsen are vivid in men's minds, as long as the long bloody years of the Second World War are remembered personally and ruefully, men will return to stand in judgment upon the Tribunal which sought to establish the verdict of human justice upon those accused of causing death, misery, and sorrow of those bitter years.

But even when the last person who experienced the war is dead, men will return to the Nuremberg court because it was a test of men's basic concepts of law, politics, and morality. Nuremberg is significant not so much because of what happened once and for all in 1946 in a Bavarian city, but because of what it has become for many men—sign and symbol of greater realities.

—William J. Bosch, *Judgment on Nuremberg:*
American Attitudes toward
the Major German War-Crimes Trials

TABLE OF CONTENTS

PART THREE

THREATS TO THE LEGACY

10 pages of photographs appear between pages 110 and 111.

PROLOGUE

ON A COLD AFTERNOON IN 1939 I CAME HOME FROM SCHOOL TO find my mother in tears. She sat on the sofa clutching several envelopes. When I asked what was wrong she simply handed them to me, too choked up to speak. They were unopened letters she had sent to her father in Czechoslovakia. They had all been returned, all stamped with the same two words: "Address Unknown." What was wrong? He had always answered before. Where was he? Her father had always lived at the same address in the city of Ostrava, the same house where she had spent her youth until her marriage to my father and their emigration to America in 1910. He would not have moved without notifying her. No wonder she was upset. In the next year our family tried frantically to find out what had happened to my grandfather. We called the Red Cross, tried to contact the government in Washington, all to no avail. The Red Cross told us that the Nazis occupying the country would not give them any information.

This was the first time I knew that something seriously wrong was going on in Europe. My mother never heard from her father again. When World War II ended in 1945 I was in Austria as an American artillery officer with our occupation forces. My mother wrote asking if I could possibly visit her hometown to find out what happened to her father. I had a jeep and a driver willing to accompany me. My request to make such a trip went all the way from my battery commander to Washington, D.C., but was turned down because it would have required my traveling through Russian lines, believed to be unsafe. Years later, after the cold war and after my mother had died, I went to Ostrava to seek information about my grandfather. I found out what I expected. He had been murdered by the Nazis at a concentration camp in Treblinka, Poland.

At the time my mother's letters were being returned, many similar incidents were happening in homes across the country. Thousands of Americans had their letters sent back also, all stamped with the same words "Address Unknown." They began asking questions too, trying to find out what happened to their missing relatives in Europe. Thus began the investigation that led to the trials at Nuremberg.

INTRODUCTION

I COULD SMELL THE STENCH OF DEATH AS I WALKED THROUGH THE streets of Nuremberg on my way to the Palace of Justice. Beneath the rubble of the shattered city lay the bodies of 20,000 air raid victims. In that macabre setting the first international trial in history for crimes against humanity and crimes of waging aggressive war was under way.

This book tells why the Nuremberg trials matter today and how much they affect our lives in the twenty-first century.

Ever since the trial of some of the major Nazis began in 1945, experts have debated whether the event was the greatest trial in history, a beacon of justice for all the world to follow, or merely the wreaking of vengeance by the Allied victors over Hitler's top brass with little meaning for modern times. These remain intriguing questions for historians but what matters to us now is not just the trial itself but rather its impact on law and society, the Nuremberg legacy.

As I sat in the press gallery I knew I was witness to a historic moment but I had no idea how much it would mean in the next century. Hermann Goering, number two man to Adolf Hitler, sat thirty feet away. With him in the defendants' dock were Rudolf Hess, Joachim von Ribbentrop and the other high Nazis. Hitler was dead so they blamed everything on him.

I thought to myself: this cultured nation, so rich in music, literature, and science—land of Beethoven, Bach and Brahms, birthplace of Goethe and Schiller—how could it have produced leaders so barbaric? How could these few Nazis have persuaded and organized so many others to aid and abet their atrocities? Then another thought struck me, frightening in its implications. Who am I? I am of the same species—the human race. Is there a beast in me too? Am I capable of the same atrocities? Are we all?

Such questions plagued me then. Maybe I was too young and too naïve to figure it out. I was twenty-four years old, just out of the Army, a cub reporter for the American newspaper in Europe, *The Stars and Stripes*, still too inexperienced to cover this big case by myself.

Much has been written of the evidence presented at the Nuremberg trials. To think back on the evidence still sends shivers down the spine: bulldozers shoving thousands of white, naked corpses into mass graves; lampshades made from the skin of murdered victims; inmate-slaves forced to carry huge stones out of a quarry until they died of exhaustion; inmates forced to undress and jump into ice-cold water so Nazi doctors could test how much cold a human could stand before freezing to death; mounds of dead or dying bodies stacked up in little pyramids about the concentration camps. The scenes of horror went on and on.

What has not been told is the significance in today's world of the decision by the Allies to conduct a full and fair hearing of the Nazi leaders. Only after many years as a lawyer and judge in America, and after conversations with hundreds of Germans then and now in East and West Germany, have I come to realize the true meaning of that decision and the record it created.

My story begins in the spring of 1945, months before the Nuremberg trial began. In the waning days of World War II, I was a forward observer for a battery of field artillery, attached to General George Patton's Third Army. As we advanced into Austria to meet the Russians coming from the eastern front, unexpected events awaited us.

That summer of 1945 the four Allies—England, France, the Soviet Union and the United States—met in London to decide the nature of the first international trial for war crimes. No one had ever faced such charges in court before. Robert H. Jackson, a U.S. Supreme Court justice turned prosecutor, persuaded the Allies to make a historic decision: to give the Nazi defendants a genuine trial, not a show trial or a sham, but a trial instilled with due process and justice.

Jackson turned out to be the principal architect of the entire proceeding. He gave the trial its legitimacy with his victory at the pre-trial conference, and rightly earned the status of an international hero. He began the trial with a passionate opening statement that stunned the audience. Nowhere in the literature of Nuremberg is there a finer description of Hitler's rise to power and the atrocious crimes he foisted upon the world. Beyond its grand scope, there was an extraordinary factor about the opening statement whereby Jackson, as prosecutor, actually pleaded with the judges to be fair.[1]

One of the first important precedents set at Nuremberg was to carry prosecution to the top. "The common sense of mankind," Jackson said,

> demands that the law shall not stop with the punishment of petty crimes by little people. It must also reach men who possess themselves of great power and make deliberate and concerted use of it to set in motion evils which leave no home in the world untouched.[2]

The Nuremberg trial exposed the nature of the Holocaust and Hitler's wars of aggression, but this book was not written to cover the evidence presented in the courtroom. Instead I have tried to examine the trial in a new light after sixty-odd years, the good and bad of it, and its unexpected legacy, from the rare perspective of a young journalist at the scene, who was so inspired by the drama being played out before him that after returning home, he changed the direction of his life to become a trial lawyer himself and later a judge.

Few Americans realize that immediately after the main trial by the International Military Tribunal there followed twelve other Nuremberg trials, supposedly of lesser Nazis but nevertheless of major historical value. Among them was the case of Alfried Krupp, Hitler's biggest financial supporter, a trial this writer covered for *The Stars and Stripes* newspaper in 1948. Krupp was hardly a "lesser" figure. Only a clerical error allowed him to escape prosecution in the first trial. In the charged atmosphere of 1946 the International Criminal Tribunal would very likely have convicted Krupp and had him executed for crimes against humanity, including the use of slave labor. Instead a more lenient court two years later gave him twelve years in prison, subsequently commuted to time served.

Now the Krupp case has suddenly taken on new significance. Some of America's biggest corporations, such as Unocal, Exxon, Mobil and Coca-Cola, are being sued in our federal courts for allegedly abusing human rights while doing business in foreign countries headed by repressive governments. The plaintiffs base their claims on precedent set in the Krupp case at Nuremberg.[3]

For years some of our best historians have been belittling the Nuremberg legacy and predicting the early demise of the trial's use as precedent. "Why did its hope blaze so brightly and then burn out," asked Joseph E. Persico in his book *Nuremberg, Infamy on Trial,* "the flame of its example reduced thereafter virtually to historic ash?"[4]

Robert E. Conot, author of *Justice at Nuremberg,* adds this lament: "Nuremberg has become an abstract concept rather than a dire precept."[5]

How wrong they were! This book is written in response to those pronouncements of Nuremberg's doom. Rather than burning out, the ideas spawned at Nuremberg—new concepts of justice and human rights—have spread across much of the world and have become more evident than ever before. Those of us who were there in the courtroom and then watched the legacy grow over the past half century have a duty to challenge such critics and set the record straight.

These pages will show what Nuremberg says to our time, and that the trial has produced positive changes in law and society. In this new century, Nuremberg's impact on our lives grows stronger every day. Some will say it is still too early to judge. They want more time to make a valid judgment of Nuremberg's value. But the time for review is now, because the precedents set in that old German courthouse have become too powerful to be transitory. They have affected millions of people— many of whom never heard of Nuremberg. From the poor villagers of Burma who are denied human rights to a charged courtroom in Baghdad where Saddam Hussein was brought to justice; from the hallowed chambers of the United States Supreme Court to a black man on trial in Mississippi; from the executives of big business to any doctor in America who contemplates research; from United Nations headquarters to the tiny nation of Rwanda: Wherever men and women seek justice in their courts, Nuremberg looms large.

Today Nuremberg touches aspects of our society in ways beyond our ken in 1945. Human rights, racial discrimination in America, medical ethics, the concept of fair trial, the ethics of big business—all have come under Nuremberg's influence. In international trials for human rights abuses in Yugoslavia, Rwanda and Sierra Leone, Nuremberg precedent rules the courtroom. Before he was finally hanged, Saddam Hussein was given a trial with the presumption of innocence, rather than summary execution. The new International Criminal Court at The Hague in the Netherlands adopted Nuremberg's precedent as its guide for trial procedure. And interviews with hundreds of German young people show that the evidence elicited at Nuremberg awakened the Germans to the past and played a part in the postwar development of a peaceful democracy.

The Nuremberg legacy is strong but since the attack of 9/11 that legacy has come under serious threat. As of this writing, the Bush administration has allegedly used the war on terror as "a blank check when it comes to the rights of the Nation's citizens."[6] There are many who say the policy has harmed America's image as a defender of human rights.[7] How far the administration has gone along this path becomes the subject of the book's final chapters.

PART ONE

————

NUREMBERG REDUX

CHAPTER ONE

———

WITNESS TO THE HOLOCAUST

IT WAS APRIL 1945. THE SECOND WORLD WAR WAS COMING TO A quick end in Europe. As the 71st Infantry Division advanced across southern Germany toward Austria I began to hear the stories. The men talked of Nazi gas chambers and torture and concentration camps. I was skeptical. It was all hearsay, maybe. Rumors abound in wartime. Who would do such things?

I was a forward observer with B Battery, 607th Field Artillery Battalion, attached to General Patton's Third Army. The assignment meant that I was to go forward with the infantry company commander and call for fire from our four 105-millimeter howitzers whenever he wanted it. On our right flank, the Seventh Army was engaged in bitter fighting in Nuremberg but our artillery was not called in. General Eisenhower wanted us to make a straight line to Austria.[1] Our orders were to meet the Russians there, coming west. By the end of the month the Germans were surrendering in droves. Many of them wanted to know if they could help us fight the Russians. We told them they were crazy if they thought we were going to do that. The regular army Germans were giving up but we had to be careful of Waffen SS strongholds.

The Waffen SS was the combat arm of Hitler's elite SS organization (the *Schutzstaffel*) commanded by one of the most hated of all Nazis, Heinrich Himmler. The SS, I found out later, committed revolting brutalities, murdered hostages, massacred Jews and ran the concentration camps. The Waffen SS troops were the fighting units of the organization and were supposedly restricted to purely military operations. With the regular German Army (the Wehrmacht) crumbling, the Waffen SS was composed mostly of fanatic teenagers sworn to fight to the death. They had no backup support but they had guns and ammunition.[2] Hiding in the woods in small units, the Waffen SS youth could be dangerous.

As we crossed the border and started through the Austrian country-side, the company commander devised a clever system to conduct the campaign with a minimum of casualties. He found out that I spoke some German, and seeing the weakening nature of the opposition, he took me aside and laid out the plan. The Austrian telephone system was still working well in most towns. As we advanced toward Vienna, I was to phone ahead to the Nazi command post—usually a city hall—of each city or village, and ask to speak to the German officer in charge. I would tell him in my broken German that we were Americans coming in with heavy artillery ready to fire on his command post. Unless he raised the white flag of surrender we would blast the place. The idea seemed odd. This was not part of our training at artillery school in Fort Sill, Okla-homa. I agreed to try, and practiced my little speech in German. What followed was indeed a strange way to fight a war. As soon as we arrived in a community with a telephone I would ring up the military commander in the next town down the road. Often I had the assistance of a fright-ened but willing Austrian civilian.

"*Halten sie weisse Fahne hoch!*" I shouted into the phone. "*Weisse Fahne hoch!*," which meant "Raise the white flag high!" They seemed to understand, for in a few minutes we would see a white sheet go up and we would move in to capture the village without firing a shot and, more importantly, without losing any men. We moved rapidly from town to town this way.

One time we had a problem. The SS commander on the phone sounded like a fanatic. When I finished my speech he exploded with a string of obscenities, followed by a slamming down of the phone. I called for a single round of artillery on his headquarters. Shortly after-wards the white flag went up.

Near Lambach, Austria we found that the stories of the concentra-tion camps were true. North of the city the 5th Infantry Regiment came upon hundreds of men, women and children, mostly Hungarian Jews, who had been held in a concentration camp at the Gunskirchen Lager. Some were dead, some dying of starvation. Many lay in a dense patch of pine woods, abandoned by their Nazi guards who left them without food and water when the German army retreated. The guards had fled as the 71st Division approached. The inmates tried to flee in search of food, and the Americans found many crowding the trails near the camp area. They had been living for months on a slice of bread and a bowl of soup each day.[3] The Americans evacuated the survivors to a hospital in Wels. I saw enough and heard enough to realize that I had become a witness to what was later called the Holocaust.

In May the city of Steyr, about eighty miles west of Vienna, fell to the 71st Division without the firing of a single shot. Located near the Enns River, Steyr had a population of about 40,000, and it seemed as though the whole city turned out to give us a warm reception. They treated us like liberators, not enemies. As we drove through town in a column of jeeps and trucks and howitzers, the citizens of Steyr lined the streets cheering. We had never been greeted this way anywhere in Europe. The Austrians hung out of second- and third-story windows waving and smiling at us. What happened to the war? Wasn't it supposed to be still going on? My telephone lineman, Floyd Reid, was a mountaineer from West Virginia. Seated in the back of our open jeep, Reid sensed the friendly mood of the crowd. He picked up a banjo he kept under the seat and began to play a hillbilly song. The Austrians laughed and cheered all the louder. I was worried about snipers from one of the windows, and we kept our carbines and pistols at the ready but no incidents occurred.

We thought we would pass through Steyr and go on to Vienna. General Dwight Eisenhower, the Allied Commander in Europe, had other ideas. He sent down word that the Russians would take Vienna and we were to stay in position and wait for them. This was a big disappointment because we had imagined capturing Vienna and celebrating the end of the war in that romantic city. Instead we holed up in the woods outside Steyr and waited. Our position was on the southernmost flank of the Allied western front. I had orders not to call for artillery fire because the shells might fall on the Russians coming from the east.

So we waited. Several days went by with no sign of the Russians. My forward observer platoon consisted of four men: a jeep driver, a radio operator, a telephone lineman and myself. We were growing restless. The Russians hadn't shown up and we were tired of sitting around. Somehow I wrangled permission to move forward. The four of us climbed into the jeep and took off to look for the Russians. As we drove east we passed long lines of German prisoners walking westward. They were guarded by two GIs riding in a jeep behind them with machine guns at the ready. The Germans waved as if they were happy to see us. They were glad to know they were going to be prisoners of the Americans rather than of the Red Army, who they feared would treat them with brutality. As we passed the GIs, they yelled "The war's over!" We didn't know whether to believe them because that rumor had been going around for days, always turning out to be false.

We didn't see any Russians that day so we returned to our headquarters. Along the road more GIs waved and yelled at us: "The war's over! The war's over!" At headquarters the news was confirmed. My driver had a flask of whiskey in the glove compartment and the four of us shook hands and had a drink together. The next day the Russians finally arrived and a meeting took place on the banks of the Enns River. At first our commander, Colonel Sydney C. Wooten of the 5th Infantry Regiment, tried to talk with their commander, but the colonel could not understand Russian and the Russians did not know English. They stood there gesturing with their hands, trying to communicate, to no avail.

The two officers wanted so much to converse, both well aware that this was a historic moment. They had important matters to discuss, such as who would occupy what. The precise lines of the occupation zones of the Soviet and American forces would be decided later at a higher level, but in the meantime these two regimental commanders had to agree on the immediate details of territorial possession. A Russian officer came forward and tried to speak in German. Someone whispered to Colonel Wooten that the 5th Regiment had an artillery forward observer who could speak a little German. So I was summoned and the Russian and I were able to converse in a limited manner, enabling the two commanders to make some sense to each other. Soon a Russian interpreter arrived and the language problem was resolved.

It was a momentous occasion. The Red Army had closed with the Americans in the south. The Germans between us had been squeezed into unconditional surrender. Smiles and handshakes and embraces all around. Songs and vodka. The Russians had women soldiers in their ranks. GIs gave them flowers. Later, Major General Willard G. Wyman, commanding general of the 71st Division, gave a party for the Russians. Long tables were set up in the woods with tablecloths and real dishes. The war was definitely over. Soon the camaraderie would be over, too. In six months the greatest trial in history would start at Nuremberg.

CHAPTER TWO

─────────

THE DEFINING MOMENT

THE NUREMBERG TRIALS ALMOST NEVER HAPPENED. AS WORLD War II drew to a close, strong opposition to the trials came from men of power on both sides of the Atlantic. In London, Winston Churchill, the British prime minister, was burning with the suffering of the British people at the hands of Hitler's aerial attacks. Churchill said the Nazis did not deserve a trial; a trial would only give them a chance to spout their Nazi propaganda. Hitler and his gang had forfeited any right to legal procedure. After a summary hearing, they should be taken out in the yard and shot by a firing squad.[1] In Washington, the United States Secretary of the Treasury, Henry Morgenthau, Jr., took the same position. Morgenthau had more power than the other cabinet members. He was a close friend and adviser to President Franklin D. Roosevelt, and the president listened to what he said. Morgenthau not only wanted summary execution of the Nazi leaders; he also had a plan to destroy Germany economically to make sure that it could never rise to power again. Follow Churchill, Morgenthau advised his friend Roosevelt. The people want revenge, not a long drawn-out legal proceeding.[2]

Two camps, bitterly opposed to each other, formed in Washington. On the one side stood Morgenthau, who reportedly had Roosevelt in his pocket.[3] The other side came from the War Department and its adamant Secretary of War, Henry Stimson, who insisted on a trial with due process. In opposing Morgenthau, Stimson believed that to execute the Nazis without trial would sow the seeds of another world war. Stimson was desperately looking for a plan that would impress Roosevelt. That is when Murray Bernays came on the scene. Bernays, relatively unknown at the time, had been a successful New York lawyer but now found himself working in the War Department with the rank of lieutenant colonel and head of the Special Projects branch. He was a specialist in problems involving the treatment of American prisoners in German hands and had worked closely with various projects involving the war in Germany. In early September, Stimson picked Bernays as the logical choice to develop a proposal for a trial that would win Roosevelt over. Meanwhile the Morgenthau plan, with Churchill's support, was gaining strength.

Roosevelt and Churchill planned a meeting in Quebec to discuss what to do with the captured Nazi leaders. Roosevelt invited Henry Morgenthau to be at his side during the meeting. Stimson was not invited. He felt snubbed, and was so upset he fired off a cable to Roosevelt in Quebec warning him that to execute the Nazi leaders without giving them the chance to defend themselves would be similar to what the Nazis were doing to their victims. It would be, he told Roosevelt, a "crime against civilization."[4] On September 15, 1944, the feared decision came down. Roosevelt and Churchill signed a summary of the Morgenthau plan. Roosevelt sided with Churchill. The Quebec meeting was over, there would be no trial.

A feeling of doom descended over the Pentagon and the offices of the War Department. The talk went around Washington. It was settled. The Nazi leaders would be executed as soon as they were captured and identified. But on the very day of the Roosevelt-Churchill agreement in Quebec, Bernays laid a six-page plan for trial of the major Nazi criminals on Stimson's desk. Bernays based his plan on the concept that Hitler's regime was a giant criminal conspiracy to conquer Europe and kill all the Jews on the continent. He branded the Nazi atrocities as war crimes. Everyone who conspired to create the Nazi movement was a war criminal and had to be tried and punished if found guilty. The plan, wrote historian Joseph Persico, was "beautiful in its simplicity."[5]

Due mostly to Stimson's tenacity, Morgenthau's victory at Quebec was short-lived. Stimson refused to give up. He was adamant that as to the agreement to shoot the Nazis without a trial, "there would be nothing of the sort done" so long as he was Secretary of War.[6] Stimson insisted on a private conference with Roosevelt. On October 3, 1944, having reviewed the Bernays memorandum, Stimson sat down with the president to make his plea for trial.

At the time Roosevelt's health was failing. Already an invalid who could not stand or walk by himself, Roosevelt was further worn out by twelve years of work and responsibility as president of the United States. In addition he was in the middle of a campaign for his fourth term with the election only weeks away. Stimson was worried that the president's illness would lead him to make a bad decision on the question of a trial for the Nazi leaders. Stimson's views were that a trial was essential both morally and politically. A trial would not only help establish America's place as a moral leader in the world but would also produce a full record of the Nazi atrocities. Morgenthau's plan to destroy Germany's industrial capacity and turn the country into an agricultural state could only lead to disaster. Stimson brought out a copy of the Quebec agreement and pointed out the folly of it to the president. By the time Stimson finished talking, Roosevelt admitted that he had made a mistake at Quebec and said that he regretted initialing the Morgenthau plan. The result was a fatal blow to the idea of summary execution.[7]

In the next few months the Bernays plan went through many changes. William Chanler, a friend of Stimson and a leading New York lawyer, suggested another part of the framework, adding Hitler's waging of aggressive war as one of the major crimes to be charged. The modified Bernays plan, however, was still riddled with flaws. One was the prospect of convicting hundreds of thousands of Nazi Party members simply by proving their organization was criminal. This lacked due process protection because it did not give the Nazis a chance to defend themselves in court. The central idea of criminal conspiracy, however, held fast. Roosevelt liked it.

Two events in Washington—Stimson's victory in persuading Roosevelt to drop the idea of executing the Nazis without trial, and the modified Bernays plan—were major steps on the road to Nuremberg. But Roosevelt still would not make a definite commitment.

In February 1945 the three Allied leaders—Roosevelt, Stalin and Churchill—met at Yalta, a Ukrainian city on the Black Sea. Victory was imminent. Questions still existed as to whether there should be a trial and if so what kind. By now the list of potential war criminals was growing. All agreed the Nazis were guilty of war crimes and had to be punished, but there was no agreement on how this should be done or what kind of punishment should be meted out. Roosevelt was sick and weary and lacked the strength to argue vigorously. The three Allied leaders left Yalta without having decided these issues. They would never meet again.

On April 12, 1945, with the Nazi surrender in Europe only a month away, and after thirteen years as President, Franklin D. Roosevelt died. Roosevelt's death changed the trial issue dramatically. Harry Truman became president and he definitely wanted a trial. As a former judge, Truman had faith in the bench and believed that a court made up of reasonable judges would conduct a fair trial and come to the right decision.[8]

On the day after President Roosevelt's death, Robert H. Jackson, associate justice of the Supreme Court, made a significant speech before the opening session of the American Society of International Law at the Carlton Hotel in Washington.[9] Referring to the proposed trial of the Nazi war leaders, Jackson called for a fair trial by American standards of justice. "You must put no man on trial," Jackson said, "under forms of a judicial proceeding if you are not willing to see him freed if not proven guilty . . . the world yields no respect for courts that are organized merely to convict."[10] The speech impressed Truman and three weeks later he named Jackson chief prosecutor of the first international war crimes trial in history.[11]

Jackson's appointment and his decision to promptly accept were remarkable for several reasons. Jackson was a genuine country boy, reared in rural surroundings in the small towns of Frewsburg and Jamestown in upstate New York. His father ran a horse stable; his mother taught school. He always wanted to be a lawyer but the sum total of his formal education was limited to high school and one year at Albany Law School. Amazingly, Jackson never went to college and never earned a law degree. He passed the New York bar exam by reading law books in the back office of a Jamestown lawyer. Roosevelt noticed Jackson, liked him and brought him to Washington, where he rose quickly through the government ranks as solicitor general, attorney general and in 1941 associate justice of the United States Supreme Court. Jackson's lack of both a college education and a law degree may not have been so unusual in Abraham Lincoln's time but was certainly rare for a Supreme Court justice in the middle of the twentieth century, and unthinkable today.

By accepting the appointment Jackson had to step down from the Supreme Court to become, in essence, a criminal trial lawyer. No

Supreme Court justice had ever done so before. Jackson readily took on the challenge because he had passionate views on stopping aggressive war. He feared civilization could not survive another world war. He saw this trial as a chance to send a message to belligerent leaders of nations—that if they waged aggressive war they would face serious consequences in court. He wanted to establish a new law that would apply to all world leaders. Waging aggressive war and the conspiracy to wage aggressive war were serious crimes. An international trial would give him the rare opportunity to do what he could not do in the rarefied atmosphere of the Supreme Court. Jackson was not so naïve as to think he could stop war and its atrocities altogether, but if he could make war less likely, and cause aggressive leaders to hesitate before launching their armies, then his venture in Nuremberg would not be in vain. In fact, it would be a giant step forward in civilization's quest for peace.

On May 8, 1945, World War II came to an end in Europe—the bloodiest war in the history of the world. In June Jackson took his staff to London to meet with the Allies on the nature of the projected trial. He knew he had a fight on his hands. There was no law, no court, no trial procedure for an international criminal trial. There was, in fact, no precedent for what Jackson had in mind, a joint tribunal that would bring the remaining Nazi leaders to justice and earn the world's respect for its commitment to due process. No one knew whether the trial would follow Anglo-Saxon law or the civil law of Europe. The victorious Allies would have to write the laws and the statutes to fit the crimes charged. Then they would have to draft the penalties to go with those statutes.

~

I was still in Germany that summer, stationed with the American occupation forces, awaiting discharge from the Army and wondering what to do with my life. The news of the Nazi atrocities had been leaking out even before the war was over. By the summer the death camp survivors were beginning to talk and the gas chambers were being discovered. The news spread in greater force of the horrible slaughter of the Jews—news from such camps as Mauthausen and Ebensee in Austria; Auschwitz and

Treblinka in Poland; Dachau and Buchenwald in Germany. The stories traveled across the Atlantic and filled the front pages of the American press. Americans were outraged. Many wondered why in the world these despicable characters deserved even a single day in a court of law. There were cries for revenge: Do away with them! Kill them! This talk of a trial is ridiculous!

Amid all the cries for revenge, one man stood up at the Church House in London and called for a full and fair trial—Robert Jackson. Justice must be done, Jackson told the delegates. A fair trial for every defendant. A competent attorney for every defendant.

The Russians, in particular, looked at Jackson in disbelief. Some members of their staff wondered if the American could be serious.

Do you mean, they asked, a fair trial for Hermann Goering, second in command to Adolf Hitler, creator of the Gestapo? A fair trial for Ernst Kaltenbrunner, Heinrich Himmler's successor as chief of the SS and Gestapo, the man in charge of exterminating all the Jews in Europe? Or for Julius Streicher, the publisher who tried to incite the Germans to annihilate all the Jews? Or for Alfred Rosenberg, official Nazi voice of anti-Semitism?

Yes, Jackson replied. A fair trial. For every defendant, justice and due process. Jackson was adamant. He wanted the world to respect this trial. Justice must prevail. The world will judge us hereafter on what we do today.

The heaviest opposition to Jackson's demand for a fair trial came from Major General Ion T. Nikitchenko, the Soviet delegate. Nikitchenko told Jackson that the Nazi leaders' guilt had already been decided and there was no reason to waste time on that question; Stalin, Churchill and Roosevelt declared the Nazis guilty at the Yalta conference and the only thing left for the Allies to do was to determine the measure of guilt and mete out the punishment.[12]

Nikitchenko's argument substantiated what Jackson had feared from the beginning: the differences in trial procedure and legal philosophy might be too great to overcome. Jackson tried to explain to his Russian counterpart that in America the president had no power to convict anyone. The president could accuse someone of being guilty of crime but such an accusation carried no weight whatsoever in an American court. Likewise, the declarations made by the Allied leaders at Yalta were merely accusations and not convictions. A conviction is not valid without a judicial finding.[13]

Nikitchenko was not convinced. The idea of having to prove Goering and the rest of Hitler's coterie guilty when everyone knew they were guilty seemed nonsense to the Soviet delegate. After many sessions, Nikitchenko held to his position. "The fact that the Nazi leaders are criminals has already been established," he said on the record. "The task of the Tribunal is only to determine the measure of guilt."[14]

The debate in London went on for weeks. There were moments when Jackson became frustrated and threatened to walk out, wondering if perhaps each nation should try its own prisoners. But Nikitchenko urged Jackson to continue. The Russian said he was under orders from Stalin to plan an international trial. Jackson threw himself into the debate again. He fought like a crusader for justice. In the United States some criticized him for insisting on a full and fair trial, saying he was too soft for the job; that he didn't have the heart for a strong prosecutor. But Jackson would not budge. Finally he won out; his energy, his passion, his persuasive qualities wore down the opposition. It was settled. The trial would go forward under Jackson's vision of justice.

Jackson's victory was indeed the defining moment. Here were men believed to be the worst criminals of all time. They were charged with the murder of six million Jews and millions of others that Hitler found undesirable. In their days of pomp and power the Nazis never gave a fair trial to anyone. Now for the first time in history, the rulers of a defeated nation would be given the benefit of the rule of law and due process. In the past they were always treated by executive order. The decision was a turning point in the history of law, igniting a revolution in the law of nations. It changed the way we perceive justice, even the way we perceive each other. It changed not only international law but everyday street law as well. Jackson was making a declaration to the world that anyone accused of a crime, no matter how high or low his station in life, no matter how heinous the charge against him, is entitled to a fair trial. Today we take that proposition as an obvious, ordinary concept. But it wasn't so obvious in 1945—witness Churchill's call for immediate execution, and the cries of so many in America for revenge.

Consider that at the time in some American towns defendants were being tried for felonies without counsel.

Consciously or not, the decision influenced the way state judges like myself—who hear trials of murder and rape and robbery and drunk-driving—conduct their judicial responsibilities. I have been a criminal court judge for thirty-one years and often when I take the bench I know that somehow they are still there, the ghosts of Nuremberg, watching, monitoring, making sure the spirit of Nuremberg still lives.

～

When the news that there would be a trial reached Germany from London in early August 1945, I remember I felt proud to be an American, proud of what my country stood for and the high moral ground it had taken. It was a moment in time, as Jackson pointed out, that ranks beside that earlier moment in history when human beings stopped punishing each other by the hue and cry of the public and the thirst for revenge, and for the first time let reason and justice govern punishment. Had Churchill's call for the firing squad succeeded, had Morgenthau persuaded Roosevelt to follow Churchill's view, there would have been no Nuremberg trial, no Nuremberg legacy, and the history of civilization would have taken a different course.

Jackson won over the Allies on his concept of a fair trial but he still had to deal with another sticking point, which was his insistence on charging the Nazis with conspiracy to wage aggressive war and the actual waging of aggressive war. From the outset, Jackson hoped to make these charges the focus of his entire case. He knew this plan would run into trouble in London and he was right. When he made his proposal to the other Allies they balked. All three—Great Britain, the Soviet Union and France—appeared to desert him at first on this issue. Morally he was right but there was no law, no precedent to support him. The primary purpose of the trial, Jackson believed, was to establish the law that waging aggressive war is a crime, but no court had ever held that view. The French in particular wanted to know where it was stated that waging aggressive war was a crime. They told Jackson flatly that they did not consider a war of aggression to be a criminal act; Jackson seemed to be inventing a new crime, which meant that it was *ex post facto* law and therefore had no legal basis.[15]

Ask any American today what was the main charge in the Nuremberg trial and most would say it was about the unspeakable crimes that came to be known as the Holocaust. Yet that was not how Jackson saw it. In his view the extermination of the Jews was subsidiary to Hitler's overall goal of military conquest by aggressive means.

"I think our proof amply demonstrated that the campaign against the Jews," Jackson said in a letter to author Eugene Gerhart, referring to the Holocaust, "was intended to remove what they [the Nazis] regarded as an obstruction to instituting war and that the extermination was a part of the objective of the war."[16]

Jackson threw himself into his argument as to why aggressive war should be charged as the main crime. Waging a war of aggression was illegal, Jackson argued, because it violated existing international treaties such as the Kellogg-Briand Pact of 1928 in which sixty-three nations, including Germany, condemned war as an instrument of foreign policy. Before that pact it was fairly well established in international law that each nation had a legal right to wage war to defend the national interest. The Kellogg-Briand Pact renounced that right. War was to be justified only as self-defense against military aggression, and it was clear that in World War II Germany was the aggressor.[17] Jackson agreed aggressive war was not codified in any statute. The crime had never been defined. It does not have to be. By analogy, murder was wrong and a punishable crime long before any statute said so.

There were other disagreements of lesser importance among the London delegates, such as where the trial should be held. Some delegates argued for London; others suggested Berlin. Jackson wanted Nuremberg because it had the best available courthouse, was the site of Hitler's giant rallies and was in the American Zone, which meant the Americans would pay most of the bills. He got his way.

Disputes arose as to which captured Nazis should be charged. The Soviets wanted Hitler to be tried *in absentia* because he was the Nazi Führer, the main man. Jackson objected. He pointed out that Hitler was dead, a suicide in a bunker beneath the streets of Berlin. To try Hitler, Jackson argued, would only revive rumors that he was still alive. So Hitler was left off the indictment and was never tried. During the discussion, differences in trial procedure became obvious. The Russians were unfamiliar with the American custom of cross-examination. At one point Nikitchenko asked Jackson, "What is meant in English by 'cross-examine'?"[18]

Jackson's insistence on charging conspiracy was also a sore point. Not only was conspiracy not a part of the European legal system, but it had never been recognized as an element of international law.[19] Nevertheless Jackson insisted on including it in the indictment and made Conspiracy to Wage Aggressive War the first count. He saw conspiracy as the key to the entire prosecution, a vital part of his whole case.[20] The Russians and French had difficulty understanding conspiracy and when they did they were shocked. "The French," Bradley Smith wrote, "viewed it entirely as a barbarous legal anachronism unworthy of modern law."[21] The main concern of the French and Russians was that it was too vague and confusing. They wanted the whole idea of conspiracy to be abandoned, but by the time they came to this conclusion it was too late.

A major criticism of the trial was its failure to provide for the defendants' right to appeal their convictions to a higher court.[22] When Jackson insisted at the London Conference that there should be no appeal, he no doubt had in mind an angry, impatient public. The millions of victims of the Nazi atrocities, dead and alive, deserved finality and retribution.

Jackson was already under heavy criticism for seeking a trial that would take months to complete. Any appeal would take many more months, if not years, considering the time it would take to prepare the lengthy record, for the attorneys to prepare their briefs and for the court to review the record and briefs. The world in 1946 was in no mood for more waiting. The other Allies agreed with Jackson[23] and the result was Article 26 of the London Charter (officially known as the Charter of the International Military Tribunal), which said that the judgment of the tribunal as to guilt or innocence "shall be final and not subject to review."[24]

Somehow—and no one seems able to explain how—Jackson persuaded the other Allies to agree on the four charges of the indictment:

1. Conspiracy to Wage Aggressive War.
2. Waging Aggressive War. (The first two counts were called Crimes Against Peace.)

3. War Crimes (violations of the rules and customs of war, such as mistreatment of prisoners of war and abuse of enemy civilians).
4. Crimes Against Humanity (includes the torture and slaughter of millions on racial grounds, now known as the Holocaust).

When the assignments were handed out to the various prosecution teams, the Americans were assigned to count one (conspiracy); the British assigned to count two (waging aggressive war). Counts three and four, war crimes and crimes against humanity, were to be shared by the French and Russians. The indictment named twenty-four defendants including Martin Bormann, Hitler's secretary, who was missing. No one knew if he was dead or alive.

The Charter of the International Military Tribunal drafted at the London conference set out the constitution, jurisdiction and functions of the first international war crimes trial in history.[25] The site chosen for the trial was Nuremberg, Germany.

Jackson had faced two historic battles in London. First he had to convince an obstinate Nikitchenko to conduct a reasonably fair process; then he had to persuade the French that waging aggressive war was a crime. He did both.

CHAPTER THREE

WHO COULD BE OBJECTIVE?

OUTSIDE THE PALACE OF JUSTICE IN NUREMBERG, THE GERMANS LIVED A macabre existence. The city lay in ruins. Once a bustling metropolis, the ancient city had been shattered by an air raid from Britain's Royal Air Force earlier in 1945. Months later, Nuremberg's citizens still searched the debris for the missing and for what was left of their belongings.

The German people showed little interest in the forthcoming trial that was attracting worldwide attention. They had too many other things on their minds. Many were struggling daily for survival, spending their days in search of the necessities—food, clothing, a bar of soap, a spool of thread. Most Germans expected a sham proceeding at Nuremberg. Surely the victors would have their way no matter what they promised. The German press was still getting back on its feet under careful Allied control. My paper, *The Stars and Stripes*, conducted a public opinion poll of German citizens to find out their views on the trial. The result showed that most Germans believed all defendants would be executed after only a brief hearing.[1] So most Germans looked upon the trial with disfavor and cynicism. Not until years later when the trial record and its revelation of the Holocaust began to be taught in the schools did the German people begin to appreciate the fact of a fair trial and what it meant to their history. In 1945 and 1946 most German people were simply glad the war was over and hoped the United States would protect them from the "red menace."

At the time of the trial Germany no longer existed as a sovereign nation. The country was divided into four military zones, each occupied and controlled by one of the four Allies—the British, the French, the Russians and the Americans. In each zone two very different societies existed, the occupiers' and the Germans'. In the American zone there was the community comprised of military personnel and American civilians working in the military government. This society lived well, having taken over the best homes and offices. They played a lot, free from the social restraints back home. The other society was that of the surviving Germans, who were struggling to live and given little sympathy for their plight by Americans who suspected that all Germans were Nazis.

The nature of currency took a weird course. The German Mark fell into disrepute. Cigarettes became the primary medium of exchange. A carton on the black market sold for one hundred dollars. A pair of shoes cost eight packs of cigarettes. When Americans tossed away their cigarette butts, many Germans were not too proud to pick them up because cigarette butts were the equivalent of money. Almost anything could be purchased for cigarettes. I had a toothache in Berlin and found a local dentist but he had no gold for filling the cavity. He asked me if I could get a bit of gold for my tooth. I wrote to my mother in the States for help. She searched her jewelry box, found an old gold necklace and sent it to me. The dentist melted it down and I lived for the next fifty years with part of my mother's necklace in my mouth. The dentist's bill: ten packs of cigarettes.

Another curious social condition emerged at the time of the Nuremberg trial. When the war ended there were hundreds of thousands of American men in Germany without women, and a similar number of young German women without men. Much of Germany's generation of young men had been decimated by the war, especially the devastating battles on the eastern front such as Stalingrad and Leningrad. A new atmosphere arose now that the fighting was over. There was a desire on both sides for companionship, sexual companionship. The Americans were far from home and far from the customs and inhibitions of their hometowns. The situation was like kindling ready to burst into flame.

General Eisenhower issued a nonfraternization order. If an American soldier or officer had any social contact with a German, such as speaking to a German woman, the violation would be punished with a $65 fine. But the force of sexual attraction was too great and no military decree with a $65 penalty attached could hold back the thousands of young persons eager for contact. The fine soon became a laughing matter and the prohibition quickly broke down. Another order prohibited marriage between American military personnel and Germans. This order likewise did not last long.

American soldiers, officers and civilians working for the military suddenly found themselves living a lifestyle they never would have experienced in the States. Many lived with or had affairs with German women. The sexual revolution, which was not to occur in America until the mid-1960s, was in full swing in postwar Germany. Americans back home would have been shocked if they had known. Historian Robert Conot wrote of the situation: "Nothing would have capped Hitler's disillusionment with the German people more completely than the manner in which the German girls took to the American soldiers."[2]

Bizarre stories circulated. One enterprising American, a photographer, started an unusual business. He found out that a number of army officers who were returning home were seeking ways to bring their German girlfriends back to the States. He offered himself as a proxy. For a handsome price he would marry the woman involved and fly with her to the United States. He was a civilian, and therefore not subject to the military prohibition against marrying Germans. Once in America the couple would go to Reno immediately to obtain a divorce, leaving the young lady free to continue the relationship with her American friend. Then the photographer would return to Germany and repeat the process with another woman. It was a most successful enterprise.

I once covered an odd story about an attractive young German girl, a dental technician from Darmstadt. She fell in love with a GI from Brooklyn, but they could not marry because of the military restriction. When the Army transferred him home, the lovers wrote feverish letters back and forth trying to find a way to bring her to the United States, but she could not obtain a passport or visa. Then she conceived of a plan.

She noticed that her friends would occasionally ship objects of various sizes to their sweethearts in America. The boxes were rarely searched. She was small; why couldn't she have a friend pack her in a wooden box and ship her via airmail to Brooklyn? She had a cabinetmaker build her a box about two-and-a-half feet square with holes for air. For two weeks she practiced every night, curled up in her closed box and sleeping in that position. Finally the day came. Her friend packed her inside the box. At the Frankfurt airport the box was placed aboard the plane. As the handlers were about to shut the door they heard a strange sound coming from the box. They investigated and found a girl in her underwear curled up, struggling to breathe. She would have died from suffocation and cold if the plane had taken off. She was arrested and ordered to appear in court the next day. I watched her come into the courtroom surrounded by friends. They were laughing and cheering her on as a heroine who had risked her life for her man in America. She pled guilty to attempting to smuggle herself out of Germany. She told the German judge she did it for love, and was fined 100 marks. The story was a welcome bit of levity compared to the trial at Nuremberg.

❧

After settling in Nuremberg before the trial, Jackson proved to be more than a great advocate. He was the first among the Allies to learn of a new IBM simultaneous translation system, which was being used at the League of Nations in Geneva.[3] He dispatched his son William, an attorney on his staff, to contact IBM in New York and find out more about the novel method. Jackson then arranged to have the system brought to Nuremberg and persuaded the Allies to adopt it. As a result the Allies were able to conduct the trial in German, French, Russian and English at the same time,[4] thus speeding up the process considerably. He also oversaw the rebuilding of the courthouse and enlargement of the courtroom.[5] Meanwhile, he continued to dispatch his investigators all across Europe to gather the evidence.

But amid the preparation for trial, Jackson realized for the first time that a mistake had been made at the London Conference in selecting the defendants. In the rush to develop a list that would include all the leading Nazis, the name of Alfried Krupp, Hitler's top financier, was inadvertently omitted. The error, due to the sloppiness of the selection process,[6] worried Jackson. He had promised President Truman that he would charge individuals "who were in authority in the government, in the military establishment, including the General Staff, and in the financial, industrial, and economic life of Germany who by all civilized standards are provable to be common criminals."[7] But when Jackson studied the list of defendants in the quiet of his Nuremberg study, he noticed that not a single one represented the giant industrial machine that had thrown its massive productive capacity behind Hitler and made his military exploits possible. The head of the Krupp munitions-manufacturing firm was the logical choice to be a defendant.

The Krupps were a venerable family that traced its roots back to sixteenth-century Germany. Over the centuries they were involved in the business of weapons. Early in the nineteenth century, the family accelerated its enterprise by building a cast steel factory. They were to become Europe's leading manufacturer and supplier of guns and munitions. The Krupps armed Germany in three major wars and changed the course of German history. By the first World War, the firm had developed into a huge industrial empire that also made tanks and ran coal mines, steel mills and a shipyard that built navy ships and submarines. The owner during World War I was Bertha Krupp. The giant mortars that pounded Paris in that war were her special legacy—the American doughboys famously dubbed the weapon "Big Bertha." Bertha married a German diplomat, Gustav von Bohlen und Halbach, who took the name Gustav Krupp and also took control of the firm. Their oldest son was Alfried.[8]

Gustav Krupp ran the firm until he suffered a stroke in 1940. From then on he was in no condition to manage anything, and Alfried became sole owner and a strong Hitler supporter. During World War II, throughout Europe the Krupps managed 138 concentration camps, which they owned privately.[9] Alfried Krupp used slave labor from the camps and prisoners of war to build his factories. He looted occupied countries for his own use. An ardent Nazi, he was in every way a war criminal.

All the delegates at London wanted a member of the Krupp family to be indicted.[10] When the indictment was signed on October 6 in Berlin, Jackson named the Krupp firm in his bill of particulars. But it was unclear which Krupp he was thinking of, Gustav or Alfried. Apparently it was Gustav, for when the seating in the defendants' dock at the Palace of Justice was set up, the seat behind Goering was reserved for Gustav Krupp. The case against Gustav was overwhelming. He was implicated in the secret rearmament of Hitler's military as well as the planning of a war of aggression.[11]

However, while the wrangling was going on in London, Gustav had become a senile, incoherent old man who had to be diapered like a baby. No one bothered to investigate, and the news of Gustav's condition apparently never reached Jackson. The British delegation seemingly did not know of it because they picked Gustav to be indicted and did not even mention Alfried.[12] When the final list of twenty-four defendants came out, Alfried's name was left off and the name of Gustav Krupp appeared.

Alfried's name was originally included, but a day or two before the list was announced, someone on Jackson's staff decided that since Alfried was not in control of the firm before the war, he would have a ready defense against the charge of conspiracy to wage aggressive war. At the last minute Alfried's name was crossed off and Gustav's substituted.[13] Telford Taylor, part of Jackson's prosecution team and eventually chief counsel of the ensuing twelve trials, said he was not consulted and had no explanation for the mistake except to say it was poor planning.[14]

When Jackson and his prosecutors left London for Nuremberg they still had no inkling of the problem caused by the name of Gustav Krupp being on the list of defendants.[15] After a few weeks Jackson became aware of the mistake and discovered that Gustav Krupp could not possibly stand trial. As one writer put it: "Krupp was a senile old man whose mind could control neither his thoughts nor his bladder."[16] Thereupon Jackson did an extraordinary thing. He made a motion to substitute Alfried for Gustav. He told the court: "No greater disservice to the future peace of the world could be done than to excuse the entire Krupp family from this trial."[17]

The judges gave Jackson a difficult time on this issue and put him on the defensive. The Chief Justice, Geoffrey Lawrence, told Jackson, "This is not a football game where another player can be substituted for one who is injured."[18] Lawrence embarrassed Jackson further by asking Jackson if such a motion would be granted in an American court. Jackson had to admit that it would not.[19] Jackson pleaded with the tribunal that if they did not grant his motion to put Alfried in the defendants' dock the whole case against the German arms manufacturers would collapse. Jackson sounded desperate. Krupp represented the sinister forces that Jackson was sent to Europe to punish. The family lawyer for the Krupps argued that it was unfair to indict a man on such serious charges just because his father was too sick to stand trial.[20] Jackson must have known he was on weak ground when he made the incredible suggestion to the court that perhaps Alfried would voluntarily step into the shoes of his father.[21] Alfried Krupp would have had to have been out of his mind to accept that idea. The British opposed Jackson's motion, the first serious disagreement within the prosecution team which, until the Krupp fiasco, had shown a united front. The Tribunal rejected Jackson's motion outright and Gustav Krupp's seat in the dock remained empty. Several of the judges were shocked by the notion of substituting Alfried for Gustav at the last minute, and the American judge Francis Biddle called it "amazing."[22] In its ruling the court implied that Gustav Krupp could be tried when he recovered from his illness. He never did and died a few years later.

The Tribunal's rejection of Jackson's motion was significant to the defendants who expected a sham trial. One could imagine them raising their eyebrows at each other in amazement and thinking to themselves: "The judges actually ruled in our favor and denied the motion of the chief prosecutor. Can this be true? Can it be that we will receive a fair trial after all?"

In 1948 Alfried was finally brought to trial before a U.S. court at Nuremberg. He was convicted of various war crimes and sentenced to twelve years in prison, his vast fortune confiscated. I covered the sentencing for *The Stars and Stripes*. I looked at Krupp and wondered if he realized how lucky he was to receive only twelve years. But that was only the beginning of his luck. By 1951 the political climate had changed. The United States needed Krupp's industrial strength in the event of hostilities against the Soviet Union. Krupp was released and his fortune was restored. But for that clerical error in London, Alfried Krupp would likely have been convicted at the main trial and sentenced to death.

The early release of Alfried Krupp stained Nuremberg's reputation as the great promise of justice. Here was one of the worst of the Nazis, the man who had provided the money and weapons for Hitler's wars, who had used forced slave labor and prisoners of war to run his factories under abominable conditions, being let off as if his prosecution was all a mistake. In the ensuing years we would see many such politically motivated consequences of the Cold War.

⁓

As I entered the Palace of Justice on the Fürtherstrasse for the first time, I wondered if I was too personally involved to be able to report objectively on the Nuremberg trials. A journalist is supposed to set aside his or her own prejudices in reporting a story. I learned this at the University of Missouri's School of Journalism before I left for the Army. Before covering an event a conscientious reporter should take the time to list all the prejudices that might affect his or her story, perhaps even write them down. When the list is complete you should consciously set them aside and promise yourself that you will not let them influence your reporting. But it was hard to imagine anyone doing that in this setting.

In the first place, I was a Jew and some of these defendants supported the policy of exterminating all the Jews in Europe. That was reason enough to bow out of this job. I also had a strong suspicion, later confirmed, that my grandfather was murdered by the Nazis at the Treblinka concentration camp in Poland. In the last weeks of the war my division, the 71st, had liberated a concentration camp at the Gunskirchen Lager in Austria. I had seen the remnants of that camp. I could not bring myself to write of it to my family at home. I could not tell my mother what I suspected about her father.

Perhaps my prejudices were too strong for me to take this job. But I was too selfish to let this chance get away, so instead I went inside and took my seat in the press gallery. I put on the headphones that were lying on my seat.

Every person in the room wore headphones—or almost everyone. Rudolf Hess would often take his off and choose not to listen. At the side of each seat was a switchbox. A flick of the switch let you hear what was being said in any of four languages—English, Russian, French and German. During that summer the courthouse had been in a shambles, the result of an RAF bomb that had ripped a hole in the ceiling just before the war ended. That the building was still standing was remarkable. But by the fall of 1945 it had been rebuilt and was in excellent condition.

On the right side of the courtroom was a high, long bench where eight judges, two each from the four powers, sat facing the defendants' dock across the room. Only four of the judges had voting power; the other four were alternates to be called upon if one of the voting judges could not proceed. Six of the judges wore black robes; the two Russian judges insisted on wearing their military uniforms. On the left side the twenty-one defendants sat in two rows in a dock resembling an over-sized jury box. Lawyers, clerks and interpreters packed the room. At the back wall, opposite the press and visitors' gallery, was the witness stand. There was a story going around that the Russians objected to allowing the defendants to sit in the same witness chair used by the prosecution witnesses. Somehow the dispute was resolved.

I studied the faces of the men on trial. Hermann Goering, Hitler's heir-apparent, sat a few feet away in the defendants' dock. He looked about the courtroom as if to see who was present. Our eyes met. He glared at me for a moment. I was much younger than the others in the press gallery. I could almost tell what he was thinking. Who is this kid? What lies will he write about me? I had imagined him as fat and flabby. Germans told me that in the last months of the war he was considered a buffoon; that he had become fat and sluggish, a drug addict who painted his nails—no longer the heralded ace of the German air force during World War I. But he did not fit that description now in his light-colored uniform, stripped of all his medals. During his months in custody he had lost weight. There were no drugs to be had in prison. He looked alert, eyes clear. While we waited for the judges to take the bench, he conversed busily with the other defendants. Even in those few minutes he behaved like the leader of the pack. I thought, I am looking at the symbol of the Nazi evil.

I looked down the line at what was left of the "Who's Who" of the Third Reich. Next to Goering sat Rudolf Hess, the Deputy Führer who had flown a Messerschmidt fighter plane solo to Scotland in 1941 on a purported peace mission and ended up as a British prisoner throughout the war. Hess sat straight up and stared fixedly ahead like a robot, eyes glazed. He spoke to no one. A mental case, I thought. Probably insane. Next in line came Hitler's foreign minister, Joachim von Ribbentrop, bent over, intensely studying the papers on his lap.

After von Ribbentrop came General Wilhelm Keitel, chief of the Nazi armed forces; Ernst Kaltenbrunner, the senior surviving official of the Gestapo and the SS after Heinrich Himmler's suicide; Alfred Rosenberg, leading Nazi theorist of anti-Semitism and minister of German-occupied territories in the east; Hans Frank, governor-general of Poland; Interior Minister Wilhelm Frick; Julius Streicher, newspaper editor and the leading anti-Semite in Europe; Minister of Economics Walter Funk; Hjalmar Schacht, also Minister of Economics and president of the Reichsbank. Behind them in the second row, again left to right, were Admiral Karl Doenitz, chief of the German navy from 1943 until the end of the war and successor to Hitler briefly after Hitler's suicide; Admiral Erich Raeder, commander-in-chief of the German navy until 1943; Baldur von Schirach, the Hitler Youth leader and governor of Vienna; Fritz Sauckel, primary figure in the foreign forced labor program; Major General Alfred Jodl, chief of the Wehrmacht operations staff; Franz von Papen, once Hitler's vice chancellor; Arthur Seyss-Inquart, commissioner for Nazi-occupied Netherlands; Albert Speer, armaments minister; Constantin von Neurath, von Ribbentrop's predecessor as foreign minister; and Hans Fritsche, radio broadcaster and Goebbels' deputy for propaganda.

Some of the most notorious Nazis were absent. Hitler, of course, committed suicide, as did Heinrich Himmler, the SS leader; Joseph Goebbels, the propaganda minister; Robert Ley, chief of the labor front. Reinhold Heydrich, chief of the security service and the Gestapo, had been assassinated. Others were missing, including Adolf Eichmann, in charge of shipping Jews to the concentration camps, and Martin Bormann, Hitler's secretary.

Robert Ley and Martin Bormann in fact had been on the list of twenty-four selected at the London Conference. Ley had been a fanatic follower of Hitler. While waiting in his cell for the trial to begin, he wrote letters to Henry Ford in America asking for a job when the trial was over.[23] Alone in his cell, a few weeks before the trial opened, he committed suicide. He stuffed his mouth with strips of cloth from his underpants, and then used his jacket to somehow strangle himself.[24] Since he was dead there was no motion to try him *in absentia*.

Martin Bormann was another matter. No one knew whether he was dead or alive. Intensive searches to find him or ascertain his status were still going on. The tribunal agreed to try Bormann *in absentia* over the strenuous objection by his German defense counsel.

As a group the defendants looked gray and sallow and unworthy of all the attention. Some wore old business suits, some wore the uniforms they had on when they were captured but without their medals and ribbons and brass. I could see the marks on the uniforms where the insignia had been torn off.

Charged with aggressively planning and launching the bloodiest of all wars, the murder of millions of Jews and millions of other "undesirables," the men in the dock looked so ordinary. They were not supermen; they did not look like monsters. I was naïve to expect anything else. They looked like the rest of us.

With one of the defendants in the box I had a strange bond, unknown to me at the time. During the time of Nazi domination the most outspoken anti-Semite was a vulgar man named Julius Streicher. Before the war he prospered by founding and publishing a Nazi scandal sheet named *Der Stürmer*. He embarrassed even many Nazis with his pornographic stories on a comic-book level, mostly about rich old Jews seducing innocent German maidens. The headquarters for this outpouring of filth were located in the quaint medieval village of Altdorf, just outside Nuremberg.[25] There Streicher operated his publishing plant with modern printing presses and editorial offices. His journal was so obscene and repulsive that even many devoted Nazis could not bear to read it.[26] But Hitler delighted in Streicher's vulgarity and made him *Gauleiter*[27] of Franconia, a part of Bavaria that included Nuremberg. He rode high as *Gauleiter* and continued to publish his paper until his libels against Goering's manhood got him in trouble. Streicher made the mistake of suggesting that the pregnancy of Goering's wife Emma was the result of artificial insemination. The story angered Goering and he took action against him. Streicher was stripped of his office as *Gauleiter,* spent the rest of the war under house arrest on his estate in Franconia and ran his newspaper by telephone. The Altdorf paper kept going during the war but publication dropped from over a million to fifteen thousand.

At the end of World War II, the United States government took over Streicher's plant in Altdorf to publish the American GI newspaper, *The*

Stars and Stripes. There I started my career as a journalist upon discharge from the Army, not knowing of the plant's history, not knowing I was working in the former office of Julius Streicher, and maybe even sitting in his seat.

CHAPTER FOUR

THE CASE UNFOLDS

JACKSON CAME TO THE LECTERN FOR HIS OPENING STATEMENT. HE was an imposing figure: open morning coat, vest and striped pants, with a gold chain across his vest.

"May it please Your Honors," he began,

> The privilege of opening the first trial in history for crimes against the peace of the world imposes a grave responsibility.
>
> The wrongs which we seek to condemn and punish have been so calculated, so malignant, and so devastating that civilization cannot tolerate their being ignored because it cannot survive their being repeated. That four great nations, flushed with victory and stung with injury, stay the hand of vengeance and voluntarily submit their captive enemies to the judgment of the law is one of the most significant tributes that power has ever paid to reason.[1]

As a lawyer and judge for over forty-five years in the courtroom I have heard close to a thousand opening statements. No one ever spoke with such eloquence.

Criminal prosecutors do not usually implore the court to be fair to the defendants (that speech is left for defense counsel to make). But that is exactly what Jackson did in his opening statement. First he reminded the judges that they must not let the cry for vengeance color their judgment. "We must never forget," he said, "that the record on which we judge these defendants today is the record on which history will judge us tomorrow."[2] Then he made what is still considered a classic plea for justice, a warning that should be engraved in the minds of prosecutors and judges everywhere: "To pass these defendants a poisoned chalice is to put it to our own lips as well."[3] The meaning was plain enough. If you give these men a trial that is not fair, you degrade yourself; you betray your own moral integrity; and you lower yourself to their level of injustice. The address was hailed in the American press. *The Philadelphia Inquirer* called it "one of the greatest opening statements ever delivered before any court."[4] *The Christian Science Monitor,* anticipating the Nuremberg legacy, said the trial "may well have a significance impossible to rightly estimate at the present time."[5]

Telford Taylor said of Jackson's opening: "I know of nothing else in modern juristic literature that equally projects the controlled passion and moral intensity of many passages."[6] It was certainly a brilliant performance, eloquent, passionate, moving and thorough.

One remark must have caught the other Allies as well as the defendants by surprise. That had to do with the burden of proof required of the prosecution. In U.S. law, both in federal and state court criminal trials, a defendant is presumed to be innocent, and before a defendant can be found guilty the prosecution must overcome that presumption of innocence and prove the defendant guilty beyond a reasonable doubt. This burden is recognized as the cornerstone of the U.S. criminal justice system. It is not enough, as criminal defense lawyers often argue to a jury, that the evidence shows the defendant *might* be guilty, or is more likely than not to be guilty, or, to cite the burden in civil cases, that the preponderance of evidence weighs in favor of the prosecution. In criminal trials, the proof must be so overwhelming that there is no reasonable doubt.

What a shock it must have been to the Russians in particular when Jackson declared in his opening statement that he would give the defendants the benefit of this doctrine and ask the court to presume their innocence. "Despite the fact that public opinion already condemns their acts," he announced to a hushed courtroom, "we agree that here they must be given a presumption of innocence."[7]

There is nothing in the minutes of the London Conference to indicate this all-important principle had ever been discussed. Nowhere does the London Charter mention it. No historian says that it was ever considered. The other Allies apparently had no forewarning Jackson was going to make such an announcement. Jackson's American lawyers told me they simply took it for granted.

There is no indication that Jackson ever explained the meaning of the presumption of innocence to his counterparts beforehand. "We agree" Jackson said, but it is unlikely that the Russian judge Nikitchenko had agreed to the presumption of innocence when he had insisted so vigorously in London that there was no issue left as to guilt, and that the defendants had already been found guilty by Stalin, Roosevelt and Churchill when they met at Yalta. Jackson may not have realized it at the time, but in giving defendants the presumption of innocence he set in motion one of the most important precedents of the trial.

One passage of Jackson's opening speech that still sparks bitter controversy is the claim that this was not a trial of the German people, but only of the leaders who had duped and misled them. The German people, he said, were also victims of the Nazi evil.

> We would also make clear that we have no purpose to incriminate the whole German people. . . . If the German populace had willingly accepted the Nazi program, no storm troopers would have been needed in the early days of the Party, and there would have been no need for concentration camps or the Gestapo. . . . The German, no less than the non-German world has accounts to settle with these defendants. . . .[8]

When I spoke to a Jewish audience in Frankfurt in the summer of 2003 I quoted Jackson's remarks above. They reacted angrily. They tended to agree with Daniel Goldhagen in his book *Hitler's Willing Executioners,* that almost all Germans aided and abetted the Nazi program.[9]

Jackson's initial plan for presenting the evidence puzzled spectators and even some members of his staff. American criminal trial lawyers are used to the drama and excitement of calling witnesses to the stand and then eliciting vital evidence through examination and cross-examination. The American press was expecting just that kind of show. But Jackson's team disagreed over the use of that tactic. Jackson himself wanted a strong, reliable record that could withstand any challenge. He disfavored a trial based on live witnesses. If he could base his case on German documents signed by the defendants themselves, or those signed by Hitler to show his plans, the record would have greater strength.[10] His idea was that no one can cross-examine a record and that defense counsel would be in a weak position trying to argue against the validity of a signed document. One of the best examples of Jackson's point was the famous Hossbach memorandum—notes made by Hitler's adjutant, Colonel Hossbach, at a conference in Berlin on November 5, 1937. The notes showed Hitler's plan for waging war against Europe to gain "living space" (Lebensraum). Germany needed more land and the only way to get it was by force. This document turned out to be one of the best pieces of evidence to prove the charges in counts one and two—conspiracy to wage aggressive war, and the waging of aggressive war.[11]

Another factor favoring Jackson's argument was that the use of documents would make for a shorter trial rather than extensive questioning of witnesses to prove the same points, there being always the danger of the witness committing perjury or breaking down while testifying.

Debate broke out within the American legal team, especially between Jackson and Major General William Donovan, who had come to Nuremberg as one of Jackson's chief advisors. During World War II Donovan headed the Office of Strategic Services (OSS) in Washington. Donovan insisted on proving the case by the testimony of witnesses. Jackson was adamant that it should be mainly a documentary case.

Others on the staff also disagreed. Colonel Robert G. Storey, Jackson's executive counsel and a law professor, supported Jackson, while Colonel John Amen, a trial lawyer who was in charge of interrogating war prisoners, wanted colorful witnesses. Thomas Dodd, later to become a prominent U.S. senator from Connecticut, also argued for the drama of witnesses and cross-examination. Otherwise, Dodd claimed, Nuremberg would become a dull affair.

Jackson ultimately won out but his differences with General Donovan became bitter. When neither would yield, Donovan withdrew from the case and returned to the United States.[12]

The agreement by all four Allies to go forward with a trial had been made in late August 1945. The trial began in November, about three months later. In the United States the murder trial of one defendant usually takes at least six months to get into the courtroom from the time the complaint or indictment is issued. The amazingly short period between indictment and trial was due to Jackson's foresight.

Back in the spring of 1945 when Jackson was appointed chief prosecutor, he had already decided there would be a full trial even if he had to do it alone, apart from the other Allies. He put investigators to work scouring the continent for evidence. As the date for the trial drew closer, Jackson worried there would not be enough time to uncover the evidence. But the search began turning up amazing results.

At the London Conference in July Jackson said he was encouraged by the results of the investigation; they were exceeding his expectations. He told the Allies: "I did not think men would ever be so foolish as to put in writing some of the things the Germans did. The stupidity of it and the brutality of it would simply appall you."[13]

The prosecution opened its case with Jackson's presentation of evidence. The Allies had agreed he would handle the first count, conspiracy to wage aggressive war. As the case unfolded it became apparent that Jackson was covering the three other counts as well, that is, the actual waging of aggressive war; war crimes involving violations of the laws and customs of war including mistreatment of prisoners of war; and finally, crimes against humanity involving the murder and torture of civilians on racial, religious and political grounds. As a consequence, what came later from prosecutors assigned to the other three counts became repetitious and boring.

As the weeks went by, what had been billed as an exciting trial did indeed become a bore. Interest waned. Most of the big name journalists such as Walter Cronkite, Rebecca West, Edward R. Murrow, Howard K. Smith, William L. Shirer, Drew Middleton, Eric Sevareid and others had either returned to the States or to more interesting assignments in Europe. Some would return for the last act of the Nuremberg drama. I remember specifically one afternoon when I sat in the press box during the cross examination of the former Reich Chancellor, Franz von Papen, and realized I was practically the only newsman there. The press and his own staff pressured Jackson to call live witnesses to the stand to give the case some spark. Finally Jackson acceded to their pleas and a few witnesses were called.

As the documentary evidence started coming in—letters, orders written by Hitler and others, photographs, films of the concentration camps, accounting ledgers, etc.—the tremendous value of a full trial rather than a summary proceeding began to be obvious. As the evidence mounted with record after record, the intensive pre-trial investigation began to bear fruit. One simple fact emerged: the depth and breadth of this investigation would never have occurred without the decision to go to trial, a decision that was the driving force behind the exhaustive search for evidence.

H. R. Trevor-Roper, British intelligence officer and author of the classic work on Hitler's death, *The Last Days of Hitler,* recognized as early as 1946 the value of the trial record to Germany's future. Referring to evidence brought out at Nuremberg, he said:

> Had it not been for this exposure it would have been possible for a new German movement in ten years' time to maintain that the worst of Nazi crimes were Allied propaganda easily invented in the hour of such total victory. That is now impossible. The most damning documents— the minutes of Hitler's meetings, Ohlendorf's account of the mass murder of 90,000 Jews, Eichmann's account of Himmler's dissatisfaction at a mere 6,000,000 executions, Himmler's grotesque addresses to his SS leaders, Keitel's criminal orders and shocking marginalia—these and many others have now been through the test of cross-examination; their signatures and authenticity have been confirmed. And the real nature of Nazism has been confirmed, not by the fallible testimony of report, but by the exacting scrutiny of a court of law.[14]

One of the more spectacular discoveries of the trial consisted of the voluminous records of Alfred Rosenberg. These records by Hitler's leading exponent of anti-Semitism filled forty-seven crates and detailed how the Nazis operated in the East and how they looted occupied countries. They included admissions of systematic killings and lootings.[15] An American officer found them hidden under piles of straw in a barn in Bavaria. All forty-seven crates were flown to Paris, where Jackson had set up his headquarters for collecting trial evidence. Other records and films showed the numbers murdered in the Holocaust and the nature of atrocities in the concentration camps.

Here lies the most important legacy of the trial—the record itself. In collecting and presenting these documents, the trial made a giant step in revolutionizing international law. But an even more important legacy lies simply in the enduring record it established for all the world to see. By revealing the true nature of the Nazi system, this record changed the course of German and European history.

CHAPTER FIVE

DEFENDING THE INDEFENSIBLE

A MAJOR PROBLEM WITH THE NUREMBERG TRIALS WAS THAT THE ALLIES made all the rules. They decided what law should govern and what procedure should be followed in the courtroom. The German defense counsel had no say in these decisions. The result was that the German lawyers found themselves scrambling to learn the American adversary procedure, which was vastly different from their own continental or inquisitorial system. They also had to research the law of conspiracy with which they were totally unfamiliar. Up to that time conspiracy was unheard of in European law.

Jackson recognized the problem at the outset. "From the very beginning," he said, "it has been apparent that our greatest problem is how to reconcile two very different systems of procedure."[1] Compromises were made but generally the Anglo-American adversary system requested by Jackson was adopted and the Germans, like it or not, had to follow it.

This gave rise to the criticism that the differences were so great that they denied the defendants a fair trial. Under the European continental system as it existed in 1945, most of the documentary and testimonial evidence was first presented by the prosecutor along with the indictment to a magistrate. The magistrate would then study it, and if he or she found the evidence sufficient to warrant a trial, the entire file and the indictment would be turned over to the defense and the trial judge assigned to the case. At that point both parties and the judge would be fully informed of all the evidence for and against the defendant. The trial would proceed with a judge or panel of judges, depending on the severity of the charge. There was no such thing as a jury trial; the judge or panel of judges was the only trier of fact. The judges could call additional witnesses, and usually the judges—not lawyers—questioned the witnesses. Cross-examination, which is so important in American trials, was not generally employed in Europe. The German lawyers were used to the judges playing a much more active role. The defense counsel's lack of experience in cross-examination soon became obvious. They often seemed reluctant to make a prosecution witness look bad, as if it were against protocol to do so.

Without question substantial differences existed between German and American court procedure in 1945. In the "adversarial" system used in American courts, the defendant went to trial knowing little about the prosecution's evidence except what was disclosed in a brief preliminary examination or grand jury hearing. The trial judge usually knew nothing about the case until he or she was handed the charge or indictment on the morning of trial. In America, the defendant was entitled to a jury trial. The judge played a passive role, more like a referee, deciding which evidence would be admissible and explaining the applicable law to the jury. In American trial procedure, the lawyers ran the case, and they liked the judge to stay out of it. There was a common saying among American lawyers who approved of their trial judge: "He's a good judge. He lets us try our case." The opposing lawyers were adversaries. They "fought" against each other to support their own position and to weaken the opposition's, all within rules of ethics. Out of this contest the truth was supposed to emerge unsullied by prejudicial factors. Generally these differences between American and European courts still exist today. The difference between the two systems is sometimes described this way: The European procedure is geared to establish the facts and so get at the truth; the American focus is on fair trial and the protection of individual rights. American courts often keep out the truth in the interest of fairness. Consider this common example: Police arrest a suspect for murder and take him into custody. Without advising him of his so-called Miranda rights, the officer asks the suspect if he committed the crime. The man answers: "Sure I did it and I'd do it again if I had the chance." At trial this critical confession never comes out. The judge must exclude it because the suspect was not advised of his constitutional rights against self-incrimination.

Under Anglo-American procedure defendants may testify or remain silent. They cannot be forced to testify. If they choose to testify they must do so under oath. They are never allowed to make an unsworn statement. To a degree the London Charter represented a compromise between the two systems. There is no record that any Nuremberg defendant was ever compelled to testify unwillingly, although the charter is silent on the issue of the right to remain silent. Defendants were allowed to make an unsworn statement at the end of the trial without undergoing cross-examination, and they did so.[2] Despite the compromises, the adversary system that Jackson wanted remained largely intact.

As has been stated already, the charge of conspiracy was a legal concept as unknown to the Germans as it was to the French and the Russians. The defense asked, How could there be a conspiracy when Hitler had all the power, made all the decisions, and demanded unflagging support? There was no agreement, defense counsel claimed; the defendants only followed his orders.

Under Anglo-American law a criminal conspiracy was generally defined as an agreement between two or more persons to commit unlawful conduct. Jackson thought conspiracy was vital to his case because he had no evidence that the defendants had personally murdered or tortured anyone or committed any atrocities themselves. Some had never even visited a concentration camp. That made it difficult to prove their guilt. Under the conspiracy charge, all Jackson needed to prove was that the accused agreed to the crimes alleged, which could be proved by circumstantial evidence. Proof of a formal agreement or meeting was not required.[3]

There was certainly an element of unfairness in the conspiracy charge. Defense counsel were at a definite disadvantage in dealing with a crime they had never confronted before and which had never been part of European law. To Jackson, on the other hand, conspiracy was a familiar device. He saw no unfairness in charging it.

On its surface, the charge of conspiracy seems simple enough. You plan a crime with someone else and that's it. In some jurisdictions, an overt act is also a required element. But the elements of the crime are not that simple. Such questions as what constitutes an agreement, and whether each member of a conspiracy is liable for each act and statement of every other member, are troubling for even some American lawyers. They were baffling to the Germans.

It turned out that the judges at Nuremberg were also troubled by the conspiracy charge and put drastic limits on it, restricting it to counts one and two on aggressive war only.[4]

In the end, much of what defense counsel had feared from the conspiracy charge did not work against their defendants. As Telford Taylor, a prosecutor on Jackson's team, pointed out: "The presence or absence of conspiracy may not have been as important a factor in the eyes of the judges as in those of the American and British prosecutors."[5]

There was one other major impediment to the German attorneys preparing their defense. It had to do with the right of discovery; that is, the right of each side to be given or informed of any evidence held by the other side. Under the rules of trial set out by the tribunal, defense counsel, upon proper motion, was supposed to have access to the documents the prosecution intended to place into evidence.[6] The rule seemed simple enough and fair. It was in line with the tone of Jackson's opening statement in which he stressed the need for a fair trial. But despite Jackson's eloquent words, the defendants' right to see prosecution documents beforehand was denied to them by the prosecution during the first month of trial. As the evidence was being presented on the second day of trial, the Americans gave every appearance of conducting their prosecution with little consideration for the Germans involved (defendants and defense counsel), as well as for anyone else who did not understand English.[7] For example, American prosecutor Major Frank Wallis offered in evidence six copies of document books and briefs. Presiding judge Geoffrey Lawrence interrupted Wallis to ask if he had copies for each defense counsel. Wallis had to admit that he did not and was admonished by the judge to do so as soon as possible. Shortly thereafter the Americans fell into deeper trouble with the court. It came out that the documents were in English only, not German, and not in Russian or French either. The Americans apparently had not taken into account that this was an international trial in which half the bench and half the lawyers either could not understand English or had only a minimal knowledge of the language.

Telford Taylor called this error the "sheerest folly"[8] and criticized his own prosecution team for their shortsightedness. Jackson and his staff, according to Taylor, had badly miscalculated the work required to sort through the bushels of documents and give the defendants adequate distribution before trial. There followed a month of delays before the documents problem was finally resolved.[9]

But the scope of discovery given defense counsel at Nuremberg exceeded anything given to defendants in American criminal trials at the time. The right of discovery in America was practically non-existent. A criminal trial was like a game in which the adversaries tried to surprise each other with witnesses and exhibits unknown to the other side. American moviegoers were brought up on the dramatic scene of the surprise witness called to the stand at the last moment, often accompanied by a collective gasp from everyone in the courtroom. Perhaps the most significant change in American criminal trial procedure since 1945 has been an expansion of the right of discovery of evidence. For example, each side now must turn over to the other the names of all witnesses, as well as the statements they intend to use.[10] The right to discovery given to defendants at Nuremberg, along with such due process rights as the presumption of innocence and counsel of their choice, were rights that went beyond anything allowed by the Nazis, and in the case of discovery went beyond what defendants were given in the United States at that time.

But even aside from the aforementioned problems, it was virtually impossible for the German attorneys to defend against such overwhelming facts. The prosecution evidence of atrocities and genocide was so strong that no one could ever stand before the court and argue that such horrors never happened. There it was, recorded in film and photographs, written down in meticulously kept records, all of which now comprised the voluminous documentation that would serve as the damning evidence against its authors. Jackson was right when he said he hardly needed any witnesses. The accused had been most efficient in providing proof against themselves.

On one occasion there was an effort by the defense to dispute the numbers murdered in the concentration camps. During the defense case the defense attorney for Ernst Kaltenbrunner summoned Rudolf Hoess (not to be confused with the defendant Rudolf Hess) to the witness stand. One portion of Hoess's testimony exemplifies the nature of the prosecution evidence better than any other. The defense attorney, Dr. Kurt Kauffman, questioned Hoess first:

Kauffman:　You were Camp Commandant of Auschwitz from 1940 to 1943?
Hoess:　　Yes.
Kauffman:　And in that time hundreds of thousands of human beings were put to death there, is that true?
Hoess:　　Yes.
Kauffman:　Is it true that Eichmann told you that altogether over two million Jewish people were killed in Auschwitz?
Hoess:　　Yes.
Kauffman:　Men, women, and children?
Hoess:　　Yes.

Later Hoess testified as follows, still under direct examination by his own attorney:

Hoess:　　In summer 1941 I was personally ordered to Berlin to the National Chief of the SS, Himmler. He gave me to understand—I can no longer recall the exact words—that the Führer had ordered the final solution of the Jewish problem, and that we, the SS, had to carry out this order. If we did not do this now, then later the Jews would destroy the German people. He had therefore chosen Auschwitz because it was most favorably situated with regard to transport, and the extensive grounds offered space for seclusion.

Hoess spoke in a quiet, calm voice. He showed no remorse, no emotion. When Hoess's attorney finished his direct examination, Jackson's deputy prosecutor John Harlan Amen took over. He needed to ask only one question, which was whether the written affidavit he held in his hand, signed by Hoess, was true. The prosecutor read aloud from the statement to a hushed courtroom. This statement represented the heart of the prosecution case on crimes against humanity:

Amen: "I commanded Auschwitz up to December 1, 1943, and estimate that at least 2,500,000 victims were killed and disposed of there by gassing and burning; at least a further half million died of starvation and illness, which makes a total of about 3,000,000 dead. This number represents about seventy or eighty percent of all the people who were sent to Auschwitz as prisoners; the others were sorted out and used for slave labor in the workshops of the concentration camp. The total number of victims comprises about 100,000 German Jews, and a great number of mostly Jewish inhabitants of Holland, France, Belgium, Poland, Hungary, Czechoslovakia, Greece and other countries. About 400,000 Hungarian Jews alone were executed by us in Auschwitz in the summer of 1944.

"The camp commander of Treblinka told me that he had liquidated 80,000 in the course of six months. His task was chiefly the liquidation of all Jews from the Warsaw ghetto. He had used carbon monoxide, and I regarded his methods as not very effective. So when I put up the execution buildings in Auschwitz, I began to use Zyklon B, a crystallized hydrocyanic acid which we threw into the death chamber through a small opening. It required, according to climatic conditions, three to fifteen minutes to kill the people in the death chamber. We knew when the people were dead because their screaming stopped. We usually waited half an hour before we opened the doors and took out the corpses. After the bodies had been dragged out, our special detachments took off their rings and drew the gold from the teeth of the corpses. A further improvement as compared with Treblinka was that we built gas chambers which could hold 2,000 people at a time, while the ten gas chambers at Treblinka could only take 200 each.

"The manner in which we chose our victims was as follows: Two SS doctors were employed in Auschwitz to inspect all the incoming convoys of prisoners. The prisoners had to march past them while they made their decision on the spot; those capable of work were sent into the camp, the others at once to the extermination block. Very young children, being incapable of working, were killed as a matter of principle. Often women tried to hide their children under their clothes, but when they were found they were at once sent to their death. We tried to carry out these executions in secret, but the foul and nauseating stench which rose from the incessant burning of corpses penetrated the whole area."

Is this all true and correct?

Hoess: Yes.[11]

When asked how many personnel it took to kill two thousand persons a day, Hoess calmly replied that he had about three thousand men on his staff.

Hoess was a witness for the defense and yet his testimony could not have possibly helped them, and only helped the prosecution.

Whitney R. Harris was one of Jackson's leading prosecutors at Nuremberg. His book *Tyranny on Trial,* a definitive account of the evidence at Nuremberg, was highly praised by Jackson himself when it was published in 1954. On August 4, 2006, I interviewed Harris, then in his nineties, with regard to how the Hoess affidavit came into evidence. After the prosecution rested its case, Harris had the opportunity of interrogating Rudolf Hoess outside the courtroom about Hoess's tour as commander of the Auschwitz concentration camp. Hoess gave Harris a signed affidavit describing the Auschwitz experience quoted above. Harris knew the statement was dynamite, one of the most telling pieces of evidence in the entire case. But Harris was frustrated. Under the rules of evidence the prosecution, having already rested, was not allowed to call Hoess to the witness stand for cross-examination about the affidavit.

Harris told me he was beside himself with anguish trying to figure out a way to get the statement into evidence. Unless Hoess took the stand there was no way the affidavit could be introduced. Suddenly, in the middle of the defense presentation, what seemed to Harris at the time like a miracle took place. Dr. Kauffman, attorney for defendant Kaltenbrunner, made the critical error of calling Hoess to the stand. Harris could hardly believe his luck. Now Hoess was open to cross-examination and the affidavit came out in public.[12] Hoess was tried and convicted by a Polish military tribunal and hanged, fittingly, at Auschwitz on April 7, 1947.[13]

Whitney Harris also told me that despite the horrific nature of the Hoess affidavit he will always remember one other scene which to him was the "most chilling evidence of the entire trial." It occurred as Otto Ohlendorf was on the witness stand. Ohlendorf had been chief of the *Einsatzgruppe D*, a special Nazi task force of the SS whose mission was to murder all Jews, Gypsies and political commissars. The Soviet judge, General Nikitchenko, asked four questions. Harris recalled every word of the exchange:

Nikitchenko:	In your testimony you said that the *Einsatz* group had the object of annihilating the Jews and the commissars, is that correct?
Ohlendorf:	Yes.
Nikitchenko:	And in what category did you consider the children? For what reason were the children massacred?
Ohlendorf:	The order was that the Jewish population should be totally exterminated.
Nikitchenko:	Including the children?
Ohlendorf:	Yes.
Nikitchenko:	Were all the Jewish children murdered?
Ohlendorf:	Yes.[14]

Ohlendorf was later prosecuted in one of the twelve other Nuremberg trials and sentenced to death.

❧

When all the evidence was in, the defense attorneys, having few or no facts in their favor, had to rely on other means for argument. Some raised the factual defense of denial ("I didn't do it," "I was not there and had no knowledge of the crime," "That is not my signature"). But the most troubling defenses came in the form of four legal, rather than factual, arguments: victors' justice ("The court consists only of judges from the Allied powers"); superior orders ("I had to do it or I would be shot"); *Ex post facto* ("There was no law in existence declaring what we did was criminal"); and the *tu quoque* defense ("You did it too and therefore we should be allowed to show evidence of Allied atrocities as well"). Whenever the legitimacy of the Nuremberg trials is discussed, these defense arguments form the heart of the criticisms.

VICTORS' JUSTICE

The question of victors' justice was probably the most sensitive issue of the trial.[15] Every judge on the Nuremberg bench represented a victorious Allied power. No neutral country was represented, nor was any request ever made for a judge from a neutral power. No German judge sat on the bench, nor was such an arrangement ever considered; there was no jury; neither the defendants nor their counsel had any say about the trial procedure; it was not a trial by one's peers. No Allies were on trial on charges of war crimes. Only the losers were tried.

Senator Robert A. Taft of Ohio, a leading conservative voice in the Senate in 1945, and later a strong contender for the presidential nomination in 1952, said, "The trial of the vanquished by the victors cannot be impartial no matter how it is hedged about with forms of justice."[16]

On the other hand, one of the leading German defense lawyers at the trial, Otto Kranzbuehler, defender of Admiral Karl Doenitz, expressed his approval of the process this way:

> It was clear that after the obvious crimes committed under Hitler's leadership, particularly the annihilation process against the Jews, something had to happen to discharge the tension between victors and vanquished. . . . It was the United States who insisted that expiation must be sought and found by way of a judicial trial. The International Military Tribunal proceedings did, in my opinion, perform this function. It was the painful starting point for building the relations that exist today [1965] between Germany and her Western Allies.[17]

In his memoirs, Doenitz wrote that since the trial was purely a German affair, Germans should have been allowed to handle the case. But there was no German government to turn to for help in 1945. Germany no longer existed as a nation. Furthermore, there was the disastrous experience of World War I. When President Woodrow Wilson went to the Paris Peace Conference at Versailles in 1919 he expressed opposition to an international war crimes trial of the German leaders. His mind was occupied with establishing the League of Nations, which included Germany. As a consequence the trial was turned over to the new German government.

In 1920, the Germans proposed to try accused German war criminals before the German Supreme Court in Leipzig. British Prime Minister Lloyd George persuaded the French to accept the proposal and a year later the Leipzig trials began. The Kaiser had fled to Holland and when the Allies asked Holland to make the Kaiser available for trial, the Dutch refused on the grounds that the charge against him was unknown to Dutch law. The Kaiser never left Holland and died in his castle there in 1941. The first Germans tried at Leipzig were soldiers charged with beating British prisoners with rifle butts. They were convicted but received lenient sentences. A U-boat commander was tried for sinking a British hospital ship. He was acquitted on grounds he was merely obeying superior orders. Two German officers were tried for murdering French prisoners and shooting wounded French soldiers. One of the officers denied the charges and was acquitted; the other was convicted and received two years in prison. Two other German naval officers were tried and convicted for sinking a hospital ship and attacking Allied lifeboats. They were sentenced to four years imprisonment but escaped within a few months. The prosecution record was dismal.[18] Little wonder the Allies in 1945 had no inclination to turn the trial of Nazi war criminals over to the Germans.

A second option was to include German judges, but since Nazi judges were out of the question, one would have had to seek out non-Nazi judges who had fled persecution and were now living elsewhere. It is unlikely that they would have been more impartial.

Other alternatives included a neutral tribunal to be formed from Swiss, Swedish, Portuguese, Spanish and Argentine jurists of good standing.[19] But the scale of World War II was so vast that there were hardly any real neutrals in the world. The task of locating them and reaching agreement among the Allies as to their selection would have been impossible or at the least would have caused unreasonable delay. The world was crying for action. Millions of Hitler's victims who could still speak wanted vindication and they wanted it soon.[20]

Another option was a jury trial—but what a mess it would have been trying to pick a jury. Imagine trying to find an unbiased juror in that atmosphere. Or trying to have four prosecutors representing four different nations with different versions of trial procedure and twenty-two defense attorneys come to agreement on the composition of a jury panel. Robert Jackson himself recognized the problem when the charter was signed at London:

> However unfortunate it may be, there seems no way of doing any-thing about the crimes against the peace and against humanity ex-cept that the victors judge the vanquished . . . we must summon all that we have of dispassionate judgment to the task of patiently and fairly presenting the record of these evil deeds.[21]

As for the Allied judges, the question remains whether they could set aside all they had heard, read and experienced about the Hitler regime and judge the case solely on the evidence before them. That is what an impartial judge or jury is supposed to do. In his book, *Reaching Judgment at Nuremberg,* Bradley F. Smith doubted "that the Americans, or the other judges, were free from bias or were capable of rising above the overwhelming public demand that the Nazi leaders be made to pay for their evil deeds."[22]

Despite the judges' biases and the many criticisms, the judgment of historians from both sides was that the trial was basically fair. At least three quarters of the German people at the time said they found the trial "fair" and "just."[23] No one from either side has charged that the defen-dants were "railroaded." The judges generally were considered to have been humane and reasonably impartial. No one can now argue, as some predicted, that it was just a "put-up job," or that the Nazi propaganda coming from some defense witnesses embarrassed the Allies and made the case a farce.[24] Even the majority of the defense counsel felt the trial was relatively fair and the verdict reasonable.[25]

Albert Speer, Hitler's architect and Reich minister for armaments and munitions, called the verdicts "fair enough."[26] He did not object to his own sentence of twenty years. Theodor Klefisch, attorney for the SA, Hitler's paramilitary organization, said the trial met the requirements of impartiality and justice with consideration and dignity.[27]

Yes, it *was* victors' justice and the trial had its share of injustice. But the only alternative was no trial at all, or either setting the Nazis free or executing them summarily without giving them a chance to defend themselves. The scale of terror and atrocity was so great, the world's demand for action so strong, that there had to be a judicial proceeding. To delay in order to search for a more neutral tribunal would have been an injustice in itself.

SUPERIOR ORDERS

Jackson knew the defendants were certain to raise the defense of obedience to superior orders. That defense is based on the principle that a military or civilian person in the government should not be held liable for obeying an order of a superior, especially when refusal to obey the order could have severe consequences, even death.

The Nazis operated under the *Führerprinzip*. Hitler had absolute authority. What he ordered they had to carry out without question. If the judges allowed the "superior orders" defense, Jackson's whole case could collapse. He had to find a way to counter it. During the conference in London, Jackson expressed his uneasiness to his British counterpart, Sir David Maxwell-Fyfe. The British prosecutor was also deeply concerned. He told Jackson that the defense of superior orders had to be quashed at the outset. Otherwise the only person they could convict was Hitler, and he was dead.[28]

Jackson found his way out of the dilemma by citing Germany's own military code. The German soldiers' paybook contained a commandment that no soldier should obey an illegal order.[29] When Jackson argued the issue before the court he quoted the relevant section from the German code.[30] The "superior orders" defense should not be allowed because the defendants had obeyed illegal orders that they knew to be illegal. They obeyed the orders at their peril.

The American military had a similar rule. According to the *Manual for Courts-Martial United States* (2000):

> *Inference of lawfulness.* An order requiring the performance of a military duty may be inferred to be lawful and it is disobeyed at the peril of the subordinate. This inference does not apply to a patently illegal order, such as one that directs the commission of a crime.[31]

But Jackson was still troubled. Despite his passionate hatred of what the Nazis stood for, he wanted to be fair. He thought it might be unfair to ask the court to eliminate the defense altogether, so he suggested a compromise at London that the Allied representatives accepted. The court could receive evidence of obeying superior orders offered by the defense but such evidence could be used only in mitigation of sentence; that is, to reduce the punishment. It would not be allowed on the issue of guilt or innocence.[32] Almost half a century later the Yugoslavia Tribunal used the same principle as precedent in the first international war crimes trial since Nuremberg, conducted at The Hague in the Netherlands.

As expected, most of the Nuremberg defendants objected to any elimination of the superior orders defense. After all, this was their strongest argument and their case would stand or fall on it. They wanted the plea of superior orders to be accepted as a complete defense.

When Alfred Jodl, chief of operations on Hitler's military staff, read the indictment for the first time he seemed bewildered by the charges of aggressive war. "I don't see how they can fail to recognize a soldier's obligation to obey orders," he said. "That's the code I've lived by all my life."[33]

Field Marshal Wilhelm Keitel, chief of the German army, said, "For a soldier, orders are orders."[34]

The "Nuremberg Principle" as to superior orders has since come under criticism by Telford Taylor himself. Once again, as in the *ex post facto* debate, Taylor shows remarkable frankness. He is not reluctant to criticize his own prosecution.

The principle is "flawed," Taylor said in his book *The Anatomy of the Nuremberg Trials*. It fails to give standing to a defendant who did not know and had no reason to know the order was illegal. Taylor would change the principle to read along these lines:

If the defendant did not know, and had no basis for knowing, that the order he had obeyed was unlawful, the defendant should not be held liable at all. If he knew that the order called for unlawful acts, the defendant should be found guilty and allowed to rely on duress or other factors only as a matter of mitigation.[35]

With regard to the evidence of atrocities and the crimes against humanity, the Nuremberg Court could hardly be faulted for refusing to allow the defense of superior orders. Such orders were blatantly illegal. Who could ever argue to a court: "I did not know the order to gas a thousand Jews was illegal"?

On the other hand, with regard to the military men on trial for waging aggressive war—Keitel, Raeder (commander in chief of the German navy until his retirement in 1943), Doenitz, and Jodl—they were expected to know that the Kellogg-Brian Treaty had somehow made waging aggressive war a crime. Waging aggressive war had never before been declared to be criminal.

After the trial, a Michigan congressman, Rep. George Dundero, denounced the Nuremberg Principle of superior orders as an attack on the sanctity of orders from a superior officer, which could encourage mass disobedience by American soldiers. He feared that scores of U.S. military personnel would refuse to obey orders on the ground that they believed the orders to be illegal and raise the Nuremberg Principle in their defense. Dundero severely criticized the trial for prosecuting German military officers who were only obeying orders.[36]

The Nuremberg Principle was novel in the international setting, but the basic principle was not new in American law. In 1851 Supreme Court Chief Justice Roger B. Taney held that "it can never be maintained that a military officer can justify himself for doing an unlawful act, by producing the order of his superior. The order may palliate, but it cannot justify."[37]

During the Civil War, Henry Wirz, a Confederate officer, commanded the prisoner-of-war camp at Andersonville, Georgia. He treated the prisoners inhumanely, causing about 14,000 Union soldiers to die at his camp from lack of food and medicine. After the war Wirz was tried for murder and conspiracy. In his defense he showed the court proof that he was following the orders of his superior. The defense was rejected and he was found guilty.[38]

In the year 2005 the issue of obeying superior orders as a defense arose again in the case of American soldiers facing court-martial on charges of torturing Iraqi prisoners at the Abu Ghraib prison outside Baghdad. One of the first defendants to be tried was Corporal Charles Graner, whose court-martial was held at Fort Hood, Texas. Graner's counsel entered the same defense that the Nazi defendants raised at Nuremberg, arguing that Graner was merely acting on orders of his superiors. Surely the ghosts of Nuremberg were present there, unseen witnesses for the prosecution. The military court rejected Graner's defense, applying Nuremberg precedent.[39]

EX POST FACTO LAW

The term *ex post facto* refers to criminal law that is passed or created after the act in question was committed. If a person commits an act at a time when there is no law against it, the person should not be held liable. The rationale for this principle is that it is unfair to prosecute a person for criminal conduct if at the time of committing the act the person did not know his or her conduct was illegal. No crime without law, no punishment without law, the Romans said: *Nulle crimen et nulla poena sine lege.*[40] In America the prohibition against *ex post facto* law is stated in the Constitution[41] and is generally upheld by American courts, although it is not international law and several nations do not recognize it.

It was not written in any statute, the critics said, that to wage aggressive war was a crime. The nations of Europe had been making war for centuries and no one ever told them it was a crime for which individual leaders could be put to death. At the London Conference, the French representative, Professor André Gros, made precisely this objection when he heard Jackson propose it. "We do not consider as a criminal act," he told Jackson, "the launching of a war of aggression."[42]

The British and Soviets also opposed Jackson on this issue, concerned that if making war was a crime, they might be considered guilty also for their actions: the British against Norway, and the Soviets against Poland, Finland, Romania, and the Baltic countries.

One of the harshest criticisms of the Nuremberg trial is that the tribunal relied on illegal *ex post facto* law and therefore the convictions of twelve Nazi defendants for either conspiring to wage aggressive war or actually waging aggressive war were tragic mistakes. Of all the attacks made against Nuremberg in the last sixty years none has received more attention and more support than the alleged application of *ex post facto* law.

When Jackson came to London for the pretrial negotiations, he realized his greatest problem was to overcome the critics who said he was relying on *ex post facto* law. His vision of the trial depended on the charge of waging aggressive war. Everything else, all the crimes against humanity, the extermination of the Jews, were subsidiary to this single crime—they all resulted from Hitler's military ambitions.[43] Jackson had to win this point if he were to succeed.

But the other Allies at the London conference wanted to know what laws the Nazis had broken and how Jackson defined aggressive war.

The lack of a definition did not concern Jackson. Hitler had invaded Poland in 1939; Norway, Belgium, Luxembourg and the Netherlands in 1940; Greece, Yugoslavia and the Soviet Union in 1941; all without justification. Jackson used Hitler's own words as a definition: the expressed intention to use force if necessary to gain more living space *(Lebensraum)*. Hitler's attacks were aggressive war under almost any definition. Hitler had defined the term himself by his own actions.

But the other part of the *ex post facto* argument needed a careful response. Jackson came to the trial armed with his research. First of all he cited the Kellogg-Briand Peace Pact of 1928, in which Germany along with sixty-three other nations signed an agreement condemning war. The pact renounced war as an instrument of national policy.[44] The problem with using the pact was that it was not a criminal code or statute with any punishment for violations. The pact in no way assigned personal liability for any national leader who violated the treaty. There was no warning of consequences. Hitler had violated the Treaty of Versailles, the Locarno Pact, The Hague Rules of Land Warfare of 1907 and the Geneva Conventions of 1929. But those treaties did not list the penalties for violations.[45] Never before had a treaty violation been used as a criminal charge against a national leader. Furthermore, Jackson's reliance on the Kellogg-Briand Pact became vulnerable when it was pointed out that sixty-four nations signed the treaty exactly because it avoided any definition of "aggressive war" or any agreement as to individual penalties.[46]

Still another hurdle Jackson faced was the fact that nations had continued to wage war without repercussion or punishment long after the Kellogg-Briand Pact. Those nations were never charged with war crimes. No court was set up in the past to try national leaders for waging aggressive war.

Back in America prominent voices attacked Jackson's strategy. One of the first came from Senator Taft of Ohio. Ten days before the hangings at Nuremberg, on October 5, 1946, Senator Taft made a speech to the nation at Kenyon College in Ohio. He deplored the sentences and suggested that exile—similar to that imposed upon Napoleon—would be better. Then he criticized the trials which he said "violate the fundamental principle of American law that a man cannot be tried under an *ex post facto* statute."[47] He felt the Nuremberg trial was therefore a departure from the ideals of the American Constitution.[48]

Supreme Court Justice William O. Douglas, a liberal voice on the U.S. Supreme Court at the time, joined the attack:

> No matter how many books are written or briefs filed, no matter how finely the lawyers analyzed it, the crime for which the Nazis were tried had never been formalized as a crime with the definiteness required by our legal standards, nor outlawed with a death penalty by the international community. By our standards that crime arose under *ex post facto* law. Goering *et al.* deserved severe punishment. But their guilt did not justify us in substituting power for principle.[49]

In the Nuremberg Court, defense counsel pounced on Jackson's position, arguing:

> . . . that no sovereign power had made aggressive war a crime at the time that the alleged criminal acts were committed, that no statute had defined aggressive war, that no penalty had been fixed for its commission, and no court had been created to try and punish offenders.[50]

These critics can find support today by the fact that "aggressive war" has still never been clearly defined. International lawyers and diplomats cannot agree how to define it. In 1974 the United Nations offered this definition:

Aggression is the use of armed force by a State against the sovereignty, territorial integrity or political independence of another State, or in any other manner inconsistent with the Charter of the United Nations.[51]

But this definition, like all the others offered so far, has never been accepted by the international community.

The arguments against *ex post facto* law reflect the nature of the opposition Jackson had to face when he went to London to draw up the indictment. He was convinced his case was not based on *ex post facto* law and that he did not need a better definition of aggressive war. But he had to win two battles. He first had to win at London by convincing the other Allies, and then again in the courtroom by convincing the judges. But there was a third fight he wanted to win also: to persuade the American critics to his view. "Let's not be derailed by legal hair-splitters," Jackson told the delegates in London. "Aren't murder, torture, and enslavement, crimes recognized by all civilized people? What we propose is to punish acts which have been regarded as criminal since the time of Cain and have been so written in every civilized code."[52] In Nuremberg he told the court:

> It is true, of course, that we have no judicial precedent for the Charter. But International Law is more than a scholarly collection of abstract and immutable principles. It is an outgrowth of treaties and agreements between nations and accepted customs. . . . The law, so far as International Law can be decreed, had been clearly pronounced when these acts took place.[53]

Sir Hartley Shawcross, Great Britain's chief prosecutor, faced the *ex post facto* argument in his opening statement at Nuremberg: "I suppose the first person ever charged with murder might well have said: 'See here, you can't do that. Murder hasn't been made a crime yet!'"[54]

On November 19, 1945, before the evidence got underway, defense counsel made their motion to dismiss on *ex post facto* grounds.[55] The tribunal overruled the motion with its own argument in favor of the prosecution:

> To assert that it is unjust to punish those who in defiance of treaties and assurances have attacked neighboring states without warning is

obviously untrue, for in such circumstances the attacker must know that he is doing wrong, and so far from it being unjust to punish him, it would be unjust if his wrong were allowed to go unpunished.[56]

The American judge Francis Biddle viewed the issue this way:

> The *ex post facto* argument . . . issued from a lack of understanding of the theory of *ex post facto,* or of existing international law. The rubric *nullem crimen et nulla poena sine lege* did not mean that a crime had to be defined and its punishment fixed by statute before the offender could be tried. . . . Murder and treason were punished by courts in the middle ages long before they were incorporated into statute.[57]

The decision of the Nuremberg tribunal sealed the matter as far as the trial was concerned. But for half a century the debate has gone back and forth. If Nuremberg was based on *ex post facto* law, it tainted the trial's reputation. The use of *ex post facto* law meant the tribunal had wrongly convicted twelve Nazi defendants on counts one or two, and that some of them may have been sent to the gallows on that illegal ground.

Then in 1992 an amazing thing happened. Telford Taylor revealed his own opinion on the matter. He conceded that the court's judgment on counts one and two relied on *ex post facto* law. This admission had tremendous significance because of Taylor's fine reputation. When Jackson left Nuremberg to return to the Supreme Court, he turned the prosecution of the twelve remaining U.S.-conducted trials over to Taylor. After all the Nuremberg trials were completed, Taylor went back to New York and had a distinguished career as a law professor at Columbia Law School and as author of numerous books. In 1992 he published one of the outstanding accounts of the trial in *The Anatomy of the Nuremberg Trials.* In it, Taylor made this remarkable statement:

> People might well differ about the wisdom of declaring that initiation of aggressive war is an offense under international law, but surely there would be nothing unlawful about creating such a principle *for the future.* However, the Charter drew no such distinction, and unquestionably the Charter and the Tribunal's judgment applied counts One and

Two to prior actions of the defendants and thus inflicted *ex post facto* punishments.[58]

With these words, the chief deputy prosecutor seems to be admitting in effect that he helped prosecute and send defendants to the gallows on *ex post facto* law.

Despite his views on the court's use of *ex post facto* law, Taylor nevertheless believed that while it would not be outrageous to punish the Nazi perpetrators of atrocities, it would be outrageous not to punish them at all.[59] In the epilogue to his book, Taylor explains his position further:

> Arguments in support of punishing individuals *ex post facto* for violations of the crime against peace can be made, but, if conducted on a plane devoid of political and emotional factors, will be won by the defense. But in 1945 those very factors were overwhelming. Peoples whose nations had been attacked and dismembered without warning wanted legal retribution, whether or not this was "a first time." The inclusion of the crime against peace vastly enhanced the world's interest in and support for the trials at Nuremberg.[60]

Taylor's meaning is clear. Under the shocking circumstances of the time there had to be a trial. The acts the Nazis committed were so horrible that something had to be done about them. The Allies could not simply let them walk away.[61] *Ex post facto* or not, the trial was a necessary response to Hitler's infamy.

From Taylor's admissions as to *ex post facto* law it certainly appears the critics must have it right. In 1995, *The New York Times* columnist Max Frankel joined the chorus. "Don't misunderstand," Frankel wrote,

> the sins of the Nazis and their contemporary successors are unforgivable and deserve to be avenged. But in an anarchic world where there is no authority to define the crimes or individuals who lead them, those deeds are not unlawful. No one has been authorized to write such laws or to appoint judges and prosecutors and to raise the taxes to pay jailers and executioners. In the evolution of human institutions, there are major missing links. . . . The indictments were grounded in a post-war agreement among Allied diplomats who realized that they were invoking a retroactive jurisprudence that would surely be unconstitutional in an American court.[62]

In spite of the court's decision, respected names—Senator Taft and Justice Douglas, and more recently Taylor and Frankel—seem to say the trial was tainted by *ex post facto* law. However, though the concept of *ex post facto* law seems simple enough on the surface, it needs examining underneath.

To repeat, the rationale is that it is unfair to charge individuals for committing a crime when at the time they did the act they had no reason to believe what they were doing was criminal. Persons have a right to be informed in some manner that the act they are about to commit is a crime; usually it is a statute that informs them, but that is not the only way.

The Nazi leaders knew that what they were doing was criminal. They needed no warning, no statute, no treaty, to inform them that invading the rest of Europe for *Lebensraum* was criminal. On August 22, 1939, just days before invading Poland, Hitler told his top civilian officials: "I shall give a propagandistic cause for starting the war—never mind whether it be plausible or not. . . . In starting and making a war, not the right is what matters but victory."[63]

The Nazi leaders knew, before any written law existed on the subject of waging war, that they were violating the law, morally and legally. The *ex post facto* principle requires that the perpetrator believes he is acting in good faith, that he is law-abiding. No one can argue Hitler thought he was acting in good faith by his wanton invasions of foreign lands. Propaganda minister Joseph Goebbels boasted in September 1944 that he was number one on the Allied list of war criminals. The death camps, the gas chambers, the extermination of the Jews, these atrocities were all part of Hitler's plan to wage aggressive war. The Jews were in the way. He had to get rid of them to succeed. Jackson made that clear in the evidence he presented of Hitler's conferences.[64] The issue of *ex post facto* law at Nuremberg has a simple answer: Those who know that they are doing wrong when they act should be ready to accept appropriate punishment.[65]

However one views the *ex post facto* argument, it would be wrong to claim that it was unjust to try these men.[66] The defendants expected to be summarily hanged or shot for their atrocities. Instead, they got a trial and a reasonably fair one.[67]

TU QUOQUE

Jackson faced another major dilemma in drawing up rules for the admissibility of evidence: the defense of "we did it but you did it too," the so-called *tu quoque* defense. He knew the defendants would try desperately to show the Allies had also committed war crimes while fighting Hitler and Japan. Atrocities had been committed on all sides.

The defense wanted to bring out evidence that Winston Churchill had committed war crimes when, in the last months of the war, he ordered the bombing of specifically residential, working-class areas of German cities, in order to demoralize the enemy. Dresden was one of the most blatant examples. The British policy of terror bombing killed some 300,000 German civilians, and another 780,000 were seriously injured. They were not military targets.[68]

President Truman ordered the atomic bombing of Hiroshima and Nagasaki. Critics called these acts "wanton destruction of cities, towns . . . villages, . . . devastation not justified by military necessity"—to quote in part the charter's definition of war crimes.[69] In the last months of the Allied campaign in Italy, an American soldier gunned down defenseless German prisoners. He claimed he was under orders of his superior officers. This was another U.S. atrocity that the defense could bring out at trial.[70] And if the main charge in the indictment was to be the waging of aggressive war, what about Russia's invasion of Finland in 1940, or other acts of Soviet aggression against Poland and the Baltic states?

Allowing the Allies to avoid exposure of their atrocities was considered another example of victors' justice. But one can hardly imagine Truman and Churchill and Stalin being tried in the same proceeding. That is, in effect, what the defense wanted to do. It would border on the absurd to have the Allied judges at Nuremberg trying their own heads of state. Whatever Truman and Churchill did in defense of their people could never be compared with the perpetration of the Holocaust.[71]

But it was not only Allied acts during the war that worried Jackson. He was upset by what the other Allies were doing *after* the war. He complained to President Truman in a letter from Berlin, saying that the Allies

. . . have done or are doing some of the very things we are prosecuting Germans for. The French are so violating the Geneva Convention in the treatment of prisoners of war that our command is taking back prisoners sent to them [for reconstruction work]. We are prosecuting plunder and our allies are practicing it. We say aggressive war is a crime and one of our allies asserts sovereignty over the Baltic states based on no title except conquest.[72]

No wonder *tu quoque* troubled Jackson. The trial would turn into a fiasco if the defense were allowed to present such evidence. But to keep the evidence out would make the trial look all the more unfair. Jackson stood on high moral ground when he insisted on a fair trial. His position that justice must prevail would be even stronger if the Allies allowed their own war criminals to be tried.[73]

Nevertheless, Jackson decided that the *tu quoque* defense was simply unacceptable. The only question for the court was to decide whether the Nazis were guilty or not guilty, and what their punishment should be if found guilty. The Allies were not on trial.

Thus it was that the London Charter specifically limited the jurisdiction of the first International Military Tribunal (IMT) to the trial and punishment of the major war criminals of Germany—no one else. The framers of the IMT also had *tu quoque* evidence in mind when it decreed in Article 18 that "the Tribunal shall confine the Trial strictly to an expeditious hearing of the issues raised by the charges."[74]

One exception to the *tu quoque* rule caught Jackson and his colleagues by surprise. It involved the German Admiral Karl Doenitz. Doenitz, the man who succeeded Hitler for a few weeks at the end of the war, was charged with waging unrestricted submarine warfare; in particular, that he had ordered his crews not to rescue survivors of sinking Allied ships. Doenitz had a good lawyer. His name was Otto Kranzbuehler, a career officer in the German Navy. Somehow he was the only German allowed to wear his full Navy uniform in court. He used a unique ploy to get around the court's order that *tu quoque* evidence was not admissible. Five weeks before his client took the stand, Kranzbuehler wrote to Admiral Chester Nimitz, Commander of the U.S. Navy in the Pacific, asking Nimitz to respond to certain questions. He knew if he got the right answers he might save Doenitz's neck. Five weeks went by while

Kranzbuehler nervously waited for Nimitz to respond. Finally the time came for Doenitz to testify. Still no answer from Nimitz. Kranzbuehler could delay no longer and Doenitz began his testimony. The cross-examination by the British prosecutor Maxwell-Fyfe left no doubt Doenitz had ordered his men not to rescue survivors of sunken Allied ships but to leave them to their plight. It also showed Doenitz was well aware of the concentration camps and what went on there. The fact that Hitler had chosen Doenitz to succeed him as Führer showed how close Doenitz was to Hitler. Near the end of the war, it was Doenitz—not Goering, not Bormann—who was second in command. Doenitz appeared doomed. If the evidence had stopped at that point, Doenitz would likely have been found guilty of the charge and sentenced either to a long prison term or execution.

What happened next had all the elements of a movie drama. The affidavit from Admiral Nimitz arrived before the defense rested, just in time to be introduced into evidence.[75] Surely Nimitz hated the Nazis as well as anyone, but he had his honor and his loyalty to the Navy. He answered Kranzbuehler's questions forthrightly. In his affidavit Nimitz surprised the court by saying that the American Navy had also waged unrestricted submarine warfare in the Pacific. He confirmed that U.S. submarines also did not rescue survivors if such action put the American submarine in danger.

Kranzbuehler had a clever argument to counter the charge of *tu quoque* evidence. He told the judges he respected their position but this was not a case of *tu quoque:*

> I in no way wish to prove or even maintain that the American admiralty in its U-boat warfare against Japan broke international law. On the contrary, I am of the opinion that it acted strictly in accordance with international law.[76]

So he was not accusing the U.S. Navy of doing wrong. His argument was not that since the Americans committed illegal warfare, Doenitz should be excused from his wrongful acts. Instead, he argued that both navies did the right thing under international law. The court took Nimitz's affidavit into evidence over objection, and accepted Kranzbuehler's argument.

When the French judge Donnedieu de Vabres read the verdict on Doenitz, he said, "The Tribunal is of the opinion that the evidence does not establish with the certainty required that Doenitz deliberately ordered the killing of shipwrecked survivors."[77] American Judge Biddle wanted to acquit Doenitz altogether but he was outvoted. In his memoirs Biddle reveals his thoughts during deliberations:

> I thought we would look like fools if we condemned Admiral Doenitz for doing toward the end of the war what Admiral Nimitz had begun when the United States entered it . . . eventually I voted not guilty but my other colleagues thought that there was enough evidence to warrant some punishment and he was given ten years.[78]

Closely tied to the criticism for not allowing *tu quoque* evidence was the criticism of the western Allies for allowing Stalin's Soviet judges to participate at Nuremberg. German observers and even American commentators denounced the idea.[79] The Stalin regime had a reputation for ruthlessness, comparable to that of the Nazis, for inflicting atrocities on civilians. The Soviet Union was also a totalitarian regime that had launched its own acts of aggression against Poland, the Baltic States and Finland.[80] There was also the matter of the Nazi-Soviet Pact of 1939, in which the two powers agreed that Hitler would have no Soviet opposition to his aggression. With Russian judges on the bench and Russian lawyers working with the Allied prosecution team, the Nazi-Soviet Pact became a delicate matter. Jackson made only passing reference to it in his opening statement. Otherwise the Allies practically ignored it so as not to embarrass the Russians.[81]

Any attempt to bar Soviet judges and prosecutors from the trial was out of the question in light of the tremendous losses suffered by soldiers and civilians of the USSR at the hands of the Nazis. They deserved to be there. In 1945 the Russians were still our allies. At the same time the moral and legal integrity of the proceedings began to weaken when the representatives of one totalitarian regime "waxed eloquent in their condemnation of the vanquished leaders of another."[82] By the end of the trial it became apparent, both from evidence revealed in court and the reports in the press, that both the Nazi and Soviet regimes were led by ruthless dictators.

The trial presented German counsel with a monumental challenge on two fronts. First they had to adjust to unfamiliar law; second they had to try to counter overwhelming facts against their clients. For the most part, the evidence of Nazi atrocities and their intent to wage aggressive war was so strong that even the most experienced lawyer steeped in the Anglo-American legal system could not have saved them.

One of the main reasons for the ineffectiveness of German counsel was their lack of training in cross-examination because cross-examination was not part of the German trial procedure. In fact they did not handle direct examination well either.[83] In addition they had to withstand severe criticism in Europe for choosing to defend the despised leaders of the Third Reich. They knew their reputations could be forever tainted by doing so. Nevertheless, with two or three exceptions, the German lawyers generally performed in a competent, professional manner and upheld the dignity of the court. Without them the Nuremberg trials could have been a disaster. At the close of the trial the presiding judge, Lord Geoffrey Lawrence, thanked defense counsel for their dedication to the ideals of the legal profession.

CHAPTER SIX

JACKSON VS. GOERING! THE TITLE FIGHT

WHAT A BATTLE IT PROMISED TO BE. JACKSON VS. GOERING! THE PRESS billed their confrontation in the courtroom like a prizefight. After months of waiting through what had become a boring trial, the two heavyweights were about to meet. Hitler was not available to take the stand but this was the next best thing. With Hitler gone, Goering emerged as the leading man in this drama. I studied Goering carefully every time I went into the courtroom and wondered how he would stand up under vigorous cross-examination by masters of the art.

Even the judges were caught up in the anticipation. Sir Norman Birkett, the alternate British judge, wrote to a friend:

> The first really dramatic moment of this trial will come when Goering is cross-examined by the American prosecutor, Jackson. It will be a duel to the death between the representatives of all that is worthwhile in civilization and the last important surviving protagonists of all that was evil. In a sense, the whole result of the trial depends on that duel.[1]

On the afternoon of March 13, 1946, Hermann Goering entered the witness box to begin his testimony. He knew he was in an uphill battle for his life. The prosecution evidence had already shown that as minister-president of Prussia he founded the Gestapo and started the concentration camps. On July 31, 1941, it was Goering, as Hitler's second in command, who ordered Reinhard Heydrich, head of the Security Service, to start the program of exterminating the Jews.[2]

But Goering seemed confident as he took the stand. Almost immediately he began making long-winded speeches and the court, obviously trying to show its fairness, let him go on. On direct examination, Goering did well. He gave the impression of being highly intelligent and quick of wit. Unlike his co-defendants, he admitted full responsibility for his actions and made no attempt to blame them on Hitler. His complete knowledge of the National Socialist Party and of Hitler's rise to power surprised the reporters in the press gallery. He defended Hitler's *Führerprinzip* by saying, "It is the same principle as that on which the Roman Catholic Church and the government of the USSR are both based."[3] When questioned about the legality of war crimes and crimes against humanity, he quoted Winston Churchill: "In a struggle for life and death, there is in the end no legality."[4]

When Goering finished his testimony on direct examination, Janet Flanner wrote in *The New Yorker* that she had just observed "one of the best brains of the period of history when good brains are rare," and then added that it was, however, "a brain without a conscience."[5]

As the moment approached for the cross-examination, Jackson felt the pressure. He knew millions were watching him back in the States through the news media and he knew he had to do well. He had already felt disappointment at the lack of full support from the American press. The conservative magazine *Fortune* had criticized him for allowing Russian judges to participate in the trial and said he should have followed Churchill's idea for a summary hearing and then execution. The *Army and Navy Journal* had attacked him for trying to convict professional soldiers such as Keitel, Jodl, Doenitz and Raeder, simply because they were in high command in the German military.[6] So Jackson was well aware that these journals would be quick to criticize him further if he failed the test with Goering.

Goering's performance during direct examination only added to the pressure. The number two Nazi had made an impressive showing. He was not the buffoon and corrupt drug addict that many had characterized him to be, but rather a formidable adversary.

In spite of the mountain of evidence already introduced against Goering, Jackson did not take this cross-examination lightly. In his oral memoirs Jackson told how his strategy changed after watching how Goering responded to his lawyer's questions. His first plan was to start by confronting Goering with official documents signed by him and clearly identifying him as a principal in the Nazi crimes; there could be no denying he had signed them. But after the direct examination ended, Jackson decided to start instead by flattering Goering and, instead of humiliating him, encourage him to demonstrate his Nazi attitudes and, in effect, hang himself.[7]

The courtroom hushed as Jackson began. His first question revealed his strategy:

> Jackson: You are perhaps aware that you are the only living person who can expound to us the true purposes of the Nazi Party and the inner workings of its leadership?
>
> Goering: I am perfectly aware of that.[8]

Jackson continued in the same vein with a long series of questions about Nazi policies. Goering responded readily with long answers. It soon became apparent that Jackson's strategy of letting Goering hang himself was not working. Instead, Goering showed himself to be a master of European history, and Jackson's questions only allowed Goering to spout Nazi propaganda, as he did when attacking the Versailles Treaty signed by the Allies after World War I. Thereupon Jackson switched his tactics to questions that could be answered yes or no or with just a few words. The problem was that Goering wanted to explain his answers. For example, Jackson asked if people were thrown into concentration camps without any chance to defend themselves in court. Jackson wanted a yes or no answer. Goering went into a long discourse. Jackson cut him off.

> Jackson: Let's omit that. I have not asked for that. If you will just answer my question, we shall save a great deal of time. Your counsel will be permitted to bring out any explanations you want to make. You did prohibit all court review and considered it necessary to prohibit court review of the causes for taking people into what you called protective custody?
>
> Goering: That I answered very clearly, but I should like to make an explanation in connection with my answer.
>
> Jackson: Your counsel will see to that. Now, the concentration camps and the protective custody . . .[9]

Before Jackson could finish his question, the court stepped in to overrule him.

"Mr. Justice Jackson," the presiding judge Lord Lawrence said, "the tribunal thinks the witness ought to be allowed to make what explanation he thinks right in answer to this question."[10]

The court's ruling angered Jackson. As a Supreme Court justice and former trial lawyer he believed he knew the rules of cross-examination and felt the court's ruling was incorrect. Jackson may have forgotten for the moment that he was not in an American courtroom. In U.S. courts, the judge will generally sustain an objection by the cross-examiner that the answer is "beyond the scope of the question" when the witness goes far beyond his answer and expounds on peripheral matters. This is what Jackson believed Goering was doing and why he objected. It is not unfair to the witness for the court to halt such exposition because, if relevant, the witness's attorney still has an opportunity to bring out the evidence on resumption of direct examination. In fact, Jackson told Goering that his counsel could do so if he wished.

But the Nuremberg trial was not being held under American rules of evidence. This was an international court in which the principal guide for the judges was the general language in Article 19 of the London Charter, which stated:

> The Tribunal shall not be bound by technical rules of evidence. It shall adopt and apply to the greatest possible extent expeditious and non-technical procedure, and shall admit any evidence which it deems to have probative value.[11]

In any case, Jackson could do nothing but accept the court's ruling. He had to let Goering proceed though he was burning inside.[12] In his mind, the court was permitting Goering to take over the case. Jackson's biggest mistake was to lose his composure and allow it to affect his performance.

In fact, Jackson came under severe criticism from the press for his performance that day.[13] The next day was even worse. Goering continued in the same vein, providing long explanations to all questions, and Jackson became even more upset. But the court did not reprimand Goering nor try to protect Jackson.

The British alternate judge, Birkett, tried to persuade the court to take a stand and told the judges the trial was becoming unduly prolonged. Birkett was an outstanding jurist in Great Britain. Before taking the bench, he had been one of the empire's greatest criminal attorneys. He represented Wallis Simpson in the divorce that made it possible for her to marry King Edward VIII. Birkett wanted the presiding judge to tell Goering that the witness stand was not the place for political speeches but Goering went on without interruption. Birkett later called Lawrence's decision to let Goering have his way close to "outrageous."[14] The only reason I could fathom for the presiding judge's failure to step in was a desire to have the trial viewed as completely fair. When Jackson questioned Goering about Germany's planning for war, Goering denied the mobilization of the army meant preparation for a military offensive:

Jackson: You mean the preparations were not military preparations?

Goering: Those were general preparations for mobilization, such as every country makes, and not for the purpose of the occupation of the Rhineland.

Jackson: But were of a character which had to be kept entirely secret from foreign powers?

With this question Jackson left himself open to a damaging retort and Goering, seeing the opening, came back with a wisecrack:

Goering: I do not think I can recall reading beforehand the publication of the mobilization preparations of the United States.[15]

That was the last straw for Jackson. He appeared to lose his temper at being answered with sarcasm. Jackson turned to the court:

Well, I respectfully submit to the Tribunal that this witness is not being responsive. . . . It is perfectly futile to spend our time if we cannot have responsive answers to our questions. . . . This witness, it seems to me, is adopting, and has adopted, in the witness box and in the dock, an arrogant and contemptuous attitude toward the Tribunal which is giving him the trial which he never gave a living soul, nor dead ones either.[16]

Lord Lawrence, seeing the state Jackson was in, adjourned court for the day. When Jackson sat down he looked like a defeated man.

On the morning of March 20, 1945, the third day of cross-examination, Jackson was still angry, still upset by the court's failure to check Goering's harangues. He went so far as to claim that by letting Goering control the proceedings the United States was being "substantially denied its right of cross-examination."[17] Lawrence tried to calm Jackson down but Jackson persisted in criticizing the court. "It does seem to me," he said, "that this is the beginning of this trial's getting out of hand."[18]

Jackson looked defiant and bitter as he resumed cross-examination, but as the day wore on he seemed to recover his composure by using the documents signed by Goering. Jackson brought out dozens of decrees with Goering's signature that showed Goering's guilt for repressive measures against the Jews. For moments during that final day of their confrontation, Jackson showed flashes of the aggressive prosecutor the world wanted to see, luring Goering into traps from which there was no escape, letting him state his denials of doing anything criminal, and then producing the signed orders that caught the Reichsmarshal in his lies. At last, even if only for that brief period, Jackson was the master, damaging Goering's image and wiping the smug smile from his face.

Next came the cross-examination by Sir David Maxwell-Fyfe, the British prosecutor, who was thoroughly prepared. Unlike Jackson, Maxwell-Fyfe immediately gained the initiative; he began with short exact questions which left Goering no room for lengthy replies. To most of Maxwell-Fyfe's questions Goering had no choice but to agree. The prosecutor showed how Goering was involved in the infamous Auschwitz concentration camp in Poland, the use of slave labor and much of the Nazi barbarity. Documents shown to Goering revealed Goering's intentions to wage aggressive war on Holland, Belgium and Yugoslavia.[19]

Mixed critiques followed the cross-examination of Goering. The British judge Birkett wrote that Jackson "despite his great abilities and charm and his great powers of exposition had never learnt the first elements of cross-examination as it is understood in the English courts."[20]

The American judge, Francis Biddle, in a letter to his wife after the second day of cross-examination, wrote:

> Bob Jackson fell down terribly in his cross-examination of Goering today. He didn't know his case, didn't really study the document about which Goering was being cross-examined. . . . His cross-examination has on the whole been futile & weak; Goering listened to every question, takes his time, answers well. Bob doesn't listen to the answers, depends on his notes, always a sign of weakness, obviously hasn't absorbed his case. . . . [21]

Telford Taylor may have given the fairest appraisal:

> [Jackson's] questioning of Goering was not an unqualified success. . . . Replying to questions about military and diplomatic matters, [Goering] scored off his interrogator repeatedly. Nevertheless Jackson achieved the essential purpose of showing Goering in his true colors and drawing from the witness a picture of the Third Reich which abundantly supported the charges in the indictment.[22]

Many associated with the case became so obsessed with the performances of Jackson and Goering that they lost track of what the trial was all about. The significance of the cross-examination was grossly exaggerated. Yes, Jackson appeared inadequate at times; yes, he fumbled the cross-examination in many ways. And yes, he seemed humiliated by the experience, by his inability to control Goering. But what was important was the strength and quality of the evidence. What was important was the unspeakable brutality and atrocious behavior of these Nazi leaders, which was proven beyond any reasonable doubt. The exchange between Jackson and Goering had little or no effect on the verdict. I have seen many criminal trials, both as lawyer and judge, where the cross-examination of a defendant by a prosecutor was poor, where the defendant on the stand appeared to be the dominant figure, the winner of the "duel." In a close case it can make a difference. But when the evidence of guilt is overwhelming as it was at Nuremberg, then the little drama between prosecutor and defendant becomes insignificant. In the quiet of its deliberations, the trier of fact, whether judge or jury, will usually see through the prosecutor's failings and render a just verdict.

The prediction that Jackson would never recover from the experience proved incorrect. Critics claimed Jackson's skills as a cross-examiner had faded during his years on the Supreme Court. But to be fair to Jackson, there are numerous examples in the record that showed that he could still bring down a defense witness with his questions. Here is one example. After Goering left the stand, his defense attorney called the Nazi State Secretary Paul Koerner, who was a former Nazi SS *Obergruppenfuehrer*. Koerner tried to paint a picture of Goering as a friend of the Jews. The exchange follows:

Koerner: Goering always showed a different attitude to the Jewish question.

Jackson: You just tell us what it was. You may go into all details. Tell us what his attitude was.

Koerner: He always showed a moderate attitude towards the Jews.

Jackson: Such as fining them a billion Reichsmarks after the fire, right after these outrages? You know that he did that, do you not?

Koerner: Yes. The Führer demanded it.

This was typical of the way the defendants avoided personal responsibility for their evil acts. "Hitler ordered it." Then Jackson showed why Goering's witness could not be believed:

Jackson: You were interrogated at Obersalzberg, the interrogation center, on the 4th of October of last year by Dr. Kempner of our staff, were you not?

Koerner: Yes.

Jackson: And you stated in the beginning of your interrogation that you would not give any testimony against your former superior, Reichmarshal Goering, and that you regarded Goering as the last big man of the Renaissance, the last great example of a man from the Renaissance period; that he had given you the biggest job of your life and it would be unfaithful and

disloyal to give testimony against him. Is that what
you said?

Koerner: Yes, that is more or less what I said.

Jackson: And that is still your answer?

Koerner: Yes.

Jackson: No further questions.[23]

The old confidence that Jackson had at the beginning of the trial had obviously returned. His closing argument at the end of the trial, a passionate, moving speech, showed no trace of his earlier bitterness. His last
words to the court were:

> It is against such a background that these defendants now ask this Tri-
> bunal to say that they are not guilty of planning, executing, or conspir-
> ing to commit this long list of crimes and wrongs. They stand before
> the record of this trial, as bloodstained Gloucester stood by the body
> of his slain king.
>
> He begged of the widow, as they beg of you: "Say I slew them not."
>
> And the Queen replied, "Then say they were not slain. But dead
> they are."[24]
>
> If you were to say of these men that they are not guilty, it would
> be as though to say there has been no war, there are no slain, there has
> been no crime.[25]

The New Yorker called the speech a "masterpiece."[26]

CHAPTER SEVEN

JACKSON'S BREACH OF ETHICS

Many years after the trial it was revealed that an extraordinary incident had occurred during a recess in the cross-examination of Hermann Goering. The details are hard to believe to those familiar with legal procedure. When the court overruled Jackson's objections to Goering's answers, Jackson became so upset that he apparently lost his temper and sense of good judgment.[1] At recess on March 19, 1946, a seething Jackson, acting on his own and without consulting his staff, went straight into the chambers of the American judge, Francis Biddle, and gave the judge a piece of his mind. Biddle and his alternate, Judge John Parker, were the only persons present. Jackson accused Biddle of deliberately trying to thwart him. He told the judges that he "had not left the U.S. Supreme Court to come here and be sabotaged by my own countrymen. I'd better resign and go home."[2] In 1962, Biddle for the first time described the scene:

> After the recess Jackson, profoundly upset, came to see me and Parker. He said we were always ruling against him. He thought he had better resign from the trial and go home. . . . We did our best to soothe and mollify him, to stroke his ruffled feathers by telling him how much we all admired him, how well he was conducting the trial.[3]

Jackson was not satisfied, and was still in a huff when he left.

Jackson discussed the incident years later in an interview with his biographer, Eugene C. Gerhart: "I was very much annoyed. I didn't want any doubt that I was annoyed. It was really Judge Biddle who made me lose my temper. I wanted Mr. Biddle to know I was annoyed."[4]

A month later, a similar incident occurred. After Goering left the stand, Jackson returned to Washington for a period during the defense case, occupied with cases on his desk at the Supreme Court. During his absence, his Nuremberg staff complained to him that the judges were allowing the defense to introduce many irrelevant documents that were bogging down the trial. On April 9, 1946, Jackson returned to Nuremberg to criticize the court for admitting useless documents and wasting trial time. As soon as court adjourned that day, Jackson went to Biddle's secretary and demanded to see Biddle and Parker immediately. Again he entered the judge's chambers alone without informing defense counsel. Again Jackson complained that the court was always ruling against him and again he threatened to resign.

After Biddle's death many of his papers were placed for safekeeping with the Syracuse University Special Collections Research Center. The file contains this letter from Biddle to his wife in which he describes the visit:

> Bob Jackson came to see Parker and me after lunch in a very wild and uncontrolled mood. Apparently the criticism of his cross-examination of Goering has got way under his skin. He threatens to resign—this is not new; talks about refusing any printing of documents which he does not approve (irrespective apparently of what we order); says Lawrence always rules against the Americans (this is absurd); says immense trouble has been caused to the morale of his own organization by Katherine's [Biddle's wife] coming over (to which I say perhaps but that was authorized by the President). . . . Bob still contends that the defendants are engaged in active propaganda, and the Tribunal is falling into disrepute, that Thoma (Rosenberg's counsel) violated an order (he doesn't know the facts). Parker and I tried to cool him off, said we'd help to prevent unnecessary printing, and agreed that Lawrence is too easy-going. Bob certainly has it in for me. He's very bitter. He seems to me very unfair and unhappy. I am sorry for him.[5]

There is no question Jackson's *ex parte* contacts were gross ethical violations. A trial lawyer cannot simply barge into the judge's chambers without informing opposing counsel. On both these occasions Jackson went beyond merely berating Judge Biddle for the court's rulings; he threatened to resign and go home if the court failed to change its ways. This was a Supreme Court Justice with a national reputation for fairness, but these complaints to the judges make him seem petty.[6] However much this author would like to set aside Jackson's forays into Biddle's chambers out of respect for the justice, they hang as a cloud over his reputation for integrity.

Under current standards of our judicial system, if a criminal defense attorney were to discover after his client was convicted that during trial the prosecutor had privately discussed the case with the judge and in fact berated the judge for his rulings, there would be an immediate motion for a new trial. If the motion were denied, the matter would likely go up on appeal. There is no reason to believe the standards were any different in 1945.

At the time of the Nuremberg trial, Canon 3 of the American Bar Association's Canons of Professional Ethics regarding *ex parte* communications between lawyers and judges read as follows:

> A lawyer should not communicate or argue privately with the Judge as to the merits of a pending case, and he deserves rebuke and denunciation for any device or attempt to gain from a Judge special consideration or favor.[7]

That Jackson fully intended to abide by the rule is evidenced by the fact that before the trial he advised the judges not to hold sessions with only prosecutors present.

Whitney R. Harris sat beside Jackson during the cross-examination of Goering. When I asked Harris about Jackson going into Biddle's chambers without informing defense counsel, Harris said he never knew of the incident. "Jackson was an honorable man," Harris said, "I can't believe he would do such a thing." When asked about the ethics of such conduct in general, Harris said he considered it "despicable" for a prosecutor to discuss the case with the judge outside the presence of defense counsel, then or now.[8]

Jackson gained an unfair advantage over the defense every time he spoke to Judge Biddle privately about the case. He violated a basic tenet of the adversarial system he had helped to install at the trial.

What makes these breaches of conduct particularly serious is that there is no evidence defense counsel ever knew of them. If they had they would have objected immediately. Jackson's attorneys never knew of them either.[9] If they had they would have certainly counseled Jackson on the impropriety. Apparently both Jackson and Biddle kept these contacts to themselves.

When defense counsel finally discovered the contacts years later, it was too late to seek any remedy. The International Military Tribunal was dissolved. There was no court left for any motion for new trial, appeal or relief by way of writ of habeas corpus.

Roger Barrett, a thirty-year-old Chicago lawyer before entering military service, served as one of Jackson's chief aides. As the attorney in charge of all documents he was with Jackson during the pre-trial conference in London and at Jackson's side throughout the trial. After Nuremberg, Barrett went on to forge a distinguished career in Chicago as a trial lawyer. I interviewed him when he was ninety years old, enjoying semiretirement and in moderately good health. "I was shocked," Barrett said, "when years later I learned of Jackson's private contacts with the judges. Had I known I would have certainly said something to Bob about it."[10]

Jackson's defenders might say in his defense that the case was being tried in Europe and therefore American ethical standards did not apply. Under the European procedure (also called inquisitorial or continental) the prosecutor in a criminal case had a different role from that in American courts. In Europe prosecutors had a closer relationship to the judge, often sat on the same level, and private contacts with the judge were not generally considered improper. But as we have pointed out, Nuremberg was not a European trial nor was it being conducted under the inquisitorial system. Due to Jackson's urging, Nuremberg was more Anglo-American than European, more adversarial that inquisitorial. Prosecution and defense sat at the same level. Whatever the procedural system at Nuremberg, one thing is clear: pressuring the trial judge privately about the case was not and is not the American way.

Biddle must also shoulder the blame for not cutting off the conversations at the start. Under the code of judicial ethics a judge should refuse to communicate with an attorney about a case in progress unless all counsel are present.[11] Any judicial decisions by Biddle in Jackson's favor made after the improper prior contact would have made the German defense attorneys, had they known of it, suspicious of favoritism and would have created the impression in their minds that the judge was aligned with Jackson's side.

Whenever an attorney comes into a judge's chambers alone and begins to discuss a case in progress or a case pending, the judge's duty is clear. He or she should immediately admonish the attorney that the judge cannot discuss the case without opposing counsel's presence and politely (or not so politely) ask the attorney to leave. From his own memoir it is apparent that Biddle failed to follow this maxim. Instead he allowed Jackson to go on at some length without stopping him and in his own words did his best "to soothe and mollify him, to stroke his ruffled feathers."[12]

At the time of the Nuremberg trial Robert Jackson and Francis Biddle both had reputations of the highest moral and ethical character. Jackson had previously been attorney general of the United States, the highest law office in the land, and was a Supreme Court Justice for four years prior to Nuremberg. Biddle had also served as attorney general and during Roosevelt's administration was chairman of the National Labor Relations Board in Washington. An examination of their relationship and the nature of the atmosphere in the Nuremberg legal community may help explain why they committed such serious transgressions in this important case.

Jackson and Biddle had been intimate friends and colleagues in Washington for years. Jackson helped Biddle rise in the federal legal hierarchy. Since Jackson was close to President Roosevelt, the president often discussed appointments with him.[13] When Roosevelt promoted Jackson from solicitor general to attorney general, Jackson played a part in having Biddle appointed to succeed him. When Roosevelt picked Jackson for the Supreme Court, Jackson again was in Biddle's corner and Biddle succeeded Jackson as attorney general. During Biddle's term as attorney general, Jackson demonstrated their friendship by making a speech in Philadelphia honoring Biddle.[14] But at Nuremberg the relationship gradually deteriorated. Biddle often ruled against Jackson on procedural matters and this annoyed Jackson. Years later Biddle expressed his regrets that they were no longer close friends:

> We would see each other occasionally in Washington after the trial, and it was friendly, there was no tension. But we were not again intimate. He may have associated me with some disappointment he had suffered abroad. A friend said he had changed since Nürnberg. It would have been more revealing to suggest that he had there abandoned something

which his friends had loved in him. Until he died in 1954 I did not realize how much I cared for him.[15]

In Washington Jackson always held the superior position; Biddle was always a step behind. In the much-publicized Supreme Court case of *Ex Parte Quirin*[16] involving the prosecution of German saboteurs who invaded the United States in 1942 in an attempted espionage mission, Attorney General Biddle personally argued the United States position before the Supreme Court. Associate Justice Jackson joined in the unanimous opinion in the attorney general's favor. In Nuremberg, however, the roles were reversed. Now Biddle, as a judge, was the superior officer. It was Biddle's turn to judge and rule on Jackson's arguments. This switching of positions likely increased the friction between them. Biddle implied as much in a letter to his wife in the United States in which he wrote: "I have felt his opposition from the beginning, and it springs chiefly, Herb [Wechsler] thinks, from the reversal of our positions."[17]

The trouble began with Truman's appointment of Biddle as lead American judge on the Nuremberg Tribunal, which transpired as follows. President Roosevelt died on April 12, 1945. Six weeks later President Truman's secretary phoned Biddle informing him that Truman wanted his resignation as Attorney General, effective the end of June.[18] Biddle had to comply, of course, but Truman knew Biddle was hurt by the indignity of the call and wanted to make amends. So he offered Biddle the job as Nuremberg judge. The appointment rankled Jackson. Biddle was an able lawyer, but Jackson did not regard him as someone truly outstanding, the type he wanted for the most important trial in history. Jackson wanted Truman to appoint his colleague on the Supreme Court, Owen Roberts, who had just retired. Although Truman had recently appointed Jackson chief prosecutor, Jackson did not enjoy the same camaraderie with Truman as he had enjoyed with Roosevelt. He could not persuade Truman to choose Roberts.

One other factor about Biddle's appointment upset Jackson. It concerned Biddle's wife, Katherine. The Biddles were very close. When they were apart he would write her long letters revealing his deepest feelings. Francis Biddle did not want to go to Germany without her. When President Truman offered him the Nuremberg position, Biddle said he would go on one condition—that his Katherine accompany him.

But Nuremberg still lay in ruins, its urban infrastructure largely demolished. Normal conveniences and supplies were lacking. Because many major German cities were also seriously damaged, General Eisenhower ordered that Americans serving in Germany could not bring their wives or families. That order included judges, lawyers and high military officers taking part in the Nuremberg process. But apparently Truman still felt a sense of guilt for the brusque manner in which he had fired Biddle, and so he made an exception in Biddle's case[19] and gave him a special letter of authorization that would allow him to bring Katherine to Nuremberg. (But even with Truman's letter she could not join him until the spring of 1946.) The incident turned out to be a sore point with Jackson who, as chief of the American delegation in Nuremberg, was in charge of enforcing the ban on wives.[20] He did not like making exceptions. Since the military in Germany could not bring their wives it would damage morale to let the VIPs bring theirs.[21]

Jackson had to endure a few more annoyances related to Biddle before the work could begin in Nuremberg. He was eager to bring all the parties together. He had urged Biddle to come to Europe as soon as possible by taking a plane from New York. Instead, Biddle chose to travel in relaxed style on the luxurious ocean liner *Queen Elizabeth*. Jackson was furious.[22]

Then Jackson learned that Biddle was maneuvering to become president of the court. Jackson considered that unacceptable because it would increase the appearance of an American-dominated court. He had to block Biddle's plan so the court would have a more balanced international look.[23] Biddle was disappointed over being deprived of the chief judgeship but understood Jackson's reasoning. He acceded to the British judge, Lord Geoffrey Lawrence, as chief of the tribunal.

The pattern of improper communications between Jackson and Biddle began shortly after Biddle arrived in Nuremberg. Jackson committed the first of several ethical indiscretions by initiating contact with the trial judge. On October 21, 1945, he met privately with Judges Biddle and Parker and their advisers. No defense counsel were present. At that session he told the judges he wanted to run the administration of the court with his own prosecution organization instead of leaving the administrative machinery to the tribunal. What Jackson meant by running the administration included such functions as assigning counsel for the defendants and issuing summonses for defense witnesses. Jackson's staff had been in Nuremberg for six weeks by that time and had the personnel and experience to handle matters whereas the judges did not. In support of his argument Jackson improperly commented on the strength of the defense case. He told the judges he did not think defense counsel would want many witnesses since they would not dispute the fact that war crimes had been committed; their defense would be that certain defendants did not commit the crimes and they would simply lay all the blame on Hitler.

Biddle objected. He said the court needed to conduct its own administration to preserve its independence and impartiality. But Jackson responded with another statement he should never have made in that private setting. He told Biddle and Parker this was not an ordinary trial and some of the traditional rules of impartiality and independence of the tribunal had already been swept aside when the Russian General Nikitchenko switched from the role of negotiator-prosecutor at London to become a judge at Nuremberg. Biddle rejected Jackson's argument outright.[24]

Jackson's request to take over certain administrative duties may not have been so serious when considered by itself. But when he argued to Biddle outside defense counsel's presence that the defense was weak and some of the due process protections should be set aside in his favor, this clearly breached ethics and cannot be overlooked.

Jackson violated another common rule of ethics on the Saturday evening before the trial opened on Monday, November 20, 1945. That weekend Andre Vishinsky, the Soviet Union's foreign minister, visited Nuremberg, and Jackson decided to host a banquet in his honor. Only judges, prosecutors and their top assistants were invited. Defense counsel were excluded. No American prosecutor today would consider holding such a party; no American judge would consider attending. It is hard to believe Jackson did not realize how improper this gathering was in bringing judges and prosecutors together for an evening of food and liquor and friendly conversation. It seems unlikely that Jackson was unaware this behavior was wrong in light of his vast experience as a trial lawyer, solicitor general, attorney general and Supreme Court justice.

At the end of the dinner, Vishinsky stood up and lifted his glass for a toast. "Here's to the conviction and execution of all the defendants who go on trial Monday morning," he announced. The audience was stunned.

Jackson must have felt embarrassment. The U.S. alternate judge, John Parker, did not touch his lips to his glass. He leaned over to an American prosecutor and said, "I will not drink a toast to the conviction of any man . . . before I hear the evidence."[25]

Drexel Sprecher, now deceased, served as a prosecutor at Nuremberg throughout the main trial as well as the twelve trials of lesser figures that followed. During the main trial he attended several parties where only prosecutors, judges and staff were present, never defense counsel. He told me that under the circumstances no one thought they were doing anything wrong.[26]

When the trial began, the relationship between Jackson and Biddle deteriorated further. Biddle had a habit of whispering to the other judges while the court was in session. Apparently he was not aware his whispering on the bench could be heard in the courtroom. Jackson's people told him they could hear Biddle criticizing the prosecution attorneys for poor preparation. Jackson also heard that outside the courtroom Biddle was panning his staff of lawyers.[27]

In retrospect it seems that Jackson's rash decision to break with propriety and enter Biddle's chambers alone was the culmination of a series of unpleasantries between the two men before and during trial. When he felt that Biddle was ruling unfairly against him, Jackson evidently could take no more and his resentment exploded.

~

Aside from his improper contacts with Judge Biddle, Jackson arguably breached his duty as a prosecutor in another stage of trial.

The London Charter authorized the death penalty: "The Tribunal shall have the right to impose upon a defendant on conviction, death or such other punishment as shall be determined by it to be just."[28]

Many Americans, enraged by the Nazi atrocities, expected Jackson to make a strong argument for the death penalty, at least for the worst offenders. In emotional tones, the other Allied prosecutors called for the tribunal to order execution of the Nazi leaders where appropriate.

Considering the enormity of the crimes, incredible in scope and cruelty, surely this was a case that warranted the extreme penalty if there ever was one.

However, because of his own personal beliefs Jackson never asked for the death penalty. It may come as a surprise to Americans today, but never in his powerful opening or closing addresses to the court did Jackson ever mention penalty. By deliberately remaining silent, Jackson did what no prosecutor or judge should do: he allowed personal feelings to interfere with official responsibility. Jackson's client was the United States of America. He had a duty to represent his client to the best of his ability. He had a duty as well to follow the law, including the law in a case that authorized the death penalty. Some legal experts say that where there was overwhelming evidence of guilt, Jackson had a duty to argue for the death penalty; that he violated that duty when he did not and instead allowed his personal beliefs to govern his remarks. President Truman asked Jackson to be chief prosecutor. We shall never know what the feisty Truman would have said if Jackson had told him he had no intention of asking for the death penalty—no matter how strong the evidence.

Four years after returning to Washington, Jackson disclosed for the first time his personal feelings on the subject. He told his biographer, Eugene Gerhart, that he did not believe in the death penalty and therefore did not ask the court to execute the major Nazi criminals. "A completely civilized society," Jackson said, "would never impose the death penalty. . . . So long as we give the example of deliberately taking life legally as penalty for crime, we keep alive a spirit that violence is all right."[29]

Jackson made mistakes, had his faults, committed indiscretions. But as one who was there and watched his legacy grow over the years, I still think of Robert Jackson as an American hero for what he did at Nuremberg. He was never given the acclaim he deserved. More than any other person of his time he elevated the standard of justice in the world. He was the dominant force in what is still considered the greatest trial in history. His eloquent words—"To pass these defendants a poisoned chalice is to put it to our own lips as well"—will be remembered as a classic plea for justice. After the trial he was nominated for the Nobel Peace Prize and many thought he should have won it.[30] Jackson stands as a giant in the history of the law—flawed, yes, but his stature intact.

CHAPTER EIGHT

DELIBERATIONS, VERDICTS, SENTENCES

STARTING JUNE 21, 1946, FOR EXACTLY THREE MONTHS, THE FOUR judges and their four alternates deliberated the case.[1] Although only the four judges representing each ally had voting power, the alternates took active roles in the deliberations. A verdict required three votes. A tie meant acquittal. Judge Biddle later revealed that the Russians acted under instructions from Moscow and voted every defendant guilty as charged.[2]

On August 31, 1946, the tribunal heard the final pleas from the defendants. As was the custom in Europe the defendants were allowed to speak without having been sworn. On orders from Chief Justice Lawrence the speeches were short, lasting from three to twenty minutes. All defendants spoke with dignity and feeling. There were no histrionics, no shouting or disruptive scenes. Rudolf Hess, who had not testified under oath, surprised everyone by deciding to speak. Reading from a prepared statement, at first Hess spoke intelligently. He charged some witnesses with lying and said some of the affidavits were forged. Then he began to sound weird. He said a mysterious force had put the defendants in an "abnormal state of mind," which was why they acted as they did. He explained that he did not take the stand in his defense because his attorney refused to ask him the right questions. After about twenty minutes he became almost incoherent. Goering, seated nearby, tried to get him to stop but Hess went on. Lawrence told him his time was up and Hess concluded with these words: "I do not regret anything. . . . No matter what human beings may do, I shall some day stand before the judgment seat of the Eternal. I shall answer to Him and I know He will judge me innocent."[3]

When the court adjourned that day, no one knew when it would return with the judgment and verdicts.[4] As the weeks went by, tension grew over the judgment. I remember working on the *Stripes* copy desk waiting anxiously for the news of the verdicts to break. Bets were waged among the staff on who would get what. Almost no one bet on acquittal. At the Palace of Justice rumor had it that the tribunal would deliver its judgment around the middle of September 1946. The deliberations, of course, were held behind closed doors and all the disagreements and compromises were kept private. However, Judge Biddle kept copious notes and in his book, *In Brief Authority,* he reveals how minds changed and changed again during the discussions.

One of the biggest arguments arose over the first count, the charge of conspiracy to wage aggressive war. The French wanted the conspiracy count thrown out. Back in London the French had ultimately succumbed to Jackson's argument that waging aggressive war was a crime even though it had never been written down as a statute; but conspiracy was going too far. It had never been a part of international law. The French argued that the charge violated a fundamental principle of international law because it had never been defined as a crime in Europe, and to punish an individual for it was "shocking" to them.[5] Biddle was inclined to agree. Counterarguments came from the Russian judge, Nikitchenko, and the British alternate, Birkett. Nikitchenko argued for two hours that the French were not being practical; they were too theoretical, unrealistic. Just because conspiracy was a new idea in Europe was not a reason to reject it. Birkett said that to reject conspiracy would cut the heart out of the case. The Nazis had planned the war as a group and that is enough for conspiracy.[6]

Biddle finally compromised and agreed that a conspiracy definitely existed on November 5, 1937, the date of the famous Hossbach meeting between Hitler, Goering, Admiral Raeder, von Neurath and a few other military men in which plans were made for the aggressive invasion of Europe.

Another issue that occupied much of the judges' time was the charge, not against individual leaders, but against six Nazi organizations for committing war crimes. This charge became one of the major criticisms of the trial. The attempt to prosecute leading Nazi organizations with the goal of convicting hundreds of thousands of Nazi Party members was doomed from the start. Jackson wanted to root out the hard-core Nazis in Germany. Punishing a few leaders was not enough—they did not commit these horrific deeds alone. The goal was to reach the members of criminal Nazi groups such as the Gestapo, the SS and others in two stages. The first step was to prove that the organizations were criminal at the main trial. Then, at a second hearing in an "occupation court," all that would be required would be to prove that the accused Germans belonged to that organization and were therefore criminal themselves. The plan turned out to be a humiliation for the Allies because it lacked the elements of due process. Thousands, if not millions of Nazi Party members, could be convicted without having had the chance to defend themselves at the main trial where the judgment that the organization was criminal would be made.

Biddle wanted to drop the charges of belonging to a Nazi organization altogether. He wrote:

> Analyzed, this is a startling proposal to anyone taking for granted our principles of justice. You have neither the time, the patience, nor the evidence to prove the guilt of several million Nazis. You therefore prove that a group is criminal and catch all the members that way. . . . [7]

Years later Biddle wrote that the idea of convicting accused Nazis without trial was "shocking."[8]

During deliberations, the Russians became impatient with all the talk of international law and its refinements. Nikitchenko called some of the debate "ridiculous trifles" and wanted all defendants found guilty. Finally compromises were reached, and on Monday, September 30, 1946, the Nuremberg tribunal began delivering its judgment and sentences. The tribunal handed down verdicts as to each count: conspiracy to wage aggressive war, waging aggressive war, war crimes and crimes against humanity.

Of the twenty-one defendants in the dock, eighteen were found guilty of at least one count. Goering was convicted of all four counts and sentenced to death by hanging. Hess was convicted of only the first two counts and sentenced to life in prison. Three defendants—Hjalmar Schacht, Hans Fritzsche and Franz von Papen—were acquitted of all counts and released to German authorities for further proceedings.

The convictions and sentences are summarized on pp. 88–89.

	Count 1 (conspiracy)	Count 2 (waging aggressive war)	Count 3 (war crimes)	Count 4 (crimes against humanity)	Sentence
Hermann Goering Hitler's second in command	G	G	G	G	Hanging†
Rudolf Hess Deputy Führer	G	G	NG	NG	Life
Joachim von Ribbentrop Foreign Minister	G	G	G	G	Hanging
Wilhelm Keitel Chief of German Army	G	G	G	G	Hanging
Ernst Kaltenbrunner Head of Gestapo and SS	NG	O	G	G	Hanging
Alfred Rosenberg theorist of anti-Semitism	G	G	G	G	Hanging
Hans Franck Nazi governor of Poland	NG	O	G	G	Hanging
Wilhelm Frick Minister of Interior	NG	G	G	G	Hanging
Julius Streicher propagandist	NG	O	G	G	Hanging
Walther Funk Minister of Economics	NG	G	G	G	Life
Hjalmar Schacht Reichsbank President, Minister of Economics	NG	NG	O	O	Acquitted
Karl Doenitz Chief of German Navy after 1943	NG	G	G	O	10 years
Erich Raeder Chief of German Navy until 1943	G	G	G	O	Life
Baldur von Schirach Nazi Youth leader	NG	O	O	G	20 years
Fritz Sauckel head of forced labor program	NG	NG	G	G	Hanging
Alfred Jodl Chief of Army Operations	G	G	G	G	Hanging
Franz von Papen former Vice-Chancellor	NG	NG	O	O	Acquitted

	Count 1 (conspiracy)	Count 2 (waging aggressive war)	Count 3 (war crimes)	Count 4 (crimes against humanity)	Sentence
Artur Seyss-Inquart Chief of Nazi-occupied Holland	NG	G	G	G	Hanging
Albert Speer armaments minister	NG	NG	G	G	20 years
Constantin von Neurath former foreign minister	G	G	G	G	15 years
Hans Fritzsche radio broadcaster	NG	O	NG	NG	Acquitted
Martin Bormann* Hitler's secretary	NG	O	G	G	Hanging

G: Guilty
NG: Not Guilty
O: Not accused on this count
†suicide by poisoning
*convicted *in absentia*
Hangings were carried out on October 16, 1946.

Martin Bormann was never found and in April 1973 a West German court formally pronounced him dead.

Twelve men were sentenced to hang including the absent Bormann. Ten were actually hanged. One man cheated the gallows. When the guards went to Goering's cell to bring him to the scaffold set up in the gymnasium of the Palace of Justice, he was found dead. Somehow he had obtained or smuggled a cyanide pill into his cell and bit into it shortly before he was to be marched to the gallows.[9]

On the night of the executions, I was working in the newsroom of *The Stars and Stripes* at Altdorf, just a few miles away. I recall huddling over our teletype machine as word came down of each hanging. One American reporter, struggling to meet a deadline for a New York paper, filed a story that included Goering among those hanged. Later, the embarrassed editors had to call in the first editions to revise the front page.

Once again, as in the accounts of the Jackson-Goering cross-examination, there was much exaggeration in the American press over the significance of Goering's suicide; how he had outfoxed the Allies in his final move. A *New York Times* article described the German people gloating over Goering's dramatic gesture and said it "appeared to have helped these Germans forget his crimes."[10]

Those were not the Germans I have interviewed over the years. By the last days of the war, many German people had long stopped regarding Goering as a hero. They were very much aware, upon learning of the evidence at Nuremberg, of his crimes and how, with Hitler, he had led them to disaster. They did not view his suicide as a German victory. Before his suicide, Goering predicted that the Nazis on trial would be honored as heroes of the Third Reich.[11] That never happened. Travel through Germany and you will see no statues or plaques or anything else to revere the memory of the Nazi leaders.

For fifty-nine years, the question of how Goering managed to poison himself despite strictest surveillance baffled Nuremberg historians. In 1990 West and East Germany were reunited. Various documents relating to Goering's suicide, including letters written just before the event and the U.S. Army's report of its investigation, came to light. They were released to Telford Taylor, who then presented his theory on how Goering obtained the deadly cyanide pill.[12] Taylor suggests an American first lieutenant named Jack George "Tex" Wheelis, who had formed a friendship with Goering at Nuremberg, may have been the person who provided the pill to the Nazi leader.[13]

Then, in February 2005, a former U.S. Army guard assigned to watch Goering during the trial disclosed that he was the one who gave the cyanide pill to the one-time Nazi second-in-command. Herbert Lee Stivers, 78, a retired sheet metal worker from Hesperia, California, told *The Los Angeles Times* that he had kept his role in Goering's suicide a secret since 1946 because he feared being charged by the U.S. military. At the urging of his daughter, he decided to go public after learning that the statute of limitations had run out and he could no longer be prosecuted.

Stivers was a nineteen-year-old Army private with Company D of the 1st Infantry Division's 26th regiment when he was assigned guard duty at the Nuremberg trial. He was one of the white-helmeted GIs, seen in many trial photographs, who escorted the defendants in and out of the courtroom and stood at parade rest behind them during court sessions. He said he slipped Goering a pill hidden in a pen. According to the newspaper story, Stivers said he did this at the request of a German girlfriend who told him that Goering was sick and needed the medicine.

"I wasn't thinking of suicide," Stivers said. "I would have never knowingly taken something in that I thought was going to be used to help someone cheat the gallows."[14]

As we look back at the incident now, the act of suicide pales in significance to the evidence proven at trial. Goering was dead, just like the other leading Nazis who had committed suicide—Hitler, Himmler, Goebbels, Ley. They are not remembered by the German people today as martyrs or heroes, but as among the worst criminals in history.

CHAPTER NINE

THE TWELVE OTHER NUREMBERG TRIALS

THERE WERE TWELVE OTHER NUREMBERG TRIALS IMMEDIATELY following the main one. These trials were conducted not by an international court, but by the United States acting alone under an agreement by the Allies known as Allied Control Council Law No. 10. Hence these are often referred to as the "Law Number Ten" cases. Law Number Ten established a uniform legal basis in Germany for the prosecution of war criminals "other than those dealt with by the International Military Tribunal."[1] Germany was divided, and each of the four zone commanders was authorized to bring the accused Nazis held in their captivity to trial under the Nuremberg model. Although the judges were not international, all the trials were considered international law crimes trials because they were tried under international authority. The twelve other trials, often called the "American Nuremberg trials," supposedly dealt with Nazis of lesser stature than those in the main trial, but in fact they also brought to justice men who played prominent roles in the Nazi infamy and who should have been indicted in the first trial, such as Alfried Krupp and Dr. Karl Brandt.

The first Nuremberg trial was the only one held before the International Military Tribunal (IMT). The agreement hammered out by the Allies in London in the summer of 1945 originally envisaged a series of war crimes trials before the international panel. But Jackson made it clear as the main case unfolded with its myriad of problems and especially the growing hostility with the Soviet Union, that the United States did not consider itself bound to participate in more than one such trial. One reason for limiting the IMT to one trial was the complicated machinery of that tribunal—four sets of judges and prosecutors, four languages and strange trial procedures.[2] But it was obvious to all of us there in 1946 that the main reason was the difficulty of working under increasingly strained relationships with representatives of the Soviet Union.

Unlike the main trial, which had a distinctly international flavor, the twelve trials that followed in Nuremberg had only American prosecutors and judges. The other Allies—Britain, France and the Soviet Union—held trials of their own in their respective zones of occupied Germany. When the main trial was over, Jackson returned to the Supreme Court in Washington. On October 17, 1946, the day after the last Nazi convicted at the first trial was hanged, President Truman appointed General Telford Taylor as chief prosecutor of all the succeeding war crimes trials in Nuremberg.

In twelve indictments Taylor named 185 individuals as defendants. He divided them into five categories: (1) professional men such as doctors and judges; (2) industrialists and financiers; (3) SS officers and police; (4) military leaders; and (5) government ministers and cabinet members.[3] The trials adopted the original London Charter with few exceptions and followed the same trial procedure.

Many of the German lawyers who defended the twenty-two defendants before the International Military Tribunal stayed on to apply their valuable experience to the other trials. When Jackson left, most of the lawyers on his staff followed him back to the United States; the American lawyers who came over to assist Taylor were unfamiliar with the procedures, and thus at a disadvantage.[4]

All twelve trials were conducted between 1946 and 1949 and are summarized here with their popularized names.

PROFESSIONALS

The **"Medical Case"** charged twenty-three German doctors with performing ghoulish experiments on concentration camp inmates. The lead defendant was Karl Brandt, Hitler's personal physician, who held the highest medical position in the Nazi government—Reich Commissioner for Health and Sanitation. The trial began on December 9, 1946. Hitler had demanded that his doctors support his racial hatred policies with a scientific rationale called "racial hygiene," and the doctors on trial acted accordingly. Evidence showed the doctors performed such experiments as shooting victims with poison bullets to test the effect of the bullets.[5] Victims were also deprived of oxygen, injected with malaria and typhus, and forced to drink sea water for weeks, again to see how long they could live under such conditions— all this in the name of medical science.[6]

One experiment at the Dachau concentration camp was particularly revolting and challenges credibility. Victims were submerged in cold water until their body temperature was reduced to a point where they all died immediately. After a year of experimenting, the doctors had improved their technique to where the bodies could be kept alive and rewarmed with "animal heat." The experimenters would attempt to revive a male victim, almost frozen to death, by having a group of women closely surround him until he could respond by having sexual intercourse.[7]

One series of experiments was conducted for the purpose of helping the Luftwaffe determine how much its flyers could withstand at the below-zero temperatures of high altitudes to find the most effective way to treat flyers who had been badly frozen. Victims were forced into chambers that duplicated conditions at high altitudes. Many victims died as a result and others were seriously injured. In the same series of experiments the doctors forced victims to remain outdoors naked for many hours at below-freezing temperatures. Brandt and three other doctors were involved in a so-called "euthanasia" program in which elderly persons, the mentally incompetent, deformed children and others unable to work were secretly executed by lethal injections. Their relatives were told they died from natural causes.[8] The doctors involved in these experiments came from highly cultured communities. The evidence proved again that culture and education are no guarantee against uncivilized behavior. Sixteen defendants were convicted. Seven were sentenced to death including Brandt, and the rest received prison terms.

One of the most infamous of all the Nazi doctors escaped capture and prosecution. Dr. Joseph Mengele was an SS officer and physician at Auschwitz. Mengele gained lasting notoriety as the uniformed captain who headed up the "selection process" of newly arrived Jews at the camp. With riding crop in hand, he quickly decided who would go to the gas chambers and who was fit for slave labor. Known as the "Angel of Death," Mengele also performed experiments of questionable scientific value on Auschwitz inmates. After the war, avoiding capture, he hid and worked as a simple laborer under assumed names in Germany for about ten years, and then escaped to South America. He died in Brazil by accidental drowning in 1979, although this was not generally known until 1986.[9]

The **"Justice Case"** charged sixteen judges and lawyers with perverting the German judicial system by using the legal process for "enslavement and extermination on a vast scale."[10] One example involved the defendant Oswald Rothaug, presiding judge of the Nuremberg Special Court from 1937 to 1945. Rothaug had presided over the case of a Jewish man named Katzenberger who was sixty-eight years old and head of the Jewish community in Nuremberg. Katzenberger was being tried under the Nazi "racial pollution" laws for having intercourse with a young "Aryan" girl. When the question arose as to the lack of evidence, Rothaug replied: "It is sufficient for me that the swine said that a German girl had sat on his lap," and sentenced Katzenberger to death.[11] Twelve of the sixteen on trial were convicted and given prison terms.

SS OFFICERS AND POLICE OFFICIALS

The **"RuSHA Case"** charged fourteen SS officers with carrying out systematic genocide. The name "RuSHA" is an acronym for the Race and Settlement office of the SS Elite Guard *(Rasse und Seidlingsharptaunt)*. The indictment stated that the common objective of the defendants was to "safeguard the supposed superiority of Nordic blood and to exterminate and suppress all sources which might dilute or taint it."[12] The evidence showed the kidnapping of "racially valuable" children from the occupied countries so they could be "Germanized," and showed also the responsibility of the SS for extermination of Jews throughout Germany and German-occupied Europe. Five defendants were released as having already served sufficient time in custody. Eight were convicted and sentenced to various prison terms. Taylor called the sentences "excessively lenient."[13]

The most serious of all the cases was the **"Einsatzgruppen Case"** in which twenty-two SS officers were charged with having aided and abetted in the murder of two million victims. The defendants were members of SS extermination squads which had the mission to kill all Jews in the occupied areas during the invasion and occupation of the Soviet Union.

The case was rightly called the biggest murder trial in history.[14] The prosecution, headed brilliantly by twenty-seven-year-old Benjamin B. Ferencz, who was handling his first case, needed no witnesses because the captured documents told the story and thus the prosecution finished its case in two days. The evidence showed that in Russia alone the *Einsatzgruppen* slaughtered approximately one million Jews and others. The principal defendant, Otto Ohlendorf, admitted that his special group had killed some 90,000 Jews in the Ukraine and the Crimea. Ohlendorf defended the killings, even the slaughter of Jewish children, by explaining it was a "military necessity."[15] The defense took 136 trial days, claiming that the defendants were acting under superior orders. This defense was rejected on the issue of guilt but allowed on the issue of punishment.

Presiding Judge Michael Musmanno said that the evidence of homicide in this case "reaches such fantastic proportions and surpasses such credible limits that believability must be bolstered with assurance a hundred times repeated."[16] The gruesome evidence of this case brought up the same question that had haunted my mind when I entered the Nuremberg courtroom for the first time. How can men born of such a cultured society commit such horrible crimes? Judge Musmanno must have had my question in mind when he said at sentencing:

> The defendants are not untutored aborigines incapable of appreciation of the finer values of life and living. Each man at the bar has had the benefit of considerable schooling. Eight are lawyers, one a university professor, another a dental physician, still another an expert on art. One, as an opera singer, gave concerts throughout Germany before he began his tour of Russia with the *Einsatz* commanders. This group of educated and well-bred men does not even lack a former minister, self-unfrocked though he was.[17]

The judge then sentenced Ohlendorf and thirteen other defendants to death by hanging. Two others received life sentences and five received prison terms of ten to twenty years.

(I have a fond memory of Judge Musmanno. He had a lot to do with the rest of my life. I stopped in his court one day to watch the trial. When court adjourned he noticed me sitting in the back row and invited me to join him in chambers. He was curious about me and my job with *The Stars and Stripes.* We agreed that nothing in our conversation was for publication even though we never discussed the case. Judge Musmanno was a friendly, gregarious soul. He had come to Nuremberg from the Court of Common Pleas in Pennsylvania. He was tired from a long day of listening to dreadful evidence and just wanted to sit back and talk about life in the States and how it compared with conditions in Germany. His day being over, he opened a drawer in his desk, pulled out a flask of brandy, set two shot glasses between us and we had a drink together. I asked him about his career as lawyer and judge, and he answered easily. Sixty years have passed since I had that drink with Judge Musmanno in his chambers. I never saw him again but I recall his excitement about law as a career and was inspired by his passion. That evening he opened my eyes to the fascination of the law to such a degree that a few years later I entered law school at Stanford University.)

The **"Pohl Case"** was another trial involving murder and other inhumane acts by the SS, so-named because of its lead defendant, Oswald Pohl, head of the SS Economic and Administrative Department. The case charged eighteen defendants with forcing concentration camp inmates into slave labor under often extreme physical conditions. Pohl and three other defendants were sentenced to hang; eleven received prison terms ranging from ten years to life; three were found not guilty. After petitions for reconsideration were reviewed, the court reduced one death sentence to life imprisonment; three other prison terms were reduced.[18]

THE INDUSTRIALISTS

Three trials charged leading German businessmen with having financed Hitler's military schemes and participating in the Nazi slave labor program at the concentration camps.

In December 1947 the **"Krupp Case"** brought twelve executives of the giant Krupp industry to trial along with the owner, Alfried Krupp. As lead defendant, Krupp finally faced justice after avoiding prosecution in 1945. Krupp was the biggest name in German industry. In his opening statement, Taylor said, "Of all the names which have become associated with the Nuremberg trials, I suppose that none has been a household word for so many decades—indeed for half a century—as that of Krupp."[19]

The most serious charges against Krupp involved waging aggressive war. Although Krupp was neither a military officer nor a government minister, the charges were based on the theory that he had aided and abetted Hitler's wars with financial and industrial support. Unlike the orderly tone of all other Nuremberg trials, the Krupp case erupted into disorder when defense counsel objected to a ruling by the court. When the court refused to hear additional argument, all defense counsel rose and left the room in protest. The presiding judge, H. C. Anderson of the Tennessee Court of Appeal, ordered their arrest and placed them in custody for contempt of court. They were released the next day, but when one of the defense counsel refused to apologize he was banned from further participation. The defense was so upset by the court's ruling that from then on all defense counsel and defendants adopted an attitude of passive resistance and none of the defendants ever testified.[20]

Krupp's lawyer was Otto Kranzbuehler, the same man who managed to get Admiral Doenitz off with a low term in the main case. When the prosecution rested its case, Kranzbuehler and his co-counsel moved for a judgment of not guilty as to the aggressive war charges. No one expected the court's response. To the utter surprise of everyone in the courtroom the court granted the defense motion and all charges of aggressive war were dismissed against Krupp and his associates for lack of sufficient evidence. Presiding Judge Anderson explained why. In a separate opinion Anderson wrote that the charge of planning or waging aggressive war must be limited to leaders and policymakers and could not be extended to private citizens like Krupp who participate in the war effort but have little voice or control in the conduct of the war.[21] This was a new definition of the aggressive war charge. Since the Krupp case no one has been charged in any of the succeeding war crimes trials with waging or conspiring to wage aggressive war. This is because definition of the crime is so difficult that no definition has been accepted in international law. The new International Criminal Court at The Hague is still trying to figure it out. Nevertheless, Judge Anderson's opinion stands as an important guide in forming such a definition in the event anyone is ever charged with the crime in the future.

The acquittal of Alfried Krupp and all his co-defendants on the serious aggressive war charges showed once again that the Nuremberg trials were not a sham, but for the most part genuine trials with conscientious judges having the courage to render an unpopular verdict, which this one certainly was.

As to the slave labor charge against Krupp, however, the facts were simply too strong for him to deny. So he resorted to the only alternative—the defense of necessity. He claimed he was warranted in forcing thousands of victims into a state of involuntary servitude in his factories, exposing them daily to death or great bodily harm and working them in an undernourished condition because if he refused, Hitler would strip him of the plant and all his property.[22] They would all lose their jobs. The defense of necessity was, of course, rejected forthwith.

Krupp was convicted of using concentration camp inmates and prisoners of war as slave labor for his own profit and of looting property in foreign countries. He was sentenced to twelve years in prison and confiscation of all his property. His colleagues received prison terms up to twelve years. As mentioned earlier, three years later (in 1951) the Americans looked to Germany's industrial strength for support in the event of war against the Soviet Union. Krupp was released, his fortune restored and he was back in business. Between politics and justice, it was politics, as it often does, that had the upper hand.

In the "Flick Case," steel magnate Friedrich Flick and five associates were charged with seizing foreign factories, as well as using forced labor and committing other crimes against humanity. Three defendants were acquitted. Flick was sentenced to seven years in prison. The two other defendants received lesser terms.

The "I.G. Farben Case" charged twenty-three business executives with looting properties in invaded countries, responsibility for Hitler's slave labor program and helping Hitler wage aggressive war. I.G. Farben was Germany's largest chemicals and synthetics combine. When the Nazis established their notorious concentration camp at Auschwitz in Poland, Farben built a synthetic rubber plant nearby at Buna with the intent of forcing Auschwitz inmates to work for the company.

Mendel Flaster is a survivor of the Holocaust who was forced to work at the Farben plant at Buna. In 2005, sixty years after Auschwitz was liberated, I located him at his home in San Diego. He had been aware that he was making parts and tools at Buna for the Nazi military forces but he also knew that if he refused to work he would be executed.[23] Flaster was nineteen years old in December 1939 when he was taken from his home in the village of Grybow, Poland, near Cracow, and placed in a concentration camp. He was at the Auschwitz complex for two years, most of the time as a Farben factory worker under SS guards.

At Buna the inmates worked from dawn to dark with a half hour break for lunch. For breakfast he received a cup of coffee and a piece of bread. At noon the lunch consisted of a thin soup made from carrots, cabbage or turnips. Supper was usually the same, sometimes a piece of moldy bread made from flour and sawdust, and on special days a bit of margarine with the bread. Flaster was beaten many times by the SS men. One day while working at a machine cutting airplane parts, an SS guard accused him of slackening on the job. The guard struck Flaster with a stick, causing Flaster's hand to be caught in the iron-cutting machine while it was still operating. Two fingers were sliced off and after cursory medical attention he was put back to work. Flaster might have been a witness at the Farben trial on the issue of slave labor but in 1947 he could not be located.

Of the twenty-three defendants charged in the I.G. Farben case, ten were acquitted. The other thirteen were given sentences ranging from eighteen months to eight years in prison.[24] All were acquitted on the charge of waging aggressive war.

MILITARY

In the **"Hostage Case"** twelve German Army generals were indicted for war crimes committed during the invasion and occupation of Yugoslavia, Albania, Norway and Greece. The principal charge was the murder of thousands of Yugoslav and Greek civilians. Two of the defendants never came to trial. One became too ill and another committed suicide prior to arraignment. The evidence showed that the defendants had ordered the residents of certain villages slaughtered and their homes burned to the ground because of partisan action in those towns. One order directed the execution of one hundred civilian hostages for every German soldier killed by the partisans. Two defendants, Wilhelm

List and Wilhelm Kuntze, were sentenced to life in prison. Six other generals received prison terms of seven to twenty years. The court acquitted two defendants because of their lack of command authority.[25]

The judgment was bitterly criticized by the press in Europe as unduly lenient—but even more so because of its rulings upholding the right of an occupying army to shoot hostages under certain circumstances and to deny civilians such as partisans, guerrillas and resistance fighters who are not part of a nation's combat personnel the same status as combat soldiers. This meant that captured partisans would not have the rights of prisoners of war.[26] With regard to the taking of hostages the court ruled:

> An examination of the available evidence on the subject convinces us that hostages may be taken in order to guarantee the peaceful conduct of the population of occupied territories and, when certain conditions exist and the necessary preliminaries have been taken, they may, as a last resort, be shot.[27]

This ruling raised a furor and turned out to be one of the most controversial decisions of all the trials. As a result, the *U.S. Army Field Manual* now prohibits the taking of hostages.[28] With regard to prisoners taken in combat, the American judges stated:

> We think the ruling is established that a civilian who aids, abets or participates in the fighting is liable to punishment as a war criminal under the laws of war. Fighting is legitimate only for the combatant personnel of a country. It is only this group that is entitled to treatment as prisoners of war and incurs no liability beyond detention after capture or surrender.[29]

In making this distinction between combat soldiers and civilians who participate in the fighting, the American Nuremberg court, perhaps not realizing the implications at the time, was making a statement of tremendous importance to future international law. Out of this case came President Bush's decision to distinguish between prisoners of war who have definite rights, and unlawful enemy combatants who have none. The differences between the rights of prisoners of war and the rights of enemy combatants have become the center of a debate in America in the twenty-first century. Before 2004 the Bush administration took the position that those prisoners classified as un-lawful enemy combatants have no right to challenge their classification in a U.S. court. But in the landmark 2004 Supreme Court decision in *Hamdi* v. *Rumsfeld*,[30] Justice Sandra Day O'Connor overruled the administration and held that prisoners designated as enemy combatants do have a right to contest their status.

The **"High Command Case"** charged thirteen high German Army officers with ordering the mistreatment and murder of prisoners of war. Two defendants were found not guilty, two received life terms, one was discharged as having already served sufficient time, and the rest were sentenced to various prison terms.

The **"Milch Case"** was the only case that charged a single defendant. Erhard Milch, a field marshal in the Luftwaffe, was accused of exploiting slave labor and conducting inhumane medical experiments at the concentration camps. Milch was convicted of the slave labor charge, acquitted of the medical experiments count and sentenced to life in prison in 1947. But by the 1950s the political climate had changed with the onset of the cold war and Milch was pardoned and released in 1955.

GOVERNMENT MINISTERS

The longest of all the Nuremberg trials was the **"Ministries Case,"** which lasted seventeen months, almost twice as long as the main trial. The lead defendant was Ernst von Weizsacker, a career diplomat, who was charged along with twenty-one others, most of whom had served in Hitler's cabinet or as diplomatic officials. Hitler had named Weizsacker to be undersecretary of the German Foreign Office and in 1943 he became ambassador to the Vatican. Weizsacker and most of the other defendants were charged with aiding and abetting Hitler's aggressive wars. Seven defendants were charged with complicity in the murder of Allied aviators and the abuse of prisoners of war. The case was filed November 15, 1947, and sentences were not finally imposed until April 14, 1949, making it the last Nuremberg trial to conclude. The court proceedings actually ended in November 1948 but because of the large number of defendants and the voluminous evidence the court took five months to file its judgment of 833 pages. Weizsacker was popular in Europe and had many friends in other European countries. He was convicted on the aggressive war charges for aiding in the invasion and occupation of Bohemia and Monrovia in March 1939, and also convicted of complicity in deporting Jews to enslavement and extermination in concentration camps. If Weizsacker had been tried by the International Military Tribunal in 1946 there is little question his sentence would have been much more severe. But in 1949 the cold war with the Soviet Union was accelerating. He was sentenced to seven years in prison, later commuted to time served. Other defendants received sentences ranging from three years, ten months, to twenty-five years.

~

Thus the Nuremberg trials, thirteen in all, came to an end in the spring of 1949. The twelve American Nuremberg trials, although cast in the shadow of the main trial, were also important because they established lasting precedents in various fields. Several deserve special attention; the "Medical Case" for its influence on the ethics of medical practice by creating a code of conduct that governs how American doctors must treat their patients; the "Krupp Case" for its impact on big business by providing the basis for lawsuits against major American corporations for violating human rights abroad. (The Medical and Krupp cases will be treated in detail later.) The "Hostage Case" was important for its effect on the law of war and its distinction between prisoners of war and unlawful enemy combatants. This case also made a significant contribution to the Nuremberg legacy by defining the concept of universal jurisdiction. This is the principle, now accepted, that certain crimes are so serious that they are universally recognized and may be prosecuted by any country holding the perpetrator, no matter where the crime was committed.

But like the main trial, perhaps the most valuable contribution of the twelve other trials was to provide a permanent and authoritative record of the Holocaust and of the barbarism to which civilized human beings can descend.

For most of the years of the Nuremberg trials, when not in the courtroom or reporting in the field, I worked on the copydesk of *The Stars and Stripes*. I could sense the gradual waning of interest in the trials between 1945 and 1949. As the years passed, stories coming out of the Nuremberg courtroom began to retreat to the back pages. Many times a story that would have been considered newsworthy in 1945 or 1946 would not be printed at all. There was an ominous factor that contributed to this drop of interest in the trial. The specter of the cold war hung over the city. The possibility of major hostilities breaking out between the western Allies and the Soviet Union became more real each year and the relationship that had started out on fairly decent terms in 1945 gradually turned tense and unfriendly. The situation was reflected in the division between American and Soviet personnel working at the court. I wanted to make contact with the Soviet journalists but I was told that they were under orders not to socialize with the Americans. This was certainly a drastic change from that day in May 1945 when we celebrated the meeting of our armies on the banks of the Enns River in Austria.

Also reflecting the changing tide of events were the light sentences and early release of those Nazi defendants sentenced to long terms. Several leading Nazis managed to evade prosecution altogether. Even Telford Taylor, a fierce prosecutor to the end, admitted to being disheartened by the American public's lack of interest.[31]

When the war ended in Europe the United States declared a policy of "denazification" in the occupation of Germany. The idea was to destroy the Nazi Party and remove all active supporters of Nazism from important public or private jobs. The denazification policy was initiated on the assumption that Jackson and Taylor could not possibly prosecute all the major or sub-major Nazis at Nuremberg.[32]

The goal of prosecuting millions of Nazis was turned over to German officials but the task was so enormous that it simply collapsed of its own weight. The German courts charged 3.5 million persons with being major offenders, offenders, lesser offenders or followers, but only 9,600 ever spent any time in custody. By 1949 all but 300 had been freed.[33] Many American officials regarded the denazification proceedings as a whitewash.[34]

By 1950 Taylor was lecturing in the classroom at Columbia Law School. Robert Jackson was back on his seat at the Supreme Court, beginning to think about the momentous case that lay ahead—the challenge to racial segregation in America's public schools. Francis Biddle went back to his homes in Washington and Cape Cod for a life of writing and lecturing, never again to return to the bench. All had played major roles in reshaping international law.

Some precedents of the trials were immediately obvious. The waging of aggressive war is "the supreme international crime." Mass atrocities against human beings belonging to a particular racial or religious group are "crimes against humanity." No ruthless dictator of the future could ever again claim that such crimes had no precedent or that they were *ex post facto* law.

The trials were a triumph of good over evil. Despite the flaws, the trials set a standard for fair trial and respect for the rights of the accused. They showed how the rule of law could be used to punish, if not prevent, the atrocities of war. They showed how low a highly civilized nation could sink under oppressive leadership. They exposed the true nature of the Holocaust, which might never have been revealed with such specificity had there been no trial. They established that it is no defense for alleged war criminals to claim they were only obeying orders. They prevented the Nazi leaders from becoming martyrs, which might have happened had there been no trial. They showed that four great nations with different languages, different legal systems and trial procedures, different customs and policies, could join together to conduct an international trial. They sent a message to warlike or sadistic leaders to be wary or they too might be brought to justice. As President Truman said:

> I have no hesitancy in declaring that the historic precedent set at Nuremberg abundantly justifies the expenditure of effort, prodigious though it was. This precedent becomes basic in the international law of the future.[35]

The Nuremberg principles were immediately accepted by the people of West Germany and for the most part incorporated into their basic law, the Bonn Constitution. In 1948 the United Nations recognized the Nuremberg principles when the General Assembly adopted the Universal Declaration of Human Rights.

But there were other precedents that were not so manifest at the time, other precedents that were still to take form. In 1949, when the last trial was over, it was still too early to judge the true worth of the Nuremberg trials. The world would have to wait another half century to make a fair assessment. The world would have to wait for the Nuremberg legacy.

CHAPTER TEN

VICTIMS' RIGHTS

AT ALL THE NUREMBERG TRIALS, THE COURT'S ATTENTION WAS focused on the defendants and their punishment. No mention was made of help for the victims. No part of the sentencing process attempted to alleviate the suffering of the millions ravaged by Nazi cruelty.

The question has arisen over the years as to whether the Nuremberg courts could have done more to recognize victims' rights. Consider first the arrangement of the four charges of the indictment in the first trial. Jackson chose at the outset to make two charges the main ones: count one, the conspiracy to wage aggressive war, and count two, the waging of aggressive war. The fourth and last charge covered the crimes against humanity. Jackson wanted to make Hitler's launching of war the lynchpin of the entire case, and he had good reasons for doing so. But this approach may have made the extermination of Jews, Romany (Gypsies) and others appear to be less important. After all, what most enraged the world about Hitler was the record of the Nazis' wanton atrocities—the death camps, the gas chambers, the murder and torture of millions of human beings. Americans demanded retribution and wanted the Nazi leaders to be held accountable for their horrific acts. If there were to be a trial, that trial should reveal and document the scope of the Nazi bestiality. The American people in 1946 were more incensed with the "crimes against humanity" than whether Hitler had waged an illegal war. Some experts argue that the Holocaust should have been the foremost charge.[1] When Jackson decided to make aggressive war the main charge, the Holocaust seemed to be relegated to second place.[2] Indeed, at first glance it seems to belittle the tragedy of the Holocaust by implying that waging an aggressive war was the worst and first of Germany's multiple crimes.

In defense of Jackson it must be pointed out that it was Hitler's illegal invasion of Poland in September 1939 that led to the extermination

of Polish Jews in the gas chambers. If the Nazis had confined their mis-
deeds within German borders, the full enormity of the Holocaust, and
the Nuremberg trial as well, might never have taken place. Over ninety
percent of the Jews murdered in the concentration camps had lived in
countries that Hitler invaded illegally.[3] These facts give logic to Jackson's
mindset. Hitler's military plans came first. The result of Hitler's plans, so
Jackson reasoned, was the Holocaust.

After the war, the survivors of the Holocaust were in tremendous
need, not only for material goods and money but more importantly for
relief for their physical and mental suffering. Thousands of survivors
were being treated in hospitals. Many did not survive and among those
who did, thousands experienced deep depression. The London Charter
gave no guidance for aiding victims except for a provision giving the
court the right to order return of stolen property taken by any convicted
person.[4] That was the sole reference to reparations.

No precedent existed in international law for giving aid to victims.
The court's jurisdiction covered only the defendants being tried. The
German people were not defendants and the court could not order
them to make reparations. This was not, as Jackson pointed out in his
opening statement, a trial of Germany or the German people. The court
could not order the German government to do anything, because no
such government existed. In showing the world what the Nazis did, in
exposing the gruesome realities of the Holocaust and in punishing the
guilty, the Nuremberg trial was one small step to assuage the victims'
pain. Whatever other help the victims received was left for another time.

Almost fifty years after Nuremberg, the next international war
crimes court was established in May 1993 by the United Nations—the
tribunal for the former Yugoslavia. The Yugoslav tribunal was created
to investigate and prosecute widespread violations of humanitarian
law within the territory of the former Yugoslavia, especially in Bosnia,
Herzegovina and Kosovo. Its statute represented an advancement,
however small, in considering the victims of war crimes.

The Yugoslavia statute, besides following the Nuremberg precedent
in empowering the court to order the return of stolen property, took an
additional step toward aiding the victims and recognizing their rights:
"The work of the International Tribunal shall be carried out without
prejudice to the right of victims to seek, through appropriate means,

compensation for damages incurred as a result of violations of international humanitarian law."[5] This was not a giant step. It merely gave victims the right to seek help through other means. But it was a step forward in that it gave official sanction to the rights of victims. The phrase "compensation for damages" could be interpreted to include damages for medical and psychological suffering. The statute creating the International Criminal Tribunal for Rwanda in 1998 contained similar language. The Yugoslavia and Rwanda tribunals made strides but, like Nuremberg, did not include any specific provision for rehabilitation of victims.

The giant step finally came in 2002 in the Statute of the International Criminal Court established at The Hague in the Netherlands. In embracing the new statute, 191 nations recognized the rights of war crimes victims. That statute for the very first time entitled war crimes victims and their families to go to the court to seek reparations for the sufferings inflicted on them.[6] Article 79 of the ICC statute provides for establishing a trust fund for "the benefit of victims of crimes within the jurisdiction of the Court and of the families of such victims."[7] The court will act as a mediator between the convicted persons, the court and the victims with respect to any damage, loss or injury to the victims.[8] The Victims Trust Fund of the ICC will provide direct reparations to victims to help them rebuild their lives. The fund will accept donations from governments, organizations and individuals.[9] This innovative provision of the ICC is an excellent example of what Nuremberg might have done had it made victims' rights a top priority.

In criticizing Nuremberg for its oversight of victims, however, one must remember that victims' rights is a relatively new concept in jurisprudence. In 1946 American courts paid little attention to the rights of persons injured by criminal acts. Attention was focused on the defendant's rights. Restitution such as the return of stolen property was always ordered, as it was in the London Charter, but it was not until the 1990s that victims' rights became a major public issue. American judges were urged to give greater attention to rehabilitating the victim both mentally and physically. If a victim suffered from depression or frightening memories as a result of a crime, and was undergoing therapy to heal the mental injury, the judge could order the defendant to pay for the therapy. If a victim or victim's family wished to appear in court at time of sentencing and (without being sworn in) describe their feelings about the crime and the

criminal, the judge was obligated to permit it. There was a public percep-
tion that for too long the rights of defendants had been protected while
victims' rights were ignored. A new program in California, for example,
created a fund to help the injured victims of crime.[10]

~

In 1951, West German Chancellor Konrad Adenauer met with Jewish
leader Nahum Goldman on the subject of reparations. That meeting
started the ball rolling, although it took several decades for the German
government to acknowledge responsibility for the Holocaust and attempt to make amends to the victims. Billions of dollars in reparations
were paid out, memorials were erected, apologies were offered.

Lou Dunst is an eighty-year-old Holocaust survivor who lives in San
Diego. Lou was a prisoner of the death camps of Auschwitz and Mauthausen. In 2006 Lou told me that for the last ten years he has been re-
ceiving about $1,000 every three months from the German government.
Before 1995 he had to prove that he was either a pauper or disabled in
order to be eligible to receive reparations. That requirement no longer
applies. Now the only requirement is that every year Lou has to send in a
notarized statement that he is still alive. "Sixty-two years ago they wanted
me dead," Lou says, "Now they want proof I'm alive."[11]

In July 2006, at a time when restitution funds for Holocaust survivors were dwindling, the Hungarian government offered a new program for relatives of victims of the Holocaust. Family members could
receive $1,800 for each parent and $900 for each sibling who died in a
Nazi death camp with the complicity of Hungarian collaborators. Hundreds in Los Angeles crowded Jewish social service agencies to apply.[12]

Much would have been added to Nuremberg's reputation for fairness and compassion if it had initiated a reparations program at the beginning and created a victims' trust fund similar to the one established
later by the International Criminal Court. Money would have poured in
from all over the world in 1946, when emotional reaction to the Holocaust was at its highest, if the Nuremberg Tribunal had thought to set up
such a fund to help the survivors.

A view of Nuremberg at the time of the trials, having been devastated by Allied bombing raids. Some 20,000 bodies lay beaneath the ruins. (Telford Taylor Papers/Arthur W. Diamond Law Library/Columbia University. Photographer: Charles Alexander)

The Nazi doctors and assistants seated in the defendants' dock with counsel in the foreground. The defendants were charged with conducting inhumane experiments. (Telford Taylor Papers/Arthur W. Diamond Law Library/Columbia University.)

During the doctors' trial, prosecution witness Dr. Leo Alexander explains injuries sustained by a Holocaust survivor. (Telford Taylor Papers/Arthur W. Diamond Law Library/Columbia University.)

Karl Brandt, Hitler's physician and chief of the Nazi medical program, makes his final plea at the trial of the Nazi doctors. (Telford Taylor Papers/Arthur W. Diamond Law Library/Columbia University.)

*Fourteen Nazi judges await their trial for perverting the German judicial system
and collaborating in the worst excesses of the Hitler regime.* (Telford Taylor Papers/
Arthur W. Diamond Law Library/Columbia University.)

*Hjalmar Schacht,
Minister of Economics
in Hitler's cabinet, was
one of three defendants
acquitted in the trial of
the major Nazi war
criminals.* (Telford
Taylor Papers/
Arthur W. Diamond
Law Library/Co-
lumbia University.)

Industrialist Alfried Krupp, Hitler's biggest financial supporter, addresses the court at his trial for aiding crimes against humanity. Krupp was convicted but served only three years in prison. (Telford Taylor Papers/Arthur W. Diamond Law Library/Columbia University.)

Telford Taylor was part of Robert Jackson's prosecution team at the main trial. Later Taylor became chief prosecutor of the ensuing twelve trials. (Telford Taylor Papers/Arthur W. Diamond Law Library/Columbia University.)

The four judges and the four alternate judges as they were seated at the International Military Tribunal. The four alternates took part in all sessions of the trial but did not have voting power. Pictured from left to right: Lt. Col. A. F. Volchkov (alternate) and Maj. Gen. I. T. Nikitchenko (USSR); Justice Norman Birkett (alternate) and Tribunal President Lord Justice Geoffrey Lawrence (Great Britain); Francis Biddle and Judge John J. Parker (alternate) (U.S.); Prof. Donnedieu de Vabres and Robert Falco (alternate) (France). (Photo Credit: U.S. Holocaust Memorial Museum, courtesy of Tade Wolfe. Photographer: Charles Alexander) (The views or opinions expressed in this book, and the context in which the images are used, do not necessarily reflect the views or policy of, nor imply approval or endorsement by, The United States Holocaust Memorial Museum)

A view of the dead at the Gunskirchen concentration camp near Lambach, Austria, in May 1945. The author was attached to troops of the 5th Infantry Regiment, 71st Infantry Division, when they overran the camp. (Photo Credit: U.S. Holocaust Memorial Museum, courtesy of John Cunnington) (The views or opinions expressed in this book, and the context in which the images are used, do not necessarily reflect the views or policy of, nor imply approval or endorsement by, The United States Holocaust Memorial Museum)

Robert H. Jackson delivers the opening statement before the International Military Tribunal at the Palace of Justice in Nuremberg on November 21, 1945. (With permission of photographer Ray D'Addario and the Robert H. Jackson Center)

The author, back to camera, at work in "the slot" at The Stars and Stripes *newsdesk in 1948 in Pfingstadt, Germany. Ehrenfreund served as both reporter and copy editor for the American newspaper during the Nuremberg trials. (Author's personal file)*

American troops of the 71st Infantry Division meet the Russians near Steyr, Austria, in May 1945. Such camaraderie faded with the emergence of the Cold War. (Courtesy of 71st Infantry Division [WWII], U.S. Army)

PART TWO

THE NATURE OF THE LEGACY

CHAPTER ELEVEN

___

TOKYO: ALMOST A NUREMBERG COPY

ANY EXAMINATION OF THE NUREMBERG LEGACY MUST BEGIN WITH the Tokyo trial of the Japanese war leaders because it relied so heavily on Nuremberg precedent. In May 1946, while the first Nuremberg trial was winding down, General Douglas MacArthur and the Allied powers in the South Pacific brought to trial Hideki Tojo, prime minister of Japan at the time of Pearl Harbor, and twenty-six other Japanese defendants. No one could have foreseen that, unlike Nuremberg, which lasted a little over ten months, the Tokyo trial would last two and a half years, from May 1946 into November 1948. A total of 417 witnesses testified in person and an additional 719 submitted affidavits or depositions.[1] The defendants faced the International Military Tribunal for the Far East, the so-called Tokyo War Crimes Trial. Except for one important deviation, the ghosts of Nuremberg were there to ensure that the trial followed the Nuremberg script.

The Tokyo Charter differed from the London Charter in only a few respects. Nuremberg used a large plain courtroom, with no special trappings, hurriedly reconstructed following extensive devastation from British air strikes. But the Tokyo setting was more like a theater, with klieg lights and cameras, altogether more of a Hollywood atmosphere.[2]

Another difference pertained to the number of judges. At Nuremberg, eight judges sat on the high bench facing the twenty-one men in the defendants' dock. Only four judges had actual voting power; the other four were alternates in case a judge fell ill or could not continue for other reasons. Each of the four active judges represented one of the four Allied powers: Great Britain, France, the Soviet Union and the United States.

By contrast the Tokyo Tribunal consisted of eleven justices, each representing a nation that had participated in bringing down Imperial Japan. The bench consisted of one judge each from Australia, Canada,

China, France, Great Britain, India, the Netherlands, New Zealand, the Philippines, the Soviet Union and the United States.

Nuremberg had four prosecution teams, each with a chief prosecutor, representing the four major powers. Tokyo had only one chief prosecutor with his aides. Robert Jackson's counterpart at Tokyo was Joseph B. Keenan of the United States, Chief of Counsel by order of President Harry Truman. Since Keenan was an American, the trial appeared to have a definite American bias.

The charges at the Tokyo trial did not include the Nanjing (Nanking) massacre of 1937. The Nanking massacre, commonly called "The Rape of Nanking," was a series of atrocities committed by Japanese troops after Nanking, China, fell to the Imperial Japanese Army. That infamous incident was treated separately in another proceeding, conducted at Nanking.

Behind the scenes of the Tokyo trial, the man in charge was General Douglas MacArthur, Supreme Commander of the Allied Powers in Japan. Unlike the London Charter, which arose out of a long hot summer of negotiations, MacArthur simply issued an executive decree making the Tokyo Charter the law of the case. No discussion took place among the nations as to the nature of the charter; no wrangling as to whether the charges of conspiracy to wage aggressive war, and the actual waging of aggressive war, were *ex post facto* law; no talk of who should sit in the defendants' box or what the charges should be; and apparently no consultation as to whether Emperor Hirohito who, unlike Hitler, was still very much alive, should be charged.

MacArthur decreed that Hirohito would not be prosecuted. The other nations represented were consulted only after the charter was made public.[3] One might have expected that MacArthur's unilateral action would have prompted protest among the Allies but "both the United States and its Allies seem to have relied heavily on the precedent set by the Nuremberg Charter"[4] and as a result there was little friction. MacArthur appointed Sir William Webb of Australia as president of the Tokyo Tribunal. The trial was conducted in two languages, English and Japanese, instead of four, as at Nuremberg.

All such differences were secondary compared to what really counted: the law, the charges, the trial procedure. In these important aspects Tokyo was true to Nuremberg. The Tokyo Charter closely resembled the London Charter and the court adopted international law as interpreted at Nuremberg. Like Nuremberg, the court held the Tokyo Charter was not *ex post facto* law but an expression of international law then in existence and generally accepted. Like Nuremberg again, Tokyo ruled it was not unjust to punish an aggressor but rather that it would be unjust not to do so. The court conceded that it could not define "aggressive war," but added that Japan's unprovoked attacks could not be characterized as anything but aggression.

Despite all the criticisms leveled at the Nuremberg process, especially the application of *ex post facto* law and the use of victors' justice, Tokyo simply ignored those criticisms, made little attempt to profit by Nuremberg's mistakes and merely followed suit. Perhaps it all happened too quickly for General MacArthur and the others to step back and assess the Nuremberg experience. If they had, the Tokyo trial might have been a vast improvement. In his critique, *Victors' Justice,* Professor Richard H. Minear asked:

> Did the victors offer the vanquished a "poisoned chalice"? . . . If the trial was indeed a travesty, was it so because a lofty aim was pursued by ignoble means?[5]

The charges in Tokyo were the same as in Nuremberg. Nuremberg placed the first two counts, conspiracy to wage aggressive war and the actual waging of aggressive war, under the heading of "crimes against peace." Tokyo did the same.

Nuremberg called the third count war crimes, referring to traditional violations of the laws and customs of war. Tokyo did likewise. Nuremberg made crimes against humanity the fourth and last count and Tokyo did also, ignoring the criticism of Nuremberg that by relegating this count to last place, it was showing, to some survivors at least, disrespect for the victims of the atrocities.[6]

With regard to the defense of obedience to superior orders, the Tokyo Charter held to the same principle as Nuremberg: acting pursuant to an order of one's superior is not a defense on the issue of guilt, but if the defendant is found guilty the defense may be used in mitigation of punishment.[7]

Tokyo adopted the Nuremberg principle that individual leaders (except for Hirohito) would be personally responsible for their war crimes, still a major change in international law. The same rights of due process granted at Nuremberg were granted at Tokyo, including the right to counsel, the right to examine witnesses and the right to apply for production of all prosecution documents, names and statements of prosecution witnesses.

The Tokyo trial procedure and conduct also followed that of Nuremberg, including the rule that the tribunal would not be bound by technical rules of evidence such as certain types of hearsay.[8] The Tokyo trial also provided for the death penalty. Following Nuremberg's path, the Tokyo judges represented the Japanese enemies. No Japanese judge sat on the bench. The charge of victors' justice would haunt the Tokyo trial just as it has haunted Nuremberg to this day.

Finally, the Tokyo Charter was also remarkable for carefully making the same omissions of major rights as at Nuremberg. Tokyo provided for no right of appeal, no rule against double jeopardy. At Nuremberg the defendants had fifteen days to appeal to the Allied Control Council. At Tokyo the convicted defendants were granted ten days to appeal to General MacArthur. In both cases all pleas for clemency or appeal were denied outright. It was as if MacArthur's staff simply took the London Charter off the shelf, changed a few words here and there, and gave it a new label: the Tokyo Charter.

But in one major aspect, the Tokyo trial broke with Nuremberg precedent. One of Jackson's most praiseworthy principles was the rule of law: that no one was above the law, no matter how high his or her status, and that every head of state must be held personally accountable for his crimes. A serious departure from Nuremberg principle at Tokyo was the failure of the Allies to indict Emperor Hirohito. On the initial list of Japanese war criminals to be tried, the emperor's name led all the rest. Many of the participating nations wanted him prosecuted, including Great Britain, the Soviet Union, Australia, China and New Zealand. But MacArthur vehemently opposed indicting the emperor and so Hirohito remained a free man. It was a decision based on pragmatism rather than principle; a decision by a militarist, not a jurist. In his *Reminiscences*, MacArthur explained his position:

Realizing the tragic consequences that would follow from such unjust action, I had stoutly resisted such efforts. When Washington seemed to be veering toward the British point of view, I had advised that I would need at least one million reinforcements should such action be taken. I believed that if the emperor was indicted, and perhaps hanged as a war criminal, military government would have to be instituted throughout all Japan, and guerrilla warfare would probably break out. The emperor's name had then been stricken from the list.[9]

The President of the Court, Sir William Webb, did not like MacArthur's ruling. He showed his displeasure by implying that he wanted to commute all the death sentences to life imprisonment because, referring to Hirohito, "the leader in the crime, although available for trial, had been granted immunity."[10] And so it was that the primary leaders of Germany and Japan were never brought to trial—Hitler because he was dead, Hirohito because he was so deeply revered by his people that his trial, according to MacArthur, would have caused more warfare. At the close of the Tokyo trial, American newspapers denounced the tribunal for not having tried the Emperor.[11]

The Hirohito incident revealed another major difference between the two trials. General Eisenhower, Supreme Commander of Allied forces in Europe, played little part in the Nuremberg trial. MacArthur, on the other hand, exerted strong control in Tokyo, even deciding the nature of the charter, appointing the justices, using his influence to keep the "leader of the crime" off the indictment and controlling appeals. He was not the judge in the courtroom but in his way he presided over the trial.

Seven defendants were hanged on December 23, 1948, including Tojo Hideki, prime minister at the time of Pearl Harbor, and Hirota Koki, foreign minister from 1933 to 1936 and prime minister from 1936 to 1937. Eighteen men were sentenced to prison terms, sixteen for life. Six of those men died in prison. The other twelve were released after serving only part of their sentences. Shigemitsu Mamoru, who had been foreign minister during 1943 and 1944, received the shortest sentence, seven years. But Shigemitsu's career as a Japanese leader was not over. After serving four years and seven months in prison, he was released on November 21, 1950, and returned to his political career. In 1954 he became foreign minister again and while in office negotiated the release of all the remaining men who had been convicted in the Tokyo trial.[12]

Unlike Nuremberg, where three of the twenty-two defendants were acquitted, Tokyo acquitted no one. Despite serious disagreements among the Tokyo justices, a majority found all defendants guilty of most of the charges filed against them. One justice found all defendants innocent; another found all defendants not guilty by reason of defective procedure; and another found five defendants innocent. They were all overruled by the majority.

Eight of the eleven justices at Tokyo supported the tribunal's judgment fully. Three dissented. The strongest dissent came from Justice Radhabinod Pal of India. He had several grounds: conspiracy had not been proved; rules of evidence were biased in favor of the prosecution; aggressive war was not a crime; and the judgments were illegal because they were based on *ex post facto* grounds. Pal held that "crimes against peace," that is, conspiracy to wage aggressive war and actually waging aggressive war, did not exist before 1945 and the Allies had no right to rewrite international law. Such a trial, he said, was only a "sham employment of the legal process" out of a thirst for revenge. The trial of the Japanese leaders, he said, "does not correspond to any idea of justice."[13]

In rejecting the idea that aggressive war was a crime, Justice Pal said that the Kellogg-Briand Pact of 1928, upon which Jackson had relied so heavily at Nuremberg, had no effect on "international life."[14] It does not tax the imagination to speculate how Justice Pal would have ruled at Nuremberg.

Justice B. V. A. Röling of the Netherlands agreed with Justice Pal that "crimes against peace" did not exist before 1945 but held that the Allies had the right to make new rules. He added that the rule against using *ex post facto* law was not a principle of justice but only a rule of policy.[15]

Some defendants lodged an appeal with the U.S. Supreme Court for a writ of *habeas corpus*. Justice Jackson, who by that time was back from Nuremberg and on his old seat at the high court, voted to hear preliminary arguments but the court decided it had no jurisdiction to hear the matter because the Tokyo Tribunal was not a tribunal of the United States.[16] Jackson abstained.

In a concurring opinion Justice William Douglas attacked the Tokyo trial as a political forum, not a judicial action. Referring to General MacArthur's supervision of the trial, Douglas said the Tokyo court "responded to the will of the Supreme Commander . . . [and] took its law from the creator and did not act as a free and independent tribunal." The Tokyo proceeding, he said, was "solely an instrument of political power."[17]

The Tokyo trial was criticized as having been poorly conducted and badly organized.[18] Owen Cunningham, an American lawyer on the Japanese defense team, sat through both the Nuremberg and Tokyo trials. He reported that Tokyo was a disappointment in comparison. For example, at Nuremberg, Cunningham said, each judge had a microphone in front of him and participated directly in the trial. This was not so at Tokyo. "It is difficult," Cunningham said, "to try a case before judges who you have never even heard utter a word."[19]

Nuremberg's impact on the Tokyo proceedings was so complete that it even influenced the behavior of the Japanese defendants. At Nuremberg, except for Goering's suicide and the temporary boycott by defense counsel in the Krupp trial, the Nazi defendants and their lawyers cooperated in making the trial a success. There were no outbursts to be quelled; no one had to be shackled; all objections were made in a professional manner (unlike the behavior seen years later in the war crimes trials of the Yugoslav president Slobodan Milosevic and the Iraq dictator Saddam Hussein, to be discussed later). The Japanese defendants had obviously informed themselves as to how the Nuremberg defendants conducted themselves, and acted likewise.

Although the Tokyo trial faced many of the same criticisms as Nuremberg such as the claim of victors' justice and the use of *ex post facto* law, public reaction to the two trials was decidedly different. When Jackson won his crusade for a fair trial at the London Conference, America took over, for a time at least, the moral leadership of the world. Americans generally hailed Nuremberg for setting a new standard of global justice. No such reaction followed the Tokyo trial. One reason Tokyo never rose to Nuremberg's reputation as an international model of fair trial was due to the difference in the rank of the chief U.S. prosecutor. Joseph B. Keenan, chief prosecutor at Tokyo, had a much lower position than Jackson, a Supreme Court justice. But the main

reasons for Tokyo's lesser reputation were General MacArthur's domi-
nance of the trial and the failure to prosecute Emperor Hirohito, the
man who approved the bombing of Pearl Harbor, and whom the presiding judge, William Webb, called "the leader of the crime."[20]

One expert's review fiercely criticizes the Tokyo trial as unjust. "We
have examined lofty motives and base motives," writes Professor Minear.
"We have found its foundation in international law to be shaky. We have
seen that its process was seriously flawed."[21]

But Nuremberg proved that a flawed trial is better than none. In following the positive elements of the Nuremberg precedent, the Tokyo
trial was still worthwhile. Even if the process had many defects, it was
better to hold the trial, make the record and make the attempt at justice,
than to execute the Japanese leaders out of hand.

CHAPTER TWELVE

A GIANT STEP FOR HUMAN RIGHTS

NUREMBERG ADVANCED THE MODERN HUMAN RIGHTS MOVEMENT by A single master stroke: the invention of "crimes against humanity." The specific language in Article 6 of the charter reads as follows:

> The following acts, or any of them, are crimes coming within the jurisdiction of the Tribunal for which there shall be individual responsibility: . . .
>
> (c) Crimes Against Humanity: namely, murder, extermination, enslavement, deportation, and other inhuman acts committed against any civilian population, before or during the war, or persecutions on political, racial or religious grounds in execution of or in connection with any crime within the jurisdiction of the Tribunal, whether or not in violation of the domestic law of the country where perpetrated.

These words created sanctions for violations of human rights on an international scale. With this single paragraph, the Nuremberg Tribunal declared that citizens of the world had rights never before recognized, rights that prevail even against heads of state and top officials of a nation. Many consider this Nuremberg's greatest achievement.[1]

Of course, the idea that human beings have rights began long before 1945 and the Nuremberg Charter. Human rights developed early in world history. The Ten Commandments, for example, in proscribing certain conduct, also had the effect of positing rights for those who would be affected by such conduct. "Thou shalt not steal" meant that persons had a right to be protected against theft. Likewise, the Magna Carta of 1215, by subtracting power from the king, expanded the rights of the nobles. The Magna Carta, predecessor of our due process clauses, provided that:

No Freeman shall be taken, or imprisoned, or be disseized of his Free-hold, or Liberties, or Free Customs, or be outlawed, or exiled or any otherwise destroyed; nor will we pass upon him, nor condemn him, but by lawful Judgment of his peers, or by the Law of the Land. We will sell to no man, we will not deny or defer to any man either Justice or Right.[2]

The works of philosophers such as John Locke, Thomas Hobbes and others influenced by the ideas of the Enlightenment further advanced the cause of human rights. In 1679 the invention of the writ of *habeas corpus* in England conferred one of the most valuable rights of all: when arrested, to have that custody questioned, examined and determined as to its legality.

When Thomas Jefferson wrote that "all men are created equal, that they are endowed by their creator with certain unalienable rights," he drew upon notions of universal human rights as a basis for the Declaration of Independence. His message applied to the American people and their relationship to their new government. Jefferson's famous description of such rights and the ten amendments (Bill of Rights) to the Constitution became the true soul of the American nation. In democratic countries, there exists an unwritten contract whereby the government is obliged to protect the rights of its citizens.

In countries like Nazi Germany no such social compact existed. The state was supreme; the individual counted for nothing. Before Nuremberg, people living in totalitarian states had no protection against torture, murder and enslavement by their governments. They could be subjected to the worst of conditions—slave labor, starvation, all kinds of abuse—and had nowhere to turn for help. Repressive heads of state could breach human rights on a massive scale and get away with it because they were shielded by the tradition of sovereign immunity. There was no international recognition of human rights. Within a nation's borders, human rights could be extensively violated and there was no recourse. No worldwide collective effort with teeth, no international court with powers of enforcement was in place to respond to the injustices inflicted by a sovereign government upon its own citizens. By creating "crimes against humanity," Nuremberg extended Jefferson's idea to the people of all nations—a major step in advancing the cause of civilization.

Whether Robert Jackson realized it or not, what he did by winning his fight for such a trial was for the first time to give authority and force to the concept of international human rights.[3] He thereby created a new relationship between individuals living in oppressed societies and their governments, a new way of perceiving each other. For the first time, victims of inhumane acts committed by their leaders had a right to voice their grievances. And a new body created at the same time as the London Charter—the United Nations—promised to listen.

The new concept did not happen in a vacuum. Forty-one years earlier, President Theodore Roosevelt may have been the first American head of state to voice the idea of crimes against humanity. In his State of the Union address in 1904, Roosevelt said:

> . . . there are occasional crimes committed on so vast a scale and of such peculiar horror as to make us doubt whether it is our manifest duty to endeavor at least to show our disapproval of the deed and our sympathy with those who have suffered by it.[4]

Robert Jackson thought that the charges of waging aggressive war were the most important features of his prosecution. In this respect history has proven him wrong. It was the fourth count, the crimes against humanity, that has dominated every war crimes trial since Nuremberg and which has become the heart of the Nuremberg legacy. By charging this count of crimes against humanity, Nuremberg sent a caution to dictators everywhere that if they mistreat their people they can be brought to justice before an international court.

Just weeks after the sentences were carried out following the first Nuremberg trial, the United Nations General Assembly endorsed the Nuremberg principles on December 14, 1946. This was followed in 1948 by the American Declaration of the Rights and Duties of Man. Six months later, the United Nations adopted the Universal Declaration of Human Rights, which is often called the Bill of Rights for the World, a fitting description. These were all products of the Nuremberg precedent, all declarations by the international community that Nuremberg law was alive.

Eleanor Roosevelt predicted that the universal declaration "might well become the international Magna Carta of mankind."[5] Along with the spirit of Nuremberg, the Universal Declaration came to represent the human rights ideal in the twentieth and twenty-first centuries. Nuremberg and the universal declaration inspired the incorporation of the human rights concept into constitutions and conventions around the world. There followed a flurry of reactions: in 1948 the U.N. Convention on the Prevention of the Crime of Genocide;[6] in 1949 the Geneva Convention (No. III) Relative to the Treatment of Prisoners of War; and the Geneva Convention (No. IV) Relative to the Protection of Civilian Persons in Time of War.[7] The Geneva Conventions were four international treaties with the aim of ensuring protection for prisoners, wounded soldiers and civilians in wartime, signed at Geneva, Switzerland in 1949 by fifty-eight nations and later by most nations of the world. They derived from the organization known today as the International Committee of the Red Cross (ICRC), founded by a Swiss philanthropist, Jean Henri Dunant, in the mid-nineteenth century.

The Universal Declaration of Human Rights was adopted December 10, 1948. On August 12, 1949, the United States signed the Geneva Convention (No. III) Relative to the Treatment of Prisoners of War. As we shall see, it was this Geneva Convention which prompted the Supreme Court in 2006 to strike down President Bush's plan to deny open trials to prisoners at Guantanamo Bay, a major victory for human rights.[8] Those two documents—the universal declaration and the Geneva Convention (No. III)—became the high-water marks of a movement that was ushered in at Nuremberg. The universal declaration called upon all its signatory nations to grant to all people a cluster of rights including the right to be protected from genocide, the right to a fair trial and the right to be free from unreasonable interference with one's choice of religion or associates.

There can be no question that these declarations and conventions flowed from the Nuremberg experience. When the London Charter recognized the concept of "crimes against humanity," a new law was born protecting human rights for all people. From that moment on, despotic leaders of nations were put on notice that they could be charged, convicted and punished for committing atrocities, including even those within their national borders and against their own people.[9] They could no longer shield themselves from prosecution through the claim of sovereign immunity.

These declarations and conventions between 1946 and 1949 showed great promise of a new world order for the protection of human rights. There arose at the time a spirit of optimism, particularly among oppressed peoples and human rights activists, that Nuremberg and its progeny would surely improve the human condition. However, for the next fifty years practically nothing was done to prosecute war criminals for crimes against humanity or for anything else. In fact, after the last Nuremberg defendant was sentenced in 1949, not a single torturer or murderer was put in prison by an international court until 1997, when a Bosnian Serb pub owner named Dusko Tadic began serving his sentence. Tadic was tried by the International Criminal Tribunal for Yugoslavia (ICTY), the first international war crimes trial since Nuremberg.

Certainly the world had its share of inhumanity during that half century: Stalin's purges; China's cultural revolution; Cambodia's killing fields; Argentina's "dirty war"; massacres in East Timor; and the gassing of the Kurds by Saddam Hussein. Millions were murdered by their own governments.[10] But little was done. The Nuremberg precedent was virtually ignored.

In 1998, U.N. Human Rights Commissioner Mary Robinson, commenting on the absence of war crimes prosecution, said:

> Count up the results of fifty years of human rights mechanisms, thirty years of multibillion dollar development programmes and endless high-level rhetoric and the general impact is quite under-whelming. . . . this is a failure of implementation on a scale that shames us all.[11]

For decades following World War II, military leaders were rarely held accountable for their aggressions. Because of their political power they could instigate war and commit crimes against humanity, and if later held to account, could then retreat to live undisturbed lives in places like Panama, South America and the south of France.[12] Or, as in the case of Africa, continue their brutal ways in a culture of impunity. Interest in the Nuremberg trial declined. In the late 1960s and with the escalation of the Vietnam War, the law and concepts established at Nuremberg took on new significance. Questions arose as to America's possible criminal responsibility. Analogies were drawn between the

American action in Vietnam and that of Hitler's invasion of other European countries. In 1970 Telford Taylor asked:

> What are the Nuremberg legal principles, and what is their meaning today as applied to American involvement in Vietnam? When we sent hundreds of thousands of troops to South Vietnam, bombed North Vietnam, and moved into Cambodia, were our national leaders as guilty of launching a war of aggression as were Hitler and his generals when they invaded Poland, or Belgium, or Greece, or other countries that were way-stations on the Nazi march of conquest?[13]

Taylor's comments raised questions as to whether U.S. leaders could be guilty of war crimes.[14] But those questions soon subsided and no trials were held or even seriously considered. For decades before the 1990s many historians felt that Nuremberg had little meaning in international law. No war crimes trials took place nor did courts claim war crimes jurisdiction.[15] As mentioned earlier, relationships between the United States and the Soviet Union—so friendly on that day in May of 1945 when my division drank and celebrated with Soviet soldiers in Austria—continued to deteriorate after the trial. Countries like Czechoslovakia, Poland and Hungary became Soviet satellites. Attention shifted from war crimes trials to the looming possibility of war between the Western Allies and the Soviet Union. There were steps taken to rebuild the West German Army in case German military power would be needed to help the West.[16]

The absence of any prosecutions for war crimes for such a long time raised doubts as to whether the Nuremberg trial would ever have any genuine and lasting value to world law. In 1987, another respected historian, David Luban, said, "If one of the aims of the Nuremberg Trial was to burn the history of Nazism into the memory of mankind, we must conclude that it failed."[17]

～

Then in 1991 events took place that brought an end to the long drought in protecting human rights. War broke out in the former Yugoslavia. The Serbs were accused of committing atrocities amounting to genocide in Bosnia. News of concentration camps operated by Serbia in Bosnia-

Herzegovina with conditions similar to the Nazi camps of World War II spread across the world. The city of Sarajevo was reported to be a "bloody killing ground."[18] At first the United States appeared satisfied to leave the handling of the Yugoslav conflict to the European community. But soon the continuing reports of atrocities became too serious to ignore.

In 1993, almost half a century after the last Nuremberg trial, the international community acted for the first time to protect human rights by initiating prosecutions at The Hague for crimes against humanity committed in the former Yugoslavia. There followed human rights trials of the former Yugoslavia president, Slobodan Milosevic, since deceased, and his henchmen. There have also been trials for crimes against humanity in Rwanda, Sierra Leone, East Timor and Iraq (Saddam Hussein), all heavily influenced by Nuremberg precedent.

~

In any story of human rights since Nuremberg, the case of General Augusto Pinochet, former dictator of Chile, deserves special mention. General Pinochet seized power in Chile on September 11, 1973, in a bloody military coup that ousted the legally elected Marxist government of President Salvador Allende. Thousands of Allende supporters were rounded up, tortured and killed. Santiago's main soccer stadium was filled with political prisoners who were either shot or forced into exile. For the next seventeen years Pinochet terrorized his opponents with a mockery of human rights.

During Pinochet's rule more than 3,200 persons were either executed or disappeared (known in Spanish as *los desaparecidos*).[19] His name became a byword for government terror and abuse of human rights. Pinochet stepped down from the presidency in 1989 but remained commander of the army until 1998 when he was made senator for life. At the same time the Chilean government granted him lifelong immunity from criminal prosecution. Then a surprising event occurred, fortunate for the cause of human rights and the Nuremberg legacy.

Pinochet no doubt assumed that his grant of immunity would protect him outside Chile. In 1999 he made the mistake of traveling to London, apparently unaware that as an outgrowth of Nuremberg a new legal concept known as universal jurisdiction was in effect. Universal

jurisdiction meant that any nation had the power to arrest and prosecute someone for crimes against humanity no matter where the offense
occurred, so long as the crime was serious enough to merit such action.
Spain wanted to try Pinochet for his crimes of torture while dictator of
Chile, and asked the British to arrest him and extradite him to Spain for
prosecution under the rule of universal jurisdiction. The British took
Pinochet into custody, but bitter debate ensued in the House of Lords
as to whether they should honor Spain's request. The Pinochet case became the most important test of international human rights law since
Nuremberg itself. Robert Jackson first propounded the idea at Nuremberg that crimes against humanity were so grave that they overrode any
claim of sovereign immunity. The Pinochet case before the House of
Lords in London symbolized the problem of whether Jackson's doctrine stood up at the end of the twentieth century.[20]

But a question arose in the House of Lords that had not been considered before—whether the crimes against humanity had to occur during wartime in order to warrant prosecution. All previous trials for that
crime were held to prosecute conduct committed during war. Chile was
not at war with any nation when Pinochet ordered the atrocities. Re-
sponding to the question, the House of Lords ruled that although
Nuremberg had concerned itself only with crimes against humanity
committed in wartime, events in the world had removed the requirement of a wartime connection,[21] and so Pinochet was ordered to be extradited to Spain.

The ruling was a triumph for the Nuremberg legacy. Once again the
voice of Nuremberg made itself heard. No one is above the law. Government leaders are individually accountable for the persecution of their
subjects.

The trend was clear: the term "war crimes" was no longer adequate
for violations of human rights. From then on, the term was replaced by
"crimes against humanity." The British ruling against Pinochet was
based on three points: (1) the Nuremberg Principle that no one is above
the law; (2) genocidal crimes do not require a state of war in order to be
prosecuted; and (3) Spain had jurisdiction to prosecute Pinochet even
though his crimes occurred across the sea in Chile.

Despite the British order of extradition to Spain, Pinochet's health
was so poor that he was returned to his native Chile instead. Back in

Chile, he was stripped of his immunity and indicted on human rights charges. Prosecutors there had every intention of putting him on trial despite his age of ninety-one. However, on December 10, 2006, Pinochet died of heart failure. Many Chileans celebrated his death with demonstrations in the streets, but human rights supporters bemoaned the fact that although he was one of the most villainous figures of modern times, he was never brought to justice.

~

The Pinochet case was a modern example of the Nuremberg precedent that individuals—not states or governments—will be held personally responsible for their crimes against humanity. In 1945 Robert Jackson came to the London pre-trial conference knowing that he could not protect people from abuse of their rights unless he could find a way to reach those responsible through the courts. Before Nuremberg the doctrine of sovereign immunity had always prevailed in international law. This doctrine meant that a head of state and his chief assistants could not be prosecuted for crimes committed in the name of their government. If you must blame someone, they said, blame the government, not me. Nuremberg put an end to that idea.[22]

Jackson had pressed hard for individual responsibility. That was the only way he could get to Goering, Hess, von Ribbentrop and the rest. So Jackson did what had never been done before: he pulled aside the curtain of sovereign immunity to reach individuals for their war crimes. The idea was revolutionary in international law—a complete break with the past.[23]

Not everyone agreed with Jackson on this point. At the London Conference the French delegate took an opposite view and said that individuals could not be held responsible for acts of state. He said, "It may be a crime to launch a war of aggression on the part of a state that does so, but that does not imply the commission of criminal acts by individual people who have launched a war."[24] When the British envoy insisted on individual accountability, the Frenchman replied: "We think that would be morally and politically desirable but that is not international law."[25]

When the matter came up at trial, all judges agreed with Jackson's theory of individual responsibility. Whether or not precedent existed before Nuremberg on the concept of individual responsibility, it exists now. If there was no precedent, Nuremberg created it for all future war crimes trials. After Nuremberg no war crimes defendant could argue otherwise.[26]

Years later, in his memoirs Judge Biddle wrote:

> Curiously enough, little attention was paid to what was perhaps the Tribunal's most important pronouncement. I refer to the finding that individuals and not merely nations should be held responsible. . . . In making responsibility an individual matter . . . the Tribunal rejected the fiction of national irresponsibility.[27]

This new concept of individual accountability is gaining strength in the twenty-first century, a strongpoint in the Nuremberg legacy. Pinochet is a recent example. When he left Chile for London, he did not reckon with the Nuremberg precedent and the possibility that he could be arrested and indicted outside his own country based on the fruits of that precedent. Pinochet's story is bound to make other former heads of state take heed.

CHAPTER THIRTEEN

THE IMPACT ON RACIAL PREJUDICE

IN 1946, WHILE THE NUREMBERG TRIAL WAS IN FULL SWING, EXPOSING the terrible consequences of racial prejudice in Germany, an American lawyer named Thurgood Marshall was arguing an important case about racial prejudice before the United States Supreme Court. In the American South black children could not go to school with white children. Black people could not sit with whites on public busses or use the same public restrooms. Even American soldiers of different race, both fighting in the same uniform and for the same cause, were segregated. Many Americans may not be aware that the Nuremberg trials, by producing the deplorable evidence of the Holocaust, were an important factor in changing for the better that disgraceful period in our history. In the case of *Morgan* v. *Virginia* Marshall, then a lawyer for the National Association for the Advancement of Colored People (NAACP), was asking the court to strike down the practice of racial segregation on public busses as unconstitutional. He told the Supreme Court that Americans had not spilled their blood in a war against "the apostles of racism" in Germany only to permit racism to flourish at home. Marshall won his case. The Supreme Court voted seven to one in his favor, and segregation on public busses was officially ended. Years later Thurgood Marshall became the first African American to be appointed a justice of the Supreme Court.

When we were in battle in Europe we thought we were risking our lives not only to destroy Hitler's regime but also to put an end to the awful racism that prevailed under the Nazis. The twisted irony of America's discrimination against African Americans at home while they were fighting abroad to protect America and stop Hitler's racism, did not strike home to me until a personal incident at the end of the war.

It was the autumn of 1945. The war was over in Europe and Japan. I was still in the service, a first lieutenant in an artillery battery of the 71st Infantry Division, stationed in the American occupation zone near Nuremberg. Most of the soldiers were waiting to go home. I was also awaiting military discharge so I could start my civilian job with the European edition of *The Stars and Stripes.*

Because there was little incentive for training, our division commander sought other ways to keep the troops occupied. He organized a football league among units of the division and had uniforms sent over from the States. As no one else seemed willing to take on the job of coach, I volunteered and was assigned to the division artillery team. Thanks to an excellent quarterback and a big front line, we had a good team. We won most of our games and earned the right to play for the division championship in, of all places, Nuremberg Stadium. The winning team would get a free trip to the French Riviera and a week's leave.

As we took to the field to warm up, I looked up at the stands. They were practically empty now. Only a few GIs huddled in the bitter cold around the benches on opposite sides. But this was no ordinary football field. Images came into my mind of newsreels I had seen of this stadium, showing Hitler shouting to a hundred thousand Nazis raising their arms in the "Heil Hitler!" salute while he spouted his theories of the master race. I felt shaken by the memory. Those gigantic Nazi rallies were one of the reasons Jackson chose this city for the trial.

As the teams lined up for the kickoff my quarterback suddenly called time from the field. He came running over to me on the sidelines. It was over sixty years ago but I remember our exchange.

"What's the matter?" I asked.

"Listen, Coach, I have to talk to you."

"What is it?"

"I'm sorry, Coach." He hesitated. The reserves gathered around us. They looked as confused as I was. He looked at them and shook his head.

"Come on," I said. "What is it?"

"I'm sorry, Coach, but I can't play this game."

"Why? You injured?"

"No, but—"

He put his head down and shook his head and was silent. I could see he was struggling to get it out. The referee came over and told me to get on with the game. I took the quarterback's arm and led him away from the others so we could talk in private. "You won't like this," he said. "But I can't do it."

"This is crazy," I said. "What's troubling you?" I was already beginning to feel wretched over the thought of playing this game without him. I was not prepared to put in anyone in his place. Finally he gave me the reason.

"There's a guy out there on their team. A nigger. I can't play with niggers." I looked out at the other players. I hadn't noticed it initially during the warm-ups. Despite segregation, there was indeed a black player on the other team. "So what!" I said. I was growing angry. "What if he is?" Then it all came out. The quarterback came from a small town in Georgia where he had played on his high school football team. He had fought in combat against the Nazis and distinguished himself as a good soldier. But he was a racist through and through. His parents prohibited him from playing with black people.

I pleaded with him. This was our big game, the championship game. The black player was an American just like all of us. Any change in the lineup would jeopardize our chance to go to the Riviera.

"I know," he answered. "But I just can't do it. You don't understand how it is in the South." The referee came over again and blew his whistle. He threatened to penalize us if we didn't get started. I begged for five more minutes. Reluctantly he allowed it.

I turned back to the young man beside me and began a speech. I had to struggle to keep control but I was livid. What were we over here fighting for anyway? Some of his buddies died in this war. That black player was an American who risked his life for our country. Think of the American flag, the American Constitution. What do they stand for? They stand for a country that respects people of all colors and creeds. We fought this war so people could be free from prejudice, free from being despised and abused because of their race or religion. To refuse to play based on his own racial prejudice was to say it all doesn't mean anything; that Americans who died here died for nothing. Did he want to be like Hitler and his followers and go on hating people because of their race and the color of their skin?

"Look up there," I said and pointed to a platform at the top of the stands. "That's where Hitler stood when he made his Nazi speeches, spouting his Nazi propaganda of racial hatred. Right here is where a hundred thousand Nazis raised their arms and shouted 'Heil Hitler!' If you refuse to play in this game based on racial prejudice it would be like saying he was right and all those Nazis were right and his spirit would be up there smiling and cheering your decision."

I can't remember all I said. At times I got out of control and perhaps too emotional. But I know it was a good speech, maybe the best speech I ever made because I was speaking from the heart.

Gradually he began to listen earnestly. I could tell he was softening.

"If I play," he said, "I want you to make me a promise."

"What's that?"

"Promise me you will never let this get out to my hometown or my parents."

I asked him what would happen if it did get out.

"My dad would beat me. He would beat me real bad."

We played the game. We didn't get to the Riviera. Our quarterback played a good game but the black player turned out to be the star. We lost 20 to 14. Across town the Nuremberg trial, which would show the world the terrible consequences of racial prejudice, was just getting started.

With the Nuremberg trial and its exposure of the Holocaust came a series of reactions against racism. President Truman took the first major step in 1948 when he ordered the end of segregation in the armed forces. The United Nations followed in the same year with its Universal Declaration of Human Rights, an outgrowth of Nuremberg. The preamble to the Universal Declaration began:

> Whereas recognition of the inherent dignity and of the equal and inalienable rights of all members of the human family is the foundation of freedom, justice and peace in the world . . . [1]

Almost immediately upon resuming his seat on the Supreme Court, Robert Jackson began to show signs of how much the evidence he saw at the trial had impressed him. In 1949 he dissented in the case of *Brinegar v. United States*[2] involving the search and seizure by federal agents of property in an automobile. In his dissenting opinion Jackson seemed to recall scenes of how Hitler's storm troopers had invaded Jewish homes and businesses without warrants and seized Jewish property without cause. He warned his colleagues on the bench that "uncontrolled search and seizure is one of the first and most effective weapons in the arsenal of every arbitrary government" and that deprivation of the right to be protected against such invasions is "so effective in cowing a population, crushing the spirit of the individual and putting terror in every heart."[3] More than any other justice of his time Jackson knew the danger of a government committed to persecution.[4] Upon his return from Germany, he stressed to his law clerks (one of whom was the late Chief Justice William Rehnquist) the importance of the Tenth Amendment of the Bill of Rights, which retained police power in the individual states rather than placing such power in the hands of a central government. The amendment was important because it prevented the national government from crushing civil liberties in a single stroke as Hitler had done with his ruthless decrees against the Jews and other minority groups.[5] Long after Jackson was gone from the bench, justices of the Supreme Court continued to cite Jackson's reference to his Nuremberg experience in the *Brinegar* case.[6] Justice Rehnquist, recalling his days as Jackson's law clerk, wrote that the experience as chief United States prosecutor at Nuremberg "had a profound effect on his [Jackson's] judicial philosophy."[7]

But it was not until 1954, eight years after his return from Germany, that the Nuremberg experience had its greatest and most important impact on Robert Jackson and his role on the Supreme Court. In an opinion that shook American society to its core, the Supreme Court unanimously ruled in *Brown* v. *Board of Education* that racial segregation in the public schools was unconstitutional.[8] The idea that black children could not go to school with white children was officially cast out.

There can be no question that Jackson's experience at Nuremberg was linked to that momentous decision. In a memorandum dated February 15, 1954, before the opinion in *Brown* v. *Board of Education* was handed down, Jackson sketched out his thoughts on the desegregation of the public schools: "the awful consequences of racial prejudice revealed by . . . the Nazi regime," Jackson wrote, had caused "a revulsion against the kind of racial feeling" that had led to the Japanese American relocation cases during the second World War.[9]

That Jackson's vote to outlaw segregation in the schools was influenced by the evidence at Nuremberg is also evident in a letter he sent to Professor Charles Fairman of Stanford University. The letter was dated March 13, 1950, at a time when Jackson was pondering his approach to the constitutional question involved in the case. Jackson told Fairman he wished to draw on the professor's research and informed judgment on constitutional law. Jackson said in part:

> You and I have seen the terrible consequences of racial hatred in Germany. We can have no sympathy with racial conceits which underlie segregation policies. . . . I am clear that I would support the constitutionality of almost any Congressional Act that prohibited segregation in education. . . . [10]

Before Nuremberg and its exposure of the Holocaust, anti-Semitism was also widespread in America. Nuremberg shocked the world by gathering together and putting on public display the evidence of Hitler's atrocities against the Jews. As a consequence even many anti-Semites, shaken by the news, did not wish to be seen as approving of or encouraging the horrible racial policies of the Nazis. This is not to say that the evidence of the Holocaust crushed the forces of anti-Semitism. It did not. Strong feelings against Jews continued to exist. But the Nuremberg evidence did change the way non-Jews look at Jews.[11] Alan Dershowitz, a leading exponent of Jewish human rights, said:

> When America joined the war against Hitler, overt anti-Semitism lost its popular audience, and has never regained it. Blatant animosity to Jews was discredited to a great extent among Americans by the horrors of the Holocaust. . . . [12]

Jonathan D. Sarna, professor of American Jewish History at Brandeis University and author of *American Judaism*, wrote this note to me on the subject:

There is no doubt whatsoever that anti-Semitism declined in the post-war era. . . . It is hard to know how much the Nuremberg trials contributed to this decline, which was obviously also furthered by other factors. It will, nevertheless, be important to have your book remind us that the trials, and the publicity surrounding them, played an important role in changing America for the better.[13]

James Sheehan, professor of German history at Stanford University, says there is no question that the news of the Holocaust as disclosed at Nuremberg made anti-Semitism no longer respectable in America.[14] Ellen Ash Peters, former chief justice of the Connecticut Supreme Court, gave this eloquent description of how the Nuremberg record has affected racial discrimination and the protection of human rights in America:

Nuremberg produced a graphic record of the horrors of the systematic torture and genocide undertaken by that regime. Widespread dissemination of that appalling record increased American sensitivity to racial injustice and to other endemic infringements of civil liberties. Pictures of southern sheriffs attacking peaceful civil rights protestors bear an undeniable resemblance to pictures of SS troopers attacking Jews. Whatever Justice Jackson took from his experience at Nuremberg, the force of these analogies, even if unspoken, became a factor in awakening the judiciary in the 1960s to the need for enhanced protection of human rights in the United States. I am persuaded that the legacy of Nuremberg contributed to the heightening of judicial concern, under the leadership of Chief Justice Earl Warren, for the protection against intentional segregation and against abuses arising out of coerced confessions and illegal invasions of the personal privacy of criminal defendants.[15]

CHAPTER FOURTEEN

THE IMPORTANCE OF THE RECORD

SOON ALL SURVIVORS OF THE HOLOCAUST WILL BE GONE. THEN THERE will be no human voice to tell the authentic story of the genocide, the tortures, the gas chambers, the concentration camps. Of course, there will be many writings, tape recordings, pictures and films from various sources. Hollywood director Steven Spielberg has recorded more than 52,000 Holocaust survivor testimonies for his Shoah Foundation. These are all valuable records. But the one authentic, official record is the trial transcript. Nuremberg exposed the nature of the Holocaust with evidence carefully screened in a formalized procedure by a distinguished international court. Witnesses were examined and cross-examined by attorneys on both sides over months of trial. Experienced judges scrutinized the testimony and determined its admissibility in evidence. The result was a record of irrefutable proof that lives on as the Nuremberg legacy.

The legacy of the trial record shows how critical that one moment was when Jackson persuaded the Allies at London to have a full and fair trial. Had Jackson lost that debate, had the Allies decided to choose summary execution, there would be no record, no legal precedent, no Nuremberg legacy. The most important thing about Nuremberg is that it created the record of Nazi aggression and inhumanity, and set precedents that changed the world.

Consider, for example, over sixty years of peace and democracy in Germany, the longest such period in modern times for that nation. The Nuremberg record can be linked to that success. Certainly one can cite a number of reasons for Germany's postwar development, one of them being U.S. support. But it was the record of the Nuremberg trial that eventually opened Germany's eyes to what the Nazis did, and thereby became a major factor in the country's rapid strides to democracy.[1] By awakening the German people to the past, Nuremberg influenced their political conduct in the future.[2]

The first example of this influence came during the formation of the new German Federal Republic immediately after World War II. In drafting the basic law of the new government, the incoming German leaders showed that the evidence of the Holocaust produced at Nuremberg had a definite effect on them. The debates leading up to new law on such subjects as capital punishment and fair trials for criminal defendants demonstrated how much Germans wanted the kind of system of justice that was so lacking in Hitler's time.[3] In German courts after the Nuremberg trial one could observe an admirable sense of decency and humanity in even the most ordinary criminal courts. Nuremberg can take a share of the credit for that change.[4]

The young men and women of Germany today know what the Holocaust was about and what the Nazis did. They may not be aware of the source of their information but much of what they see and read today of the Holocaust and the Hitler regime comes from the records gathered for the Nuremberg trials. Today's German youth do not try to keep the Holocaust out of their consciousness as so many Germans did for twenty or more years after the war. Germans of the twenty-first century know what happened during the Nazi era because they learn about it in school, through television programs and various other sources. And this information did not arise from rumor or questionable hearsay. Nor was it a fabrication of the Jewish people, as suggested by some anti-Semitic factions. Proof of the Holocaust was based on the record of solid evidence produced at the trial. Many of the German people I encountered during six years of working in Germany as a journalist after World War II claimed surprise when the record unfolded at Nuremberg. But whether they were truly surprised or not, the more the Germans heard about what the Nazis did, the more they came to renounce Nazism and seek democracy.[5]

Holocaust survivors treasure the Nuremberg record because it is the best corroboration of their stories. Earlier I mentioned my friend, Lou Dunst, who is a Holocaust survivor. At 80 years of age, Lou still travels all over the country to tell his story. He is an effective, articulate speaker and in constant demand from community groups of all kinds.

Lou describes how in 1944 at the age of seventeen the Nazis took him from his home in Czechoslovakia along with his mother, father, brother and sister. They and many other Jews were packed into a rail-road car that had very little ventilation. They rode in these boxcars for several days and nights without water or food or toilet facilities. There were men and women, elderly people, children of all ages, and mothers holding their babies. Finally they came to a stop in Poland at a town called Auschwitz. By this time some of the occupants had already died or were dying from starvation or suffocation. The living were marched to a camp. Lou noticed chimney stacks with dark smoke coming out. He did not know until later the smoke came from the burning bodies of those who had recently been executed in the gas chambers.

He walked at first with his mother and his family. They were forced to run past soldiers with whips, and barking dogs bit at their legs if they didn't move fast enough. A Nazi officer and his military staff stood at the entrance waiting for the Jews. Lou later learned the officer was the infamous Dr. Josef Mengele. "Mengele never cured or treated anyone," Lou said. "He just figured out ways to kill Jews." When Lou and his mother came forward, Dr. Mengele waved his riding crop indicating one way for Lou to go and another way for his mother— one way meant slave labor, the other led to the gas chambers. Lou never saw his mother again. The rest of Lou's family were ordered in the direction for slave labor.

After a few days of living in quarantine at Auschwitz, Lou and fellow inmates were again marched into a railroad freight car. But this time there were no children, no women, no older people—only men who could work. Conditions in the freight car were as dreadful as before. After a long trip the train stopped at Mauthausen in Austria, another concentration camp for Jews. Lou was put to work doing slave labor at a construction site in the village of Ebensee, a sub-camp of Mauthausen. At Ebensee the inmates were assigned to dig a tunnel for an under-ground factory that was to manufacture missiles for Hitler's army. Lou was forced to work twelve hours a day, sometimes seven days a week, and when he came back to the camp he had to work several hours more building the barracks. In the morning he was given a cup of a dark liq-uid that was neither coffee nor tea, although the Nazi guards called it coffee. At noon work stopped for half an hour and the inmates were fed a thin soup made from turnips and potato peelings. Back at camp in the evening, supper consisted of a piece of bread, sometimes a bit of soup.

This was Lou's schedule from May 1944 until his liberation by the Americans on May 6, 1945. Some laborers died from exhaustion or starvation. Those who tried to escape or refused to work were shot immediately, their bodies hung up high as on a clothesline as an example to those who did not cooperate. One day Lou and about a hundred inmates were taken to the door of a building at Mauthausen. They were told to strip naked and then ordered into the building. When they were all inside a soldier told them to wait. The soldier left and the heavy door clanged shut. Lou knew he was in a gas chamber. He stood with the others, expecting the gas to be turned on, waiting for it to kill them. He felt helpless; there was no chance of resisting. Time passed in the room, their naked bodies pressed against each other. But nothing happened.

After half an hour the German soldier opened the door and ordered everyone out. Lou found out later that the Nazis had run out of gas that day. He was put back to work at Ebensee but soon became too weak to continue. He became a skeleton of himself. He saw other inmates collapse from fatigue or starvation. Guards would drag the dead or dying to a pile of bodies. There were several such mounds around the camp. The level of starvation was so compelling that the sight of these bodies led inmates to see them as a source of food. Word got around that the liver was the most edible organ. Lou saw inmates dig the liver out of dead inmates with their fingernails and devour it to stay alive. Lou was starving too but he could not bring himself to do this. Soon he collapsed. He too was dragged to a pile of bodies and thrown on top. Some in the pile were still alive, moaning, praying. Lou lost hope and didn't care anymore whether he lived or died. He lay back, closed his eyes and waited. Some time passed when suddenly he heard his brother's voice, shouting at him: "The Americans are here! The Americans are here! We're being liberated!" Lou didn't believe it. He didn't have the strength to react. He remembers an American soldier lifting him off the pile and placing him on a stretcher.

Lou's brother and sister managed to survive the concentration camps but his father did not. Years later Lou made his way to San Diego where he became a successful businessman. He knows that much of what he says sounds incredible, and some of his listeners are thinking to themselves: "Where's the proof?" He is glad there will always be a Nuremberg trial record to verify his story.

~

Near the end of the twentieth century in the United States and certain parts of Europe a bizarre movement arose that denied the Holocaust ever took place. Its leaders insisted that the Holocaust never happened, or if it did happen the reports were grossly exaggerated; that accounts of the murder of six million Jews and millions of others in the Nazi concentration camps were just myths concocted by the Jews themselves. Irrational as it seems in the face of the evidence, the movement gained followers, who formed chapters on both sides of the Atlantic. Once again the trial record proved its value by refuting the claims of the Holocaust deniers.

I wanted to find out for myself what the young Germans of the twenty-first century thought of the Holocaust and to what extent, if any, the Nuremberg evidence was linked to the country's remarkable postwar period of peace and democracy. So, in 2003, after being away for over fifty years, I went back. I had been invited to speak at the first joint conference of German and American judges, held in the village of Wustrau, outside Berlin. I spent many hours talking with German judges, most of them too young to have been alive during the Nuremberg trial. While in Germany I gave twelve lectures on the legacy of the trial, including one before the joint conference of judges. Most audiences consisted of university students and professors in west and east Germany. In Frankfurt I was asked to speak on three occasions, twice at the University of Frankfurt and once before an all-Jewish audience at B'nai B'rith headquarters. In my six-week tour I also lectured at universities in Cologne, Mainz, Hanover, Hamburg, Berlin, Leipzig, Halle, and Jena. In East Berlin, Leipzig, Halle and Jena, many in the audience had grown up under Soviet Communist rule. In Leipzig we drank and sang together at Johann Sebastian Bach's old hangout, the Auerbach Keller. Their feelings about the Holocaust were mixed: some felt shame, some not. Some felt guilty; others not. But on one point, wherever I went, they were agreed. They knew of the Holocaust because of the Nuremberg record and felt it was their responsibility to ensure that such a catastrophe will never shame their country again. On this matter I could sense their determination.

Here is a letter from a former graduate law student at the University of Halle. Despite his Irish name, Oisin Morris was born and raised in Germany. We came to know each other during my stay in Halle. I include a portion of his letter here because it reflects the attitude of the majority of students and young professors I met:

2 April 2004
Dear Judge Ehrenfreund:
If you grow up going to school in today's Germany it won't take long till you are confronted with the terrible Nazi crimes in the history class. From a very young age (something like 10 years) you begin to learn about the atrocities. Later, the schedule will reach right back to the end of the 1st world war to the economic crisis in the twenties to Hitler's coming to power, and from then on to all the steps that lead right into the gas chambers of Auschwitz. Schoolbooks contain pictures of gas chambers and piles of clothes of murdered Jews. In other words: you cannot leave a German school without having learned about the entire history of the 3rd Reich.

The generation of Germans that lived during the Nazi period often denied any responsibility for the things that had happened. Questions were brushed off with a mere "We didn't know anything" answer. It was only in the sixties and early seventies that the next generation would no longer accept these excuses.

Since then the Germans have made a great effort to make sure that history will not repeat itself. The basis for this are the facts that came to light with the Nuremberg trials. After the trials nobody can deny what happened during the Nazi reign.

The German criminal law makes it a criminal offence to publicly deny, approve of or minimize the Nazi atrocities.

As far as I know since the end of the war no Nazi party has ever won any election in Germany. They would not stand a chance.

Despite the fact that most young Germans do not see personal guilt (in the sense of responsibility for the past) for the things that happened long before they were born, there is a general understanding about the fact that there is a responsibility for the future. . . .

The heritage of the Nuremberg trial is that everybody regardless of nation, race and religion is responsible for making sure that never again such crimes can be committed.

Yours truly,

Oisin

Professor Florian Jessberger teaches international law at Humboldt University in east Berlin. He is widely recognized for his work in both German law and international criminal justice.[6] He writes:

3 March 2004

Dear Judge Ehrenfreund,

In principle I fully agree [with] the opinion you report as a widespread one among German law students and teachers. Indeed, one of the major merits of the Nuremberg trial and judgment (besides setting the precedent for the further development of an international system of criminal justice) was to document with [the] authority of an impartial court and within the framework of a formalized procedure, [the] nature and . . . extent [of] the crimes committed by Nazi Germany. . . . In fact this turns out to be one major function of inter-national criminal justice as a whole. And of course, this was one major, if not the major fundament [upon] which the democratization of postwar (West) Germany was built. In any case, I am happy to say that it appears as if the German government, judiciary and society today have fully accepted the legacy of Nuremberg. . . .

Warm regards from Berlin.

Florian Jessberger

The value of the Nuremberg record in blocking the movement for Holocaust denial asserted itself once again in 2000 when British historian David Irving sued author Dr. Deborah E. Lipstadt and her publisher Penguin Books for libel. Irving, a successful writer and lecturer on Hitler and the Nazi regime, claimed that Lipstadt, a professor of religion at Emory University in Atlanta, Georgia, had defamed him in her 1993 book, *Denying the Holocaust: The Growing Assault on Truth and Memory.* In the book Lipstadt described Irving as the most "dangerous spokesman for Holocaust denial" and an admirer of Hitler, and accused him of being the guru for the extreme right. She also wrote that he bends the truth to fit his extremist ideas.[7]

The trial began on January 11, 2000, at the Royal High Court of Justice in London. At the outset Lipstadt said the only issue to be decided was whether Irving was a liar in denying that the Holocaust occurred. But to much of the world the issue was much broader and had far greater consequences than simply whether one man had lied. In a larger sense the Holocaust itself was on trial. Many will say that such a question cannot possibly be taken seriously but the state of libel law in England forced Lipstadt to take the matter very seriously indeed. If the case had been tried in the United States, Irving would have had to prove that Lipstadt's written statements about him were false. In other words, the burden of proof would be on his shoulders. But under British law Lipstadt had to prove that what she said about Irving was true. Irving's principal claim was that there were never any gas chambers at Auschwitz during World War II and that the structures that tourists see there were built after the war. Lipstadt had to discredit this claim with clear-cut evidence. She had to prove what most people take for granted and this turned out to be not as easy as one might think. The stakes were tremendous: if Irving won it would mean that the Auschwitz survivors would be considered liars, and if Lipstadt won, Irving's reputation as a historian would be irreparably damaged. Penguin Books spent over a million pounds on lawyers' fees and plenty more to bring expert witnesses to London. Because of the heavy burden of proof placed on Lipstadt, the verdict was still in doubt up to the last day.[8] After thirty-two court days, Justice Charles Gray, hearing the case without a jury, handed down judgment in favor of Lipstadt and Penguin Books on April 11, 2000.[9] The British justice said the evidence was "incontrovertible" that Irving was a Holocaust denier.[10]

Lipstadt won her case by drawing largely on evidence gathered and produced at the Nuremberg trials.[11] In a letter to me, she wrote of the importance of such evidence in proving her case against Irving. "Much of the research on the Holocaust comes from that data," Lipstadt said. "We relied on data from the trials extensively."[12]

Without the Nuremberg evidence, the judgment in *Irving* v. *Lipstadt* may well have gone the other way. The consequences for Holocaust survivors and families of murdered victims would have been disastrous, especially for survivors whose stories thereafter might always be suspect. The Lipstadt decision was a defeat for those who deny the Holocaust ever occurred, but it has not stopped their campaign. On December 11, 2006, Iran hosted a conference in Teheran of Holocaust deniers from around the world. Organizers said it was to be a scholarly gathering. (In a speech in 2005, Iran's president, Mahmoud Ahmadinejad, stated that the Holocaust was either grossly exaggerated or an outright myth, and the conference apparently resulted from his remarks.) Some sixty-seven visitors came from thirty countries. David Duke, a former Ku Klux Klan leader from the United States, was among the participants.[13]

From the outcome of the Lipstadt case, Holocaust survivors may take comfort in knowing that the Nuremberg evidence will always be available if the matter comes up in court again.

CHAPTER FIFTEEN

HOW NUREMBERG
CHANGED MEDICAL ETHICS

THE NAZI DOCTORS' CASES PROSECUTED AT NUREMBERG RECORD THE worst examples in history of abuses of human beings by members of the medical profession. But the "Medical Case" went much further than to merely punish the guilty doctors for their gruesome crimes; the American judges wanted to make sure that no person would ever again be subjected to such inhumanity. As a result they wisely set in motion a new code of ethics for doctors that today governs, in its expanded form, the practice of medicine all over America. It was called the Nuremberg Code and consisted of ten principles, which can be summed up in four points:

1. Before doctors may perform any experiment on a human being, the voluntary informed consent of the subject is absolutely essential.
2. The experiment must be based on previous animal testing.
3. The experiment must avoid all unnecessary physical and mental suffering and injury.
4. The experiment must be conducted by scientifically qualified persons.[1]

For perhaps the first time in the history of medical practice, patients were given rights for their protection.

Since 1947, the Nuremberg Code has served as the foundation for all subsequent ethical codes dealing with experimentation on human beings. The legacy of the code began to emerge early. The Medical Case ended in July 1947 and a year later the United Nations Commission on Human Rights used the Nuremberg Code as the foundation for its proposals.[2] In

1949 the four U.N. Geneva Conventions sought to create a humanitarian law of war for the international community. The Geneva delegates adopted the strictures of the Nuremberg Code by protecting all military personnel, prisoners of war and specified civilians from unlawful human experimentation.[3] At around the same time the newly formed World Medical Association, acting under the influence of the Nuremberg Code, announced a modern restatement of the ancient Hippocratic Oath taken by all doctors. Under the new version, doctors now vow:

> I will not permit consideration of race, religion, nationality, party politics or social standing to intervene between my duty and my patient. I will maintain the utmost respect for human life from the time of its conception. Even under threat I will not use my knowledge contrary to the laws of humanity.[4]

In 1950 the U.N. Commission on Human Rights, chaired by Eleanor Roosevelt, relied on the Nuremberg Code as the basis for Article 7 of the International Covenant on Civil and Political Rights, which held that "no one shall be subjected without his free consent to medical or scientific experimentation."[5] Thus, within the first ten years after the "Medical Case" against Karl Brandt and his Nazi doctors, the Nuremberg Code had begun to exert its influence on medical practice for the benefit of patients.

In the following years the code affected various areas of society. Since the code did not have the authority of law, the U.S. federal government became involved in 1962 in regulating medical research. A new Food and Drug Administration (FDA) law required experts experimenting with drugs to inform patients that an experimental drug was being used on them and to obtain their consent.[6] Federal regulations adopted provisions of the Nuremberg Code in research involving fetuses. Under these regulations no scientist was permitted to obtain consent and perform fetal research unless approved experiments on animals and non-pregnant individuals were completed first. Another area addressed by federal regulations involved prisoners held in custody because of criminal behavior. These rules went even further than the Nuremberg Code by specifically prohibiting risky research even with the prisoners' consent.[7]

Up until the 1970s the requirement of informed consent applied only to human experimentation. Then in 1972, a series of court opinions changed the law of medicine dramatically.

Nuremberg's major contribution to modern medical practice came with the establishment of what was then a revolutionary doctrine: the requirement of informed consent (also called informed choice) for all medical treatment in which the doctor is going to perform an invasive procedure. If informed consent is not obtained pursuant to regulations, the patient has a right to sue for medical malpractice.[8] The informed consent doctrine was no longer limited to experiments. This outgrowth of the Nuremberg Code is today considered the most important of all patient rights.[9] The history of medical ethics and law since Nuremberg leaves no question that the modern doctrine of informed consent was born, not with the U.S. health laws or the court opinions of the 1970s, but in 1947 when three shocked American judges responded to the horrible experiments performed by Hitler's doctors. The signing of consent forms has by now become commonplace in doctors' offices all over America. But it rarely occurs to the millions of patients that this requirement had its origin in the Nuremberg trial of the Nazi doctors.

In 1986 three justices of the United States Supreme Court recognized that the original Nuremberg principles and the Nuremberg legacy were still very much alive. In the case of *United States* v. *Stanley,* an Army sergeant claimed that he had unknowingly been given drugs as part of a military experiment and sought compensation for the injuries sustained. Stanley lost his case because his proof was weak, but Justice William Brennan, joined by Justices Sandra Day O'Connor and Thurgood Marshall, wrote in dissent:

> The medical trials at Nuremberg in 1947 deeply impressed upon the world that experimentation with unknowing human subjects is morally and legally unacceptable. The United States Military Tribunal established the Nuremberg Code as a standard against which to judge German scientists who experimented with human subjects. The first principle was . . . [that] the voluntary consent of the human subject is absolutely essential.[10]

Today the Nuremberg principles are at the center of controversy re-garding the interrogations of suspected terrorists held at Guantanamo Bay, Cuba. Former interrogators report that American doctors have ad-vised them on how to increase psychological stress on the detainees in hopes of persuading them to provide intelligence information.[11] Such methods of coercive interrogation, if true, would raise the question of whether doctors aided and abetted torture and thereby violated the Nuremberg Code. A Pentagon spokesman allegedly commented that the doctors were not covered by ethics restrictions because they were not treating patients, but rather were acting as behavioral scientists.[12]

Dr. Karl Brandt and his associates had claimed that they were not treating patients either, but only acting as scientists engaged in research for the Nazi cause. The Nuremberg Court found that that did not relieve them of criminal responsibility and sent seven of the defendants to the gallows.

CHAPTER SIXTEEN

A NEW MEANING OF JUSTICE

IN THE DECADES THAT FOLLOWED THE LAST TRIAL OF THE MAJOR Nazi criminals, the word "Nuremberg" acquired a meaning far beyond geography or history; it grew to represent a commitment to justice that was gradually embraced by half the nations of the world. Nuremberg stood for the highest standards of law and due process—innocent until proven guilty, an attorney for every criminal defendant, a fair trial no matter how the grave the charge. Jackson's ideas may seem elementary to us now since they so thoroughly pervade the American justice system. Most of us who work in the legal system feel deeply the mandate of our calling—to ensure the primacy of justice—even though we may not always know how it developed. It was at Nuremberg that the concept began to gain respect and eventual acceptance.

Indeed such principles of justice as the presumption of innocence existed in American law and English common law long before Nuremberg. But they often lacked full acceptance; Nuremberg put teeth into those principles. When Jackson announced in his opening statement that the despised Nazi leaders were to be presumed innocent he was giving that concept new meaning and expanding it to an international level. Whether we are judges, attorneys, or spectators, consciously or unconsciously, the lessons of Nuremberg preside over all. By the end of the twentieth century this new meaning of justice was asserting itself in every subsequent war crimes trial.

YUGOSLAVIA

The bloodiest conflict in Europe since World War II broke out in 1991 between the peoples of the former Yugoslavia. The Yugoslav wars arose out of bitter ethnic and religious differences, mostly between Serbs on the one side, and Croats, Bosnians and Albanians on the other—but also between Bosnians and Croats within Bosnia, and Macedonians and Albanians within Macedonia. These wars took place between 1991 and 2001, finally ending with most of the former Yugoslavia left fragmented and in ruins. The fighting became so violent that the United Nations formally judged the conflict as genocide, the first war to be so termed since the carnage of World War II.

Slobodan Milosevic, elected president of Serbia in 1989, and later president of Yugoslavia in 2000, was considered the primary figure responsible for the war and the atrocities in the Balkans.[1] But Milosevic was not indicted immediately when the new Yugoslav tribunal was formed in 1993 because he was the person most valuable to the United States in its campaign for a peace agreement. Any indictment of Milosevic would have sabotaged any chance for agreement at the all-important peace conference to be held in Dayton, Ohio.

In November 1995, Milosevic came to Dayton at the invitation of the United States to meet with American negotiators and the presidents of Croatia and Bosnia to work out a plan for peace. The Dayton Agreement brought an end to the civil war in Bosnia, and Milosevic's reputation reached a high point in the West, where he was credited with being one of the prime movers of Balkan peace. The Clinton administration supported Milosevic's rule for a brief period until the late nineties, when Milosevic's reputation began a downslide. In 1998 he ordered a crackdown on the ethnic Albanians in Kosovo, the southernmost province of Serbia. For many years Kosovo had been a hotbed of tension between its huge ethnic Albanian majority and the Serbian Republic. The Albanians wanted independence from Serbia but Milosevic took repressive measures against them by means of an "ethnic cleansing" program.[2] This move led to his downfall and eventual arrest. Under his command, Serbian troops forced 700,000 people, nearly half the population of Kosovo, to flee the province. There were reports and pictures of massacres and long lines of Kosovar refugees fleeing into Albania and Macedonia. Kosovo was left in a legal vacuum and placed under United Nations administration, though still legally a part of Serbia and still seeking independence.[3] The key participants in the violence, including Milosevic, were subsequently charged with war crimes by a new court, the first war crimes tribunal since Nuremberg (the previously mentioned ICTY).

On May 25, 1993, the United Nations established the Yugoslav Tribunal as a temporary ad hoc agency to operate at The Hague in the Netherlands.[4] Its sole mission was to prosecute crimes of genocide and other war crimes in the Balkans. The new court differed from Nuremberg in that the Nuremberg Court was a military tribunal run by the four major powers occupying Germany. In contrast to Nuremberg, which was ruled by four Allied judges, the Yugoslav court consisted of eleven judges, none from Yugoslavia, thereby avoiding the "victors' justice" criticism. Three came from Asia, two from Europe, two from Africa, two from North America and one each from Latin America and Australia. Therefore, the Yugoslav Tribunal, although not a permanent body, was the world's first truly international criminal court.[5] Judge Gabrielle Kirk McDonald, a former federal court judge of the United States, was elected to preside.[6] The new court made a conscious effort to avoid the criticisms of the Nuremberg process. For example, the crime of waging aggressive war, which was criticized as being *ex post facto* law, was not charged.[7] Despite the differences, the Yugoslav court affirmed the basic principles of Nuremberg, including the rule of law and Jackson's credo: the presumption of innocence for every defendant no matter how weighty the charge. Convening of the Yugoslav court was hailed as a momentous victory for human rights. In May 1993, United States Ambassador Madeleine Albright made a stirring speech before the U.N. Security Council in which she said:

> There is an echo in this chamber today. The Nuremberg Principles have been reaffirmed. We have preserved the long-neglected compact made by the community of civilized nations forty-eight years ago in San Francisco to create the United Nations and enforce the Nuremberg Principles.[8]

On May 7, 1996, a forty-year-old Bosnian Serb named Dusko Tadic became the first defendant since Nuremberg to be tried for crimes against humanity. Tadic had been a prison guard and he was accused of murdering a dozen persons, beating and torturing scores of others and raping several women, all in the name of "ethnic cleansing." One of the counts alleged that he ordered one of the prisoners at knife point to bite off the testicles of another prisoner.[9] The trial was a significant step in the history of law because for the first time in half a century, a court had a chance to redeem the international rule of law and to prove that the Nuremberg legacy prevailed.[10] Three of the eleven judges were chosen to sit as a panel on the Tadic case. After a seven-month trial it took the judges over five months to render their judgment. Of the thirty-four counts charged, Tadic was found guilty of eleven. He was acquitted of all the murder charges as well as the castration charge. "The goal of the trial chamber," Judge McDonald said after summarizing the 301-page decision, "was always first and foremost to provide the accused with a fair trial to which he was entitled."[11] Unlike Nuremberg, both sides were allowed to appeal. The Appeals Chamber denied Tadic's appeal on all grounds but reversed the trial court's judgment of not guilty as to nine counts including the murder charges. Tadic was sentenced to twenty years in prison.[12]

Although heavily influenced by Nuremberg, the Yugoslav Tribunal represented an advance on its predecessor. In addition to points already noted, the Tadic trial clearly showed four major changes in procedure: (1) no death penalty; (2) no trials in absentia; (3) better treatment of defense counsel with regard to discovery of evidence; and (4) the right of appeal.[13]

Tadic's case was important for reviving the Nuremberg legacy and setting the tone for all succeeding trials for crimes against humanity— but the main event was still to come. At the time of the Tadic trial in 1996, Slobodan Milosevic was still a free man, still playing his role as peacemaker. In 1997 he was elected president of Yugoslavia and in 1999, during the Kosovo war, the Yugoslav Tribunal indicted him for crimes against humanity in Kosovo. His defeat in the presidential elections of October 2000 was followed by new charges of war crimes in Croatia and Bosnia, and genocide in Bosnia. But Milosevic was still not arrested. Finally, on April 1, 2001, he was taken into custody by the Serb government and two months later turned over to The Hague for prosecution. Milosevic's case was the twenty-second to be heard by the tribunal but because of his notoriety it was the first to receive worldwide publicity.[14]

The trial began on February 12, 2002, with Milosevic insisting on representing himself and refusing to recognize the legality of the court. He was actually the first head of state in history to face criminal charges before an international court[15] because Hitler had been missing from the dock at Nuremberg and Emperor Hirohito had been absent from the list of defendants at Tokyo.

During the first two years of the trial, the prosecution detailed the story of the Yugoslav wars in Kosovo, Croatia and Bosnia. The case was in its fourth year when Milosevic died in his cell on March 11, 2006. He owed it to Nuremberg that before his death he had the chance to defend himself in a court of law. The judges were criticized for the trial's many delays but much of the delay was due to Milosevic's poor health and his wrangling over procedure.

Carla Del Ponte, a Swiss lawyer who had made a name for herself by prosecuting the Mob in Europe, was the chief prosecutor of the Yugoslav Tribunal during the Milosevic case. Her goal was to prove that Milosevic was the prime mover behind the Yugoslav debacle, and to reaffirm the Nuremberg principle that even the highest government official can be held accountable for his crimes. Milosevic's demise left her cheated of victory. "The death of Milosevic," Del Ponte said, "represents for me a total defeat."[16]

Despite the setback of Milosevic's death, Del Ponte has shown she is not totally defeated. At this writing in early 2007, the Yugoslav prosecutors are busier than ever and trials of other defendants proceed in full force. Investigators continue to hunt for suspects still at large, including two top Bosnian Serbs, General Ratko Mladic and Radovan Karadzic, believed to be in hiding in Serbia, and Croatian general Ante Gotorina.[17]

Although the Milosevic case never reached a verdict, it provided important evidence for a recent landmark decision by the International Court of Justice (ICJ). Also known as the World Court, the ICJ is not to be confused with the International Criminal Court (ICC) which, as its name implies, deals with crime on a global basis, particularly crimes against humanity. The World Court tries civil cases, specializing in settling legal disputes between nations. Both courts are based at The Hague.

In 1993 Bosnia sued Serbia in the World Court for committing genocide in the Bosnian conflict. Bosnia charged that Serbian militias had slaughtered more than 7,000 Muslim men and boys at Srebrenica. In February 2007, the World Court, using the evidence in the Milosevic case, ruled that genocide did occur and that while the Serbian government did not directly order the killings, it could have and should have stopped them. No damages were due. The court also ordered Serbia to turn over for prosecution Ratko Mladic, the Bosnian Serb general who allegedly directed the Srebrenica genocide.[18]

RWANDA

First in line after the opening of the Yugoslav court was the International Criminal Tribunal for Rwanda (ICTR), also established by the United Nations. In 1994 ethnic militias massacred 800,000 Rwandans in just a hundred days while the world looked on and the U.N. Security Council wasted time debating whether genocide was taking place.

The tiny nation of Rwanda resides in the heart of Africa, sandwiched between two much larger countries, Tanzania to the east and the Democratic Republic of the Congo (formerly Zaire) to the west. The largest body of water inside the African continent, Lake Victoria, lies nearby to the northeast. Probably few Americans had ever heard of Rwanda until genocide erupted there in 1994 in a conflict between the Hutu and Tutsi tribes. The population of Rwanda was composed primarily of these two groups, the Hutu making up 85 percent and the Tutsi 14 percent.[19] The violence resulted in the large-scale killing of members of the Tutsi group by members of the Hutu tribe. The world did nothing. Indecision paralyzed the United Nations. Rwanda's prime minister-designate pleaded with the United Nations for a court to bring the offenders to justice. He asked the Security Council, "Is it because we're Africans that a court has not been set up?"[20] The grisly massacre, much of it accomplished with machetes, was depicted in the film *Hotel Rwanda*, which criticized the United States and the United Nations for initially turning their backs on the helpless Rwandans. "The genocide of the Tutsis and the moderate Hutus," said *The New York Times*, "was probably the fastest and most personally brutal in history."[21] In 1998 President Clinton went to Rwanda to apologize:

> We did not act quickly enough, after the killing began. . . . We did not immediately call these crimes by their rightful name: genocide. Never again must we be shy in the face of the evidence.[22]

On November 8, 1994, the U.N. Security Council adopted Resolution 955 providing for the establishment of the ICTR. So for the second time since the Nuremberg and Tokyo trials, the Nuremberg precedent of holding accountable those responsible for crimes against humanity was about to bear fruit. The new Rwanda court had the assignment of prosecuting persons responsible for genocide and other serious violations of international humanitarian law committed in Rwanda between January 1, 1994, and December 31, 1994. Genocide, which had not been defined at Nuremberg, was defined in the Rwanda statute as any one of a number of acts committed "with the intent to destroy, in whole or in part, a national, ethnical, racial or religious group."[23] In addition, the court was responsible for overseeing the prosecution of Rwandan citizens charged with similar crimes in neighboring states. Although the Rwanda tribunal was greatly influenced by both the Nuremberg and Yugoslavia tribunals, the internal factual situation raised new issues. First of all, the Rwanda court, unlike the others, was created at the request of the government where the crimes had occurred. Second and more important, the Rwandan situation involved an atrocity within the nation's borders. Rwanda was not at war with anyone. This scenario raised for the first time the important question of whether the international community had a right to enter an internal conflict. In the case of Nuremberg it is highly unlikely that the Allies would have prosecuted the Nazi leaders for crimes against humanity if the atrocities had occurred within Germany's borders, unrelated to a war with other nations. Nothing in international law at the time forbade a state from murdering its own citizens.

By 1994 a global community had come into being and the world had grown more sensitive to atrocity anywhere. Although Rwanda was not at war, the United Nations decided it could not simply stand by and let the slaughter go unheeded. Thus the Rwanda tribunal was born. Because of the poor conditions in Rwanda resulting from the conflict, the new court was set up in the city of Arusha in the neighboring country of Tanzania.

The United Nations decided to link the Rwanda court in Arusha with the Yugoslavia court at The Hague. This was done despite the vast distance between the two courts in the interest of promoting consistency in the law as well as reducing cost. As a result the two courts shared the same appeals chamber at The Hague and the same chief prosecutor.

Rwanda relied heavily on the Nuremberg and Yugoslavia models. The statute of the Rwanda tribunal is in most respects the same as that of the ICTY but with a few differences. The tribunal has jurisdiction to try persons for genocide and other crimes against humanity committed at any time, in peace or war. For the first time individuals were held responsible for acts committed in internal armed conflict, a significant step in the progression of international law.[24]

The Rwanda statute stipulated that all hearings shall be open to the public and that the fair trial rights of the accused, including the presumption of innocence, the right to counsel, the right to remain silent and the right to a speedy trial, shall be protected.

Rwanda also followed Nuremberg precedent by focusing on the people at the top, the principals who planned and organized the atrocities, such as senior leaders of government, the military and the various militias. Rwandan officials have estimated that as many as 20,000 to 30,000 potential defendants could be tried for genocide and war crimes. The core group of defendants consisted of about 100 to 300 persons.

The Rwanda statute, like its Yugoslavia counterpart, was careful to avoid the criticisms of Nuremberg with regard to victors' justice, the death penalty and the right to appeal. The elected Rwanda court judges did not come from any nation or ethnic group involved in the alleged crimes. They came from Sweden, Bangladesh, Russia and Senegal. The death penalty was prohibited as with all U.N.-sanctioned tribunals and the right to appeal was granted.

In September 1998 the Rwanda court sentenced former Rwandan Prime Minister Jean Kambanda to life in prison for genocide. Kambanda's conviction followed the Nuremberg precedent that the highest authorities are accountable *as individuals*. Kambanda was the first head of government to be convicted of genocide. In the twenty-first century, the Rwanda trials continue to function. In April 2005 the Rwanda tribunal found beyond any reasonable doubt that Mika Muhimana, a former government official in western Rwanda, shot mostly Tutsi victims, raped several Tutsi women and encouraged other men to rape in the town of Gishyita. The tribunal sitting in Arusha, Tanzania, sentenced the defendant to life in prison, the maximum sentence.[25]

In the same year the Rwanda tribunal convicted a retired Rwandan army officer, Lt. Col. Aloys Simba, for supplying guns and grenades that killed thousands of innocent people. The court sentenced Simba to twenty-five years in prison.[26] The same tribunal sentenced a former director of a Rwandan radio station to six years in prison for encouraging the killing of Tutsis through his broadcasts.[27]

At this writing the Rwanda tribunal is still going strong. In 2006 Paul Bisengimsna, the mayor of Gikoro, a city near the capital of Kigali, was sentenced to fifteen years in prison for his part in the slaughter of 1,000 ethnic Tutsis who had sought safety in a church.[28] On December 14, 2006, a Rwandan businessman, Joseph Nzabrinda, pleaded guilty to murder as a crime against humanity. Church officials were not immune from prosecution. On December 13, 2006, the Rwanda tribunal convicted a Roman Catholic priest for committing genocide during the mass killings of Tutsis.[29]

As in the Yugoslavia tribunal, all Rwanda convictions are being handed out under the aegis of the Nuremberg invention—crimes against humanity. The Rwanda tribunal is rushing to meet a deadline. Under the tribunal's mandate, all cases must be completed by the end of 2008. Appeals may continue until 2010. Interviewed in October, 2005, the president of the tribunal, Erik Mose of Norway, said that the court was operating on schedule and so long as it has sufficient resources the deadline will be met. In 2008 the court will start to close down.[30]

SIERRA LEONE

Sierra Leone, like Rwanda, is one of the smallest independent countries in Africa. It lies on the Atlantic coast of West Africa, bordered by Guinea on the north and east and Liberia to the southwest. Between 1991 and 2000 a brutal civil war ravaged Sierra Leone, basically over control of one of the country's richest resources, diamonds. The conflict left up to 50,000 persons killed and 500,000 injured or otherwise victimized.[31] Rebels terrorized the civilians with egregious practices of mass killing, amputation of various parts of the body, sexual slavery, abduction of thousands of children and adults and setting fire to large city dwellings and villages.[32]

In September 2002 the United Nations and the government of Sierra Leone jointly established a new international tribunal known as the "Special Court for Sierra Leone."[33] All the Nuremberg precedents of fair trial, including the presumption of innocence, were in place. The United States spent $22 million to create the court with the hope of chipping away at West Africa's custom of allowing its worst warlords to escape prosecution.[34]

On June 3, 2004, the new court opened in Freetown, Sierra Leone, with a promise from its chief prosecutor, American David Crane, that he would destroy what he called "the beast of impunity."[35] Missing from the defendants' dock was the leading suspect, Charles G. Taylor, the exiled former president of Liberia and the man accused of starting the civil war in Sierra Leone.[36] The new tribunal had indicted Taylor for crimes against humanity but at the time of trial he had been given asylum in Nigeria and was not available.

The tribunals for the former Yugoslavia and Rwanda were composed of judges and prosecutors from neutral countries who were appointed by the United Nations. The Special Court for Sierra Leone, however, embarked on an innovation called an "internationalized" or "hybrid" court because it is jointly administered by the United Nations and Sierra Leone and includes both Sierra Leonan and international judges. The court has jurisdiction over serious violations of international humanitarian law and certain Sierra Leonan criminal laws. The hybrid special court gives a dominant role to experienced judges and prosecutors but at the same time allows for involvement of local lawyers. Hopefully the system will educate the Sierra Leone lawyers and inspire their participation in war crimes trials.[37] Jurisdiction is limited to crimes committed since November 30, 1996. The international community is intently watching to see if this new concept of mixing national and foreign judges will succeed.

The first defendants were three men who led the pro-government militia accused of the indiscriminate killing of civilians and amputations of body parts including hands, arms, legs and lips.[38]

In March 2005 prosecutors for the Sierra Leone court opened their war crimes trial against members of a military junta that killed and maimed thousands of persons in the country's civil war. The defendants, Alex Tamba Brima, Brima Bazzy Kamara and Santigie Borbor Kanu were top officials of the Armed Forces Ruling Council that took over the country in 1997. The council joined another rebel group, the Revolutionary United Front, which was notorious for hacking off limbs. As of March 2005 two other groups of defendants were on trial before the Sierra Leone tribunal. One group was comprised of rebel commanders, the other of a government-allied militia.[39]

On March 29, 2006, the warlord Charles Taylor was finally captured in Nigeria where he had been living in exile. A customs official recognized Taylor at the border as he tried to escape into Cameroon. He was brought to Sierra Leone under extraordinary security to be arraigned before the U.N.-backed Special Court on eleven counts of crimes against humanity and then jailed to await trial. Desmond de Silva, the prosecutor for the Sierra Leone court, said Taylor's indictment "sends out the clear message that no matter how rich or powerful or feared people may be, the law is above them."[40] The statement sounded like the ghosts of Nuremberg having their say.

But Charles Taylor will not be going on trial in Sierra Leone after all. The Sierra Leone government requested that he be tried outside the country because his supporters were likely to cause more violence during the trial and destabilize the region once again. So, for security reasons, Taylor was flown to The Hague to be tried in the Netherlands at a specially created outpost of the Special Court for Sierra Leone.[41] The Netherlands agreed to host the trial on condition that another country imprison him if he is convicted, and Britain has given its pledge to provide the detention facilities. The court will use the new courtroom facilities of the International Criminal Court but it will still be the Sierra Leone Court. If convicted, Taylor faces life imprisonment but not the death penalty because the United Nations will not sponsor any trial in which capital punishment might be imposed. The trial should take about a year.

The San Diego Union-Tribune commented:

> It is still too early to tell if other African leaders will be brought to trial for past sins, but there are hopeful signs. . . . Africa is a continent with many problems, and many of them will not be solved as long as corrupt leaders rule and ruin nations. At least some of these are beginning to meet justice.[42]

On June 4, 2007, the first day of his war crimes trial, Taylor refused to appear in court and fired his lawyer. But as his lawyer left the courtroom, the judges ordered the trial to go on.

EAST TIMOR

The attempt by the United Nations to bring the violators of human rights in East Timor (officially the Democratic Republic of Timor-Leste) to justice is a story of frustration and disappointment. So far the influence of the Nuremberg legacy has not been strong enough to overcome the opposition.

In 1999 East Timor was a territory of Indonesia, part of the island of Timor, which is one of the southernmost islands of Indonesia and located north of Australia. For roughly 450 years East Timor was a Portuguese colony, which eventually had a population of about 800,000. In the latter part of the twentieth century, after the Portuguese left East Timor, Indonesia invaded the country and occupied it for the next twenty-four years against stiff resistance from the East Timorese. On August 30, 1999, East Timor voted for independence from Indonesia, and it was in the midst of this voting process that the trouble began. Indonesian security forces and local militia groups opened a campaign of violence and intimidation against those who favored independence. An estimated 1,400 persons were killed and another 250,000 were forced into exile after the vote.[43] The human rights violations were so bad that a peacekeeping force of U.N. troops comprised mostly of Australian soldiers landed in East Timor to halt the slaughter and forced the aggressors to flee.[44] East Timor is far from the ken of most Americans but it is a place of importance in the story of international justice because the events there marked what Kofi Annan, former Secretary-General of the United Nations, called a "developing international norm in favor of intervention to protect civilians from wholesale slaughter."[45] The idea that foreign nations could intervene in another nation's affairs to prevent crimes against humanity became another part of the Nuremberg legacy.

On October 25, 1999, the U.N. Security Council created the United Nations Transitional Administration in East Timor (UNTAET), an entity that would administer East Timor for the next several years. At this point the United Nations could have established an international criminal tribunal similar to those set up for Rwanda and the former Yugoslavia, but the decision to do so was put off. In early November 1999 the United Nations Commission for Human Rights investigated the scene in East Timor, concluded that the violence was committed by the Indonesian military and police and recommended creation of an international criminal tribunal.[46] The delay continued. Other investigations followed. The United Nations'

International Commission of Inquiry looked into the matter and it too advocated creation of an international human rights tribunal. An Indonesian human rights body, the Commission for Human Rights Violations in East Timor, also conducted an investigation with the same result.[47]

Herbert Bowman, former international prosecutor for the United Nations Mission to East Timor, writes:

> The findings and recommendations of all these investigative bodies were clear enough: The Indonesian military and government were responsible for the violence. Indonesia could not be trusted to bring those accountable to justice. A domestic East Timorese tribunal would not suffice. An international tribunal was the only reasonable solution.[48]

But the United Nations did not accept the recommendations. Secretary-General Kofi Annan said the United Nations would pursue other avenues to ensure justice would be done in East Timor. The main reason for the rejection, Bowman says, was the United Nations' desire to avoid confrontation with Indonesia, which opposed the idea of an international tribunal—for that matter, any tribunal.[49] This was one case where Nuremberg precedent lacked the strength to prevail.

So the United Nations decided to prosecute crimes against humanity in East Timor in another way. Two Special Panels for Serious Crimes were created to operate in the Dili District Court, Dili being the nation's capital, and in the Dili Court of Appeals. A Serious Crimes Investigation Unit (SCIU) was also established to direct prosecution of serious crimes. The procedural rules for this new system showed that the United Nations' rejection of an international tribunal was not a total defeat for the Nuremberg legacy. The East Timor court adopted the basic elements of due process that Jackson declared at London and Nuremberg, including the presumption of innocence.[50] Each panel would have two international judges and one East Timorese judge, thereby becoming a "hybrid" system.

Although the court mixed international and domestic law as well as international and domestic judges, it could not be considered a truly international tribunal in the sense of the ones set up for Yugoslavia and Rwanda. That is because the East Timor Special Panels were created not by a resolution of the U.N. Security Council, but by a treaty between the U.N. Secretary-General and the government of East Timor. This is an important difference. It meant that member states of the United Nations were not required to fund the court as they would be if the court had been created by a Security Council vote. A genuine international tribunal operates completely independently of any national or domestic law. This was not so in the case of East Timor. As a consequence the East Timor tribunal never had the resources it needed to function adequately. The defense was undermanned and underfunded. The defense team had no translators, no investigators and no budget for witness expenses.[51] Under the treaty with the U.N. Secretary-General the East Timor Special Panels were designed to operate as part of the country's newly established domestic justice system. A genuine international tribunal, on the other hand, operates outside the strictures of the domestic court system. In sum, the East Timor tribunal lacked the power to have the high-level Indonesian defendants extradited for trial; the Indonesian government refused to cooperate; and only lower-level defendants were ever prosecuted, and they got off lightly. The East Timor court is not to blame. The judges tried valiantly to make the system work but they never had the tools to do so. The process made a mockery of Nuremberg's promise that no one is above the law and that high officials will be held personally accountable.

Meanwhile, Indonesia set up its own ad hoc human rights tribunal to try those responsible for the devastation in 1999. Human rights supporters dismissed the court as a façade designed to ease international pressure for a U.N.-sponsored tribunal.[52] The Indonesian tribunal was characterized by the failure of the prosecution to press its case against the accused, and the shocking efforts by the military to intimidate the judges. Of the eighteen defendants tried, twelve were acquitted, and of the six convicted only one received more than the minimum sentence. All remained free on appeal. No one was placed in custody. Human rights organizations called the Indonesia trials a "sham."[53] In 2002 another obstacle to successful prosecution took place. The two countries, East Timor and Indonesia, signed an agreement to create a new Commission of Truth and Friendship. East Timor's foreign minister, José Ramos-Horta, said the agreement would

resolve all the events of 1999.[54] Seth Mydans, *New York Times* correspondent in East Timor, wrote:

> After ducking and dodging for more than five years, it appears that the
> Indonesian officers responsible for the devastation of East Timor in
> 1999 have reached safe ground and will avoid prosecution under a
> new agreement signed by leaders of both countries.[55]

The agreement provides immunity from prosecution for the main suspects. Critics complained that the two nations were putting their national interests ahead of universal principles of justice.[56] The agreement
to let the major offenders off sparked new controversy in international
justice circles.

In February 2005 hope for some semblance of justice in East Timor
stood at a crossroads. The United Nations formally declared its intent to
investigate the failure to prosecute those accused of crimes against humanity. In the preceding November the United States Ambassador to
the United Nations, John Danforth, had called upon the Security Council to see that those responsible for the East Timor bloodshed would be
prosecuted.[57] On the other hand, both Timorese and Indonesian leaders
were agreed that all charges should be dropped. On February 18, 2005,
U.N. Secretary-General Kofi Annan announced that he was appointing a
commission of experts to study why the U.N.'s 1999 resolution to try the
perpetrators of violence in East Timor had failed.[58] Then, on May 20,
2005, the U.N.-sponsored Special Panels for Serious Crimes in East
Timor closed down. The East Timor courts had tried less than one quarter of those indicted for human rights violations. Those who bore the
primary responsibility for the East Timor violence have yet to see the inside of a courtroom.[59]

As of this writing no court has been set up to replace the East Timor
panels. There is an urgent need for the creation of an international tribunal in East Timor to carry on the Nuremberg legacy. Perhaps the U.N.
investigation will lead to such a tribunal after all. But the spirit is weak.
"Observers in Dili," writes Jill Jolliffe of *The Asia Times*,

> believe that it will be difficult for the UN to revive prosecutions with
> so little enthusiasm being expressed by Timorese leaders. Judging by

the UN's factual errors in describing Timor's history, it doesn't care much either.[60]

Whatever happens, the East Timor attempt to do justice so far has been pitiful. The Nuremberg precedent that no one is above the law has been ignored—the big fish got away.[61]

∾

Other international trials of government officials who abuse their subjects are waiting in the wings. Every one of the trials speaks for the Nuremberg legacy. In Cambodia, Congo and Darfur, plans were underway in 2007 for trials alleging crimes against humanity.

CAMBODIA

The worst atrocities since the Holocaust occurred in the 1970s on the killing fields of Cambodia, a nation in Southeast Asia on the Gulf of Thailand, once part of French Indo-China. Two million lives were sacrificed to the horrible schemes of the despot Pol Pot and other key figures of the communist Khmer Rouge government. Another million died from starvation and disease. For over a quarter of a century afterwards the leaders continued to live comfortably in their own country, safe from arrest or prosecution.[62] In 1998 Pol Pot died. For years the United Nations tried to persuade Hun Sen, the new prime minister, to put those Khmer leaders who could still be found on trial for their atrocities. Hun Sen resisted. The men to be tried were his former comrades and he was a former Khmer commander himself. He is alleged to have said, "We must dig a hole and bury the past."[63] The United Nations wanted a "hybrid" court of local and international judges similar to the one chosen for Sierra Leone. But Hun Sen did not want independent international judges. For a time the United Nations gave up. Any chance of capturing the Khmer leaders living in Cambodia and bringing them to trial in another country was slim unless Cambodia cooperated, and Cambodia would not cooperate.

Finally, thirty years after the world first learned of the killings by the Khmer Rouge, the United Nations and the Cambodian government agreed to set up a joint national and international court to try the responsible individuals who were still alive. In July 2005 the new international tribunal, called the Extraordinary Chambers in the Courts of Cambodia (ECCC), was sworn in with seventeen Cambodian judges, thirteen from other countries and a budget of $56.3 million.[64]

Although Pol Pot is dead, several of his subordinates remain as possible defendants. One prominent Khmer Rouge leader, Ta Mok, who was charged with crimes against humanity by the new Cambodia tribunal, died in prison on July 21, 2006, at the age of eighty. Mok faced trial for his part in the deaths of 1.7 million Cambodians from 1975 to 1979.[65] Other defendants are living freely among survivors of one of the great atrocities of the last century. The trials are not expected to start until 2007 or possibly 2008 because there will be a year of investigation first. The plan is for a three-stage time frame: a year for investigations, a year for trial and a year for appeal. The authorities are heeding the lessons of Nuremberg: Jackson showed that the best course is to start prosecutions at the top level with only a small pool of senior figures facing trial. The Cambodia tribunal will follow that path. However, Jackson made the mistake of also trying to convict the hundreds of thousands of Nazis who were involved in Hitler's infamous policies. That attempt collapsed. The Cambodia court will not make the same mistake, and will not try to indict the thousands who helped Pol Pot carry out his inhuman devastation.[66]

The new law provides for a panel of Cambodian and foreign prosecutors and judges with Cambodians in the majority. Such Nuremberg rights as the presumption of innocence, free counsel to defendants who cannot afford it, and public trial are included; the position or rank of any suspect shall not relieve such person of criminal responsibility or mitigate punishment, and the fact that a suspect acted pursuant to a government order shall not relieve the suspect of criminal responsibility. The law also states that trials shall be fair and expeditious.[67] A large building on the outskirts of Phnom Phen will be refurbished as the courthouse. The building is part of a military headquarters, not far from a killing field where thousands of bodies were buried.

Despite the promise of justice contained in the new law, the Cambodian justice system is considered to be inept, corrupt and subject to political pressure. Human rights groups complain that Hun Sen has been given too much power.[68]

If the Cambodia tribunal ever gets rolling, there will be no shortage of evidence for trials of Khmer Rouge defendants. The U.S. Congress has seen to that. In 1994 Congress established the Cambodian Genocide Program at Yale University. Congress gave Yale the assignment of making a systematic catalogue of cases arising from charges of genocide or crimes against humanity in Cambodia. At the same time Congress directed the president to pursue a trial for the leaders of the Khmer Rouge.

Throughout Cambodia tens of thousands of skulls remain available as forensic evidence if the time ever comes for their use as exhibits in court. Some are crammed into little shrines; some buried in pots or piled in temples or simply left out in the countryside. Many other skulls have been broken or disintegrated, some eaten by cows.[69]

The Cambodia trials face major problems. Many of the defendants are old and in bad health, and not even yet in custody. If the trials are delayed, these defendants could die before ever being brought to court, as Pol Pot did, or die in the course of the trial, like Slobodan Milosevic. There is also a shortage of funds. Cambodia is a poor country where most people live on less than a dollar a day. The government may not be able to pay its share of the $56.3 million budget. Japan has pledged half the court's budget. Ten million dollars will come from Britain, France and Australia. As of June 2006, the United States had not contributed a dime to the tribunal fund because of the Consolidated Appropriations Act of 2005, which prohibits funding to countries that do not meet criteria concerning human rights and other democratic principles. The Bush administration is a longtime opponent of Cambodia's elected leader, Hun Sen, but the fact that the court will follow Nuremberg principles of due process may convince the U.S. administration to contribute.[70]

On July 10, 2006, more than twenty-seven years after the mass killings in Cambodia, formal proceedings began against the remaining leaders of the brutal Khmer Rouge regime. The prosecutor's office officially opened its investigation. On July 17, 2006, the first shipment of 383,149 pages of evidence arrived in Cambodia.[71]

In the same month seventeen Cambodians and twelve foreigners took office as judges and prosecutors selected for the trial. In January 2007 a dispute arose between the Cambodian judges and the foreign judges over procedure. Officials say the dispute is so serious that if they cannot agree, the foreigners may walk out. The central issue is over the independence of the judiciary and the Cambodian government's alleged attempt to manipulate the trial.[72]

The problems of prosecution are serious but they do not doom the Cambodia tribunal. Every war crimes trial from Nuremberg to the present has had serious flaws but each one has advanced the cause of international justice.

CHAPTER SEVENTEEN

THE INTERNATIONAL CRIMINAL COURT:
NUREMBERG OFFSPRING

NUREMBERG WAS A TEMPORARY AD HOC COURT CREATED SPECIFI-
cally to try the major Nazi war criminals and no one else. In 1949 the
court closed down operations and all personnel involved went home.
But Jackson envisioned something more: he dreamed of a permanent
court that would stand ready to bring criminal heads of state to justice.
He saw the Nuremberg trials as a forerunner to an international court
that did not need to be set up on an ad hoc basis every time a high government official was accused of committing war crimes or crimes
against humanity. Jackson hoped that the existence of such a court on a
permanent basis would deter war and atrocities, and would stand as a
constant reminder to potential war criminals that they could face serious consequences for their crimes.

In the next half century practically nothing happened to fulfill Jackson's lofty hopes. In the aftermath of World War II several countries
brought former Nazis to trial under their own laws and in their own
courts, but that was all.

On July 17, 1998, at a conference in Rome with 120 countries voting
in favor, the statute of the International Criminal Court was adopted,
often referred to as the Rome Statute. With its courthouse located at The
Hague in the Netherlands, the ICC would become the world's first-ever
independent permanent court, set up to punish individuals primarily for
crimes against humanity, a major advancement of the Nuremberg legacy.
Seven states voted against the treaty, including Iraq, Israel, Libya, China
and the United States. But two years later President Clinton signed the
treaty, a necessary step before sending it on to the Senate for ratification.
In 2002, after President Bush took office, there came another reversal of

America's position on the Rome Statute. President Bush let it be known that the administration was opposed to the new court and thereupon withdrew Clinton's signature.[1] Since then the administration has not only opposed the ICC but has actively tried to block its progress, a definite threat to the Nuremberg legacy (discussed in a later chapter).

There can be no question that Nuremberg's precedents substantially influenced the International Criminal Court. When the ICC opened in March, 2003, Jackson's principles of fair trial were written into the statute.

Henry T. King, Jr., a prosecuting attorney at Nuremberg and later professor at Case Western Reserve School of Law, was present for the swearing-in ceremony of the judges of the ICC in 2003. He wrote:

> Today we are seeing the birth of a new international institution that will deal with problems that have plagued mankind since the beginning of recorded history. The institution is the International Criminal Court ("ICC") whose birth may be recorded as March 11, 2003, when the judges for the new court were sworn in. . . . As I watched the ceremony unfold I thought of the man who started it all: Robert Jackson.[2]

Jackson's conception of war crimes and crimes against humanity, King said, were the "progenitors" of the crimes set forth in the ICC Statute.[3] First of all the Rome Statute adopted the elements of due process with the presumption of innocence that Jackson persuaded the Allies to accept at London and Nuremberg almost sixty years earlier. Nuremberg established the principle that government leaders are not immune from prosecution, and the ICC followed suit.[4]

As pointed out, Nuremberg was the first court ever to prosecute crimes against humanity. The ICC statute followed the same concept but added to the categories of crimes against humanity such acts as torture, enforced disappearance of persons and apartheid (an official policy of racial segregation).[5] Under the ICC statute, there are three ways a case may be brought before the court. The first is through invitation by a country where the government is unable to control the violence itself and lacks the facilities to bring the perpetrators to trial; the second is for a prosecutor of the ICC to initiate an investigation; and the third is referral by the U.N. Security Council. In every case the ICC will not proceed if a country is conducting its own investigation or prosecution unless the ICC finds that the national government's prosecution is inadequate to do justice.[6]

The ICC has jurisdiction over all crimes committed by the nationals of those governments that have ratified the treaty, and also of all crimes committed in the territories of governments that have ratified. In other words, although the United States has not ratified the treaty, if an American citizen commits a crime in any country that has ratified, the American would be subject to prosecution. Also, the court can try any individual responsible for crimes under its jurisdiction regardless of the person's civilian or military status, and no matter how high his or her position.[7]

The ICC does not intend to replace national courts. Under the Rome Treaty, domestic judicial systems are still the first choice for prosecution. The ICC will become involved only if the domestic courts are unwilling or unable to try the suspected criminals themselves. That could happen because of violence, lack of resources or simply a lack of political will. In any case the ICC intends to provide guidance, if requested, from any domestic court that wishes to handle the case itself.[8]

The Hague is a medium-sized Dutch city built along canals, prosperous and fairly quiet, with a good share of art galleries and museums. For many years The Hague hosted the International Court of Justice (also called the World Court), an agency of the United Nations that rules on international civil matters. With the ICC in business, The Hague is gradually heating up and the town may undergo a change due to all the new court activity.

The ICC is already producing positive results. The chief prosecutor of the ICC, Moreno-Ocampo, claims that the fact of the court's existence has already led one of Colombia's top paramilitary commanders, Carlos Castaño, to lay down his weapons for fear of ICC prosecution.[9] If true, such an outcome is precisely what Robert Jackson had in mind.

For centuries African warlords were accustomed to committing acts of cruelty on their subjects without consequences. Now the ICC and the Nuremberg legacy are changing that custom.

CONGO

In January 2007 the ICC ordered Thomas Lubanga, the Congolese warlord, to face charges of kidnapping children and turning them into soldiers and sex slaves. Lubanga was founder and leader of one of the most dangerous militias in the Ituri region of the Congo, having allegedly killed thousands and forced more than 600,000 refugees to flee. He will be the first suspect to stand trial at the permanent war crimes court.[10] The Lubanga trial should make clear to any future despots in Africa that the days of impunity are over.

DARFUR

Darfur is a region of the Sudan where more than 300,000 persons have been killed and more than two million displaced in violence that has been going on since 2003.[11] The atrocities in Darfur, the first genocide of the twenty-first century, are a glaring example of how the Nuremberg law of crimes against humanity is being ignored in certain parts of the world. Arab militias, aided by the government, are allegedly responsible for the killings in Darfur. A trial in the Nuremberg tradition is a must, but political wrangling keeps causing delays in prosecution.

The trouble in Darfur started early in 2003 when rebels took up arms against the government and ambushed the Sudanese Air Force. The Sudanese government responded by hiring local militias to wage a counter-insurgency campaign. One tribe was pitted against another. The counter-insurgents, called *Janjaweed*, came from nomadic camel- or cattle-breeding tribes of Darfur and the neighboring country of Chad. The name *Janjaweed* means bandits or ruffians, combining the words *jinn*, meaning devil, with *jawad*, meaning horse.[12] They are very poor and therefore motivated by the Sudanese government's promises of land and property.[13]

After two years of horrible bloodshed in Darfur, the United Nations took action by making a formal request to the International Criminal Court (ICC) to take over the case. If the ICC manages to overcome opposition from the Sudanese government, the Darfur case will put the world's permanent criminal court to its first major test, its first big trial. The trial would be a landmark in international law—Jackson's dream coming true. A United Nations commission led by Antonio Cassese, noted Italian law professor and veteran judge at the war crimes tribunal for the former Yugoslavia, has spent months investigating the Darfur killings in preparation for trial. However, a top Sudanese official told the Cassese commission that it will never surrender any Sudanese defendants to The Hague for prosecution.[14] So far even visits to the Sudanese leaders by British Prime Minister Tony Blair and Secretary-General Kofi Annan of the United Nations for the purpose of persuading the Sudanese to relent have been unsuccessful.[15]

Sudan's president, Omar al-Bashir, took an oath in public in which he swore "thrice in the name of the Almighty God that I shall never hand over any Sudanese national to a foreign court."[16] Tens of thousands of Sudanese marched in a demonstration supporting their president's position.

For years one of the major problems encountered by the ICC was America's stiff opposition to its operation. The Bush administration has consistently campaigned against the court on grounds that the court could bring politically motivated actions against Americans abroad. Based on this policy the United States at first made its usual objections to any trial of the Darfur perpetrators before the ICC. Then a breakthrough occurred. The U.N. Security Council agreed to make an exception for the United States and ruled that Americans abroad would be exempt from prosecution before the ICC as to any criminal behavior in Sudan.[17] This removed a major obstacle. The United States returned the favor by withdrawing its opposition to the ICC trying the Darfur case.

In Washington, Secretary of State Condoleezza Rice said it was the "extraordinary" atrocities in Darfur that prompted the withdrawal of opposition.[18] At the same time, however, the United States made it clear that it was still firmly opposed in general to the ICC and that it was only making an exception because of the continuing humanitarian nightmare occurring in Darfur.

In April 2005 prospects for a Darfur trial brightened. The United Nations turned over to prosecutors of the ICC thousands of evidentiary documents and a list of fifty-one persons to be investigated for crimes against humanity in the Darfur region.[19] But the Sudanese government continued to object and what is worse, continued to wage war against its own population in what has become one of the world's worst humanitarian disasters.

In May 2006 a Darfur Peace Agreement was signed between the Sudanese government and one of the rebel groups. The agreement was backed by the United States but failed to stop the bloodshed. In fact, experts say the violence subsequently reached its worst level since fighting erupted in 2003. The Sudanese government is said to be arming the Arab militias more than ever before. Sudanese President Hassan al-Bashir remains opposed to the deployment of U.N. troops in Darfur to stop the fighting.[20]

Although the Sudan remains opposed to an international tribunal, the chief prosecutor of the ICC continues to build his case against the Darfur perpetrators. In February 2007, Moreno-Ocampo presented close to one hundred pages of evidence to the court and asked the judges to issue summonses to the first two suspects, Ahmed Harun and Ali Muhammad Ali Abd-al-Rahman. Harun is Sudan's deputy minister for humanitarian affairs. Rahman is a militia leader who allegedly led a brutal campaign against civilians.[21] In March 2007, Sudan said the ICC has no jurisdiction to try Rahman or any of its citizens and that it would try Rahman itself.[22]

Meanwhile the genocide continued and no one was taking effective action to force the Sudan government to stop it. "The United Nations," said *The New York Times*, "has repeatedly disgraced itself by its half-hearted and inadequate response. . . ."[23]

CHAPTER EIGHTEEN

THE EFFECT OF THE KRUPP
CASE ON BIG BUSINESS

ON JULY 31, 1948, I SAT IN A NUREMBERG COURTROOM WATCHING an American judge sentence Alfried Krupp, Hitler's biggest financial supporter, to twelve years in prison, and additionally ordering the confiscation of Krupp's vast fortune. After hearing evidence for seven months, the court found Krupp guilty of violating the human rights of prisoners in Nazi concentration camps by using them in forced labor. The Krupp firm, an industrial dynasty which had armed Germany in three major wars and influenced the course of European history for centuries, was a private enterprise and only indirectly part of Hitler's regime.[1] Nevertheless, the court ruled that Krupp was guilty of crimes against humanity because he had been a willful participant in joint action with the Nazis and had benefited from the slave labor that the Nazis provided for his factories. Over half a century later in a remarkable advancement of the Nuremberg legacy, that same principle has become the basis for lawsuits against some of America's biggest corporations—Unocal, Coca-Cola, General Motors, Ford Motor Company and others—on charges of aiding and abetting abuses of human rights by foreign governments. No one among us in that Nuremberg courtroom ever imagined the trial's legacy would reach so far.

For decades after Nuremberg, a group of American lawyers searched for a way to use the Nuremberg judgments made in the cases of Alfried Krupp and other Nazi industrialists to protect foreign workers from human rights violations. If Krupp was guilty of helping Hitler, perhaps the big American corporations operating abroad—allegedly supporting dictators who are engaged in such practices as forced labor and torture—could likewise be found guilty, or at least liable in a civil suit.

The Krupp case and subsequent cases involving Nazi businessmen brought together three important principles. These principles form part of the Nuremberg legacy and have acquired even greater significance in our time. The first principle was the idea that individuals, not just states, could be held accountable for violating human rights; the second was the notion that certain egregious actions by private corporations and their leaders would be subject to international scrutiny, and that no amount of profit could justify a company's violation of fundamental human rights; and the third was that a businessman would be guilty if he willfully aided, participated in, or benefited from some activity, knowing that such activity involved or would involve the violation of fundamental human rights.[2]

Lawyers have wondered if the Nuremberg principles could be extended to cover the twenty-first-century world of big business and human rights abroad. The idea sounded farfetched at first, but the possibilities were awesome. Major American companies have done business with rogue governments all over the world. If the idea ever became a reality, it would mean a tremendous expansion of the Nuremberg legacy and a chance for justice at last for hundreds of thousands of foreign laborers allegedly being victimized by foreign governments working in concert with these corporations.

But Krupp was a criminal case, and although tried by American judges, still a case from a foreign military court. The important questions were whether the judgment against Krupp was binding under international law, and if so, whether a U.S. court would ever allow such a lawsuit against a powerful American corporation.

For years such questions lingered without an answer. Finally in 1980 a breakthrough came in the federal case, *Filartiga* v. *Pena-Irala*.[3] The lawyers found what they were looking for. The key was an obscure U.S. statute, the Alien Tort Statute, which had lain dormant for almost 200 years.[4] The language of the statute said simply:

> . . . the district courts shall have original jurisdiction of any civil action by an alien for a tort only, committed in violation of the law of nations or a treaty of the United States.[5]

As applied in the *Filartiga* case, this meant that any alien who felt his or her human rights had been violated by an official of his foreign government could sue civilly in a U.S. federal court. The *Filartiga* case was based on a charge of torture against a former officer of the government of Paraguay. The court held that the defendant, an inspector general of the police force, had violated universally accepted norms of international law by kidnapping and torturing to death a seventeen-year-old boy, Joelito Filartiga, in Paraguay. The court said that the Filartigas, who were aliens, had the right to sue in a U.S. federal court for a "tort" or civil wrong committed against their son which violated international law. The court found that the prohibition of torture by the law of nations was "clear and unambiguous."[6]

The opinion foreshadowed a new era in international human rights litigation. Suddenly the door was open for lawsuits against direct perpetrators of human rights abuses in foreign countries.[7]

Following *Filartiga*, the first attempt was made in 1996 to hold a corporation accountable through combining the Nuremberg principles, the Alien Tort Statute (ATS) and the well-accepted notion that corporations could be sued civilly. Villagers from Burma (now Myanmar) brought an ATS lawsuit in federal court against the U.S. oil giant, Unocal Corporation, alleging that the company had used forced labor to build a gas pipeline across Burma from the Andaman Sea to Thailand. According to the complaint, Burmese soldiers hired by Unocal had forcibly relocated, tortured, killed and raped villagers.[8] Among the Burmese villagers who were plaintiffs in the case (and who remain anonymous to this day for fear of retaliation) were the parents of a one-month-old baby girl who died after she and her mother were kicked into a fire by an officer forcibly evicting them from their home.[9]

Unocal and the other defendants immediately moved for dismissal of the case. The moment of truth had come at last: could corporations be held liable under the Alien Tort Statute for egregious abuses committed against foreigners? In March 1997, the federal district court ruling on the motion to dismiss became the first U.S. court to answer yes—at least in theory. The court ruled that the plaintiffs' case against Unocal could proceed, and the idea that corporations could be sued under the ATS for certain human rights violations had its first judicial endorsement.[10]

The case ran into trouble in 2000, however, when the federal district court resolved all of the claims in favor of Unocal by granting the corporation's motion for summary judgment.[11] Regarding the alleged acts of

torture, murder and rape, the court determined that the plaintiffs had
not presented the evidence that was necessary to find the corporation liable. The court wanted evidence that Unocal had "participated in or influenced the unlawful military conduct";[12] or that Unocal had
"controlled the Myanmar military's decision to commit the alleged tor-
tuous acts."[13] As for the forced labor claim, the court concluded that although Unocal knew that forced labor was being used and was
benefiting from its use, liability required evidence that the defendant actively "sought to employ forced or slave labor."[14] This ruling sounded
like defeat for the poor villagers.

But the case was not over. The plaintiffs appealed, and the legacy of
Nuremberg came to the rescue. In September 2002, the U.S. Court of
Appeals for the Ninth Circuit reversed the summary judgment rulings
on the ATS claims for forced labor, murder and rape. This meant that
the Burmese could continue seeking redress for these acts.[15] In reasoning that Unocal could be guilty of aiding and abetting the Burmese military, the appellate court relied heavily on the legal standard established
by Nuremberg and other international criminal tribunals (which themselves draw significantly on Nuremberg precedent). For example, in deciding whether Unocal's participation in the acts of forced labor was
sufficient for liability, the court relied on the Nuremberg cases of the
two Nazi businessmen who had helped Hitler's nefarious schemes, Alfried Krupp and Friedrich Flick:

> Unocal thus resembles the defendants in *Krupp,* who well knew that any
> expansion (of their business) would require the employment of forced
> labor, 9 Trials at 1442, and the defendants in *United States* v. *Flick,* 6 Tri-
> als of War Criminals Before the Nuremberg Military Tribunals Under
> Control Council Law No. 10 (1952), who sought to increase their pro-
> duction quota and thus their forced labor allocation, *id.* at 1198, 1202.[16]

The court also used Nuremberg's aiding and abetting standard of
"knowing practical assistance [or] encouragement . . . which has a substantial effect on the perpetration of the crime" to determine that Unocal could be found liable for the military's acts of murder and rape,
which were committed in furtherance of the forced labor program.[17]

In reasoning that Unocal aided and abetted the Burmese military by subjecting the village people to forced labor, the U.S. Court of Appeals said:

> We should apply international law as developed in the decisions by international criminal tribunals such as the Nuremberg Military Tribunals for the applicable substantive law. . . . [18]

The Ninth Circuit's opinion appeared to be a victory for the victims of human rights abuses by corporations, and sent a message to international businesses that they might be held responsible for violations of international law.[19] After the ruling, in fact, many thought *Unocal* would be the first case to successfully charge a corporation with aiding and abetting human rights violations in a foreign country. Unfortunately, it never became a final judgment and thus did not make new law. The decision, which was delivered by a three-judge panel, was appealed by Unocal, and the Ninth Circuit agreed to rehear the case before an eleven-judge *en banc* panel. On December 13, 2004, before the case could be heard, the parties reached a settlement that gave the Burmese villagers $30 million in direct compensation and funds to improve living conditions in their community. Following the settlement, the case was dropped. But while none of the opinions in the case are considered legally binding as a result, they nevertheless retain their persuasive power.[20]

At the end of the day, the *Unocal* settlement was a victory not only for the plaintiffs in the case, but also for the Nuremberg legacy that made it possible. Even more important, the *Unocal* case and the fact that the Unocal Corporation was willing to pay a substantial sum to the poor Burmese villagers to settle the case provide hope to those victims abroad who have suffered abuses by powerful corporations and their partners. ATS litigation may be just the legal weapon they need to hold international corporations accountable for fundamental human rights violations.

The road to accountability, however, has been challenging. As described by Paul Hoffman, co-counsel in *Unocal* and various other high-profile ATS cases, the Bush administration, for one, has been "unrelentingly hostile" toward ATS lawsuits, particularly those against corporations.[21] Terry Collingsworth, executive director of the International Labor Rights Fund, and Rick Herz, Litigation Director of

EarthRights International, who were plaintiffs' co-counsel in *Unocal*, characterize the administration's policy and efforts as a "betrayal" of the Nuremberg legacy.[22]

In *Sosa* v. *Alvarez-Machain*, the first case in which the U.S. Supreme Court considered the Alien Tort Statute, the Bush administration challenged the statute directly, arguing that it did not provide for lawsuits for violations of customary international law, and its only function was to allow courts to hear claims that Congress would specify in future legislation.[23] In its July 2004 decision, the Supreme Court disagreed with this argument and ruled that aliens could sue under the ATS for violations of certain specific, widely accepted international norms.[24] While this landmark decision left several important questions unanswered, the court clearly rejected the administration's position outright and left the door open to ATS lawsuits so long as they involved the most egregious violations of international law and were "subject to vigilant doorkeeping."[25] Meanwhile the administration continues to allege, sometimes with success, that these cases interfere with U.S. foreign policy, its ability to fight terrorism and economic investment in foreign countries.[26]

There are a number of pending cases under the ATS that deal with big corporations. The International Labor Rights Fund has a lawsuit pending against the Exxon Mobil Corporation alleging human rights violations during a gas extraction project in Aceh, Indonesia. Coca-Cola, perhaps the most international of all American corporations, is being sued on charges of human rights abuse in Colombia. A Washington, D.C. attorney, Michael Hausfeld, has filed suit against twenty-three major corporations for aiding and abetting the South Africa apartheid regime in crimes including forced labor, murder and torture. For example, one of the cases alleges that IBM supplied computers that enabled the South African government to control the black population. Hausfeld said all the cases are based on Nuremberg precedent.[27]

The law in this area may remain relatively unsettled for some time, at least until the Supreme Court addresses the question. In the meantime, no ATS case against a corporation has reached a favorable final verdict for the victims as of the end of 2006.

In spite of the legal uncertainty, however, there is room for optimism. A powerful motivation and important part of the Nuremberg legacy was deterrence: the idea that having a legal system in place to hold perpetrators of egregious human rights abuses accountable would deter potential violators. Terry Collingsworth points out:

> One of the major impacts of the success of ATS litigation is that most reputable companies now are at least considering the potential of being sued when they are designing their offshore operations and plans. But for this litigation, we wouldn't see that going on right now.[28]

The Nuremberg precedent for business law is also catching on in foreign countries. Recently lawyers in European courts have used the Krupp case to protect poor workers from violations of their human rights. In France, for example, although there is no Alien Tort Statute to help them, lawyers there have found other ways to go after big firms involved in atrocities abroad. Using the principle of universal jurisdiction, which permits lawsuits for inhumane acts committed in far off lands, French lawyers won a settlement from the French oil firm Total following a lawsuit alleging forced labor in Burma. The French case was also based on the legal concept established at Nuremberg.[29]

Before Nuremberg there was no law, no court, no jurisdiction, for bringing men like Adolf Hitler or Hermann Goering to justice for their crimes. Robert Jackson and his Allied partners had to build the legal framework for such prosecutions. Today there is no similar framework to govern the behavior of big corporations and their leaders accused of helping foreign governments abuse their people. No international law is in place to monitor what multinational firms do when they use labor in other countries. Neither the United Nations, the World Bank, the International Monetary Fund nor any other institution has any authority to pass judgment on the legitimacy of such behavior.[30]

Prosecution of corporations for abuses in foreign lands under the Alien Tort Statute still has not won full acceptance in American law. The Bush administration and big business constitute strong opposition. But the *Unocal* case is persuasive, if not legal, authority. If the cases pending win full acceptance, then a new framework for international justice will be in place, based largely on Nuremberg principles.

CHAPTER NINETEEN

NUREMBERG AND THE SUPREME COURT

IN THE TWENTY-FIRST CENTURY THE NUREMBERG LEGACY REACHED new stature in American law when the United States Supreme Court relied on the Nuremberg judgment as authority in two landmark opinions. Once again the prediction by postwar critics that Nuremberg would have little meaning to future law was shown to be mistaken.

After the catastrophe of the 9/11 terrorist attacks, the Bush administration rounded up persons suspected of terrorism from all over the world and imprisoned them at the U.S. military base at Guantanamo Bay, Cuba. The suspects were prisoners of the war on terror but they were denied basic human rights, and in the administration's view could be kept in a permanent state of imprisonment.[1] They had no right to be present at their trials, no right to know what the evidence was against them, no right to a lawyer and no rights under the Geneva Convention Article III, which guarantees that any sentences against a prisoner of war shall be "by a regularly constituted court affording all the judicial guarantees which are recognized as indispensable by civilized peoples."[2] The administration's position was that the Guantanamo detainees were not prisoners of war in the traditional sense but unlawful combatants because they did not belong to any nation's army, and therefore the Geneva Convention did not apply. Thus the suspects had no right to challenge their treatment at Guantanamo Bay before an American court.[3] Many Americans, and especially human rights groups, were enraged by the government's treatment of the detainees. They felt that the Nuremberg legacy of fair trial for every accused person was being violated and that America's image as a defender of human rights was badly damaged.

The administration was accused in the American press of imprisoning hundreds of people haphazardly without any clear idea of what to do with them, and little attempt to find out who they were or what crime they may have committed.[4] Furthermore, the Geneva Convention has always been considered to cover all prisoners, whether they are classified as prisoners of war or as "unlawful enemy combatants," such as members of the Taliban or Al Qaeda.[5]

In June 2004 there came a breakthrough. It was the denial of the right to be heard before an American judge that landed the case in the Supreme Court. Speaking for the Supreme Court, Justice Sandra Day O'Connor, since retired, dealt a setback to the administration's arbitrary treatment of suspected terrorists. Justice O'Connor ruled that U.S. citizens held as terrorist suspects could challenge their treatment in American courts and argue before an American judge that they were being held illegally.[6] In doing so she cited the judgment of the Nuremberg International Military Tribunal with regard to German treatment of Soviet prisoners of war, and quoted the Nuremberg opinion to argue that the detainees at Guantanamo still had certain human rights. She adopted the Nuremberg language, which stated:

> captivity in war is neither revenge, nor punishment, but solely protective custody, the only purpose of which is to prevent the prisoners of war from further participation in the war.[7]

Then in June 2006 came the most substantial use ever of Nuremberg law by the U.S. Supreme Court. The high court's historic decision in *Hamdan* v. *Rumsfeld*[8] left no question whatsoever that the Supreme Court regarded the judgment of the Nuremberg tribunal as precedent, and that although Nuremberg was international or foreign law, rather than American law, it was entitled to the respect of the court. Salim Ahmed Hamdan was a Yemeni who was captured in Afghanistan in November 2001 and taken to Guantanamo in June 2002. According to the government, he had been a driver and bodyguard for Osama bin Laden.[9] In the *Hamdan* case, Justice John Paul Stevens, speaking for the Supreme Court, struck down the administration's plan to put Guantanamo detainees on trial before military commissions. Stevens ruled that the military commissions were not authorized by federal statute and violated both federal and international law by trying the Guantanamo detainees without the safeguards of due process.[10] The case was of tremendous importance to the nation because it dealt with the president's power to overrule the Constitution and the Geneva Conventions in time of war. In reaching his opinion, Justice Stevens placed special emphasis on how the Nuremberg court defined the law of conspiracy.

Hamdan was charged with conspiring with members of Al Qaeda to attack civilians and commit murder and terrorism. Conspiracy was the only charge against him. "There is no allegation," Justice Stevens wrote, "that Hamdan had any command responsibility, played a leadership role, or participated in the planning of any activity."[11] A central issue before the Supreme Court was whether a military commission had the power to proceed on such a conspiracy charge. Stevens held that the offense of conspiracy with which Hamdan was charged was "not an 'offense' that by . . . the law of war may be tried by military commissions."[12] The justice pointed out that the international war crimes tribunal at Nuremberg convicted several of the Nazi leaders of conspiracy, but that was conspiracy to wage aggressive war, requiring actual participation in a concrete plan to wage war, which was much different from the charge against Hamdan. Justice Stevens' opinion went on to show that the Nuremberg court specifically refused to recognize as a violation of the law of war the kind of conspiracy with which Hamdan was charged.

"As one prominent figure from the Nuremberg trials has explained," Stevens said,

> members of the Tribunal objected to recognition of conspiracy as a violation of the law of war on the ground that "(t)he Anglo-American concept of conspiracy was not part of European legal systems and arguably not an element of the internationally recognized laws of war." T. Taylor, *Anatomy of the Nuremberg Trials: A Personal Memoir,* 36 (1992).[13]

The Supreme Court decision in favor of the detainees, in effect, rejected the president's notion that he could ignore Nuremberg precedent and decide which people deserved a fair trial and which did not. The decision was a major triumph for the Nuremberg legacy because it advanced the idea that every person has a right to a fair trial.

Since *Hamdan,* Congress passed the Military Commissions Act, an attempt to undercut both the *Hamdi* and *Hamdan* opinions (further discussed in Chapter 21, "What Happened to Due Process?").[14] But however the higher courts rule, the decisions in *Hamdi* and *Hamdan* have made one thing clear. Whether Nuremberg law is called foreign or international, the United States Supreme Court will use it as precedent when appropriate in establishing the law of the land.

CHAPTER TWENTY

THE TRIALS OF SADDAM HUSSEIN

FORMER IRAQI DICTATOR SADDAM HUSSEIN WAS CAPTURED DECEMber 13, 2003, in an underground hideout near his hometown of Tikrit. "Ladies and gentlemen, we got him," announced Paul Bremer, United States chief administrator in Iraq. Saddam had allegedly committed atrocious crimes against humanity, massacring hundreds of thousands—the Shi'ites who opposed him, the Kurds he gassed to death and the Kuwaitis he killed when he invaded Kuwait in 1990. In the campaign he waged against Iraqi Kurdish civilians in 1988, allegedly 50,000 or more civilians were killed and 2,000 villages destroyed, and deadly poison gas was used upon thousands of unarmed women and children.[1] But despite overwhelming evidence against him, Saddam Hussein was allowed to escape immediate execution and instead given a chance to defend himself in a court of law.

How different was the reaction to Hussein's capture from the capture of the major Nazi war criminals. In 1945 the cries for disposing of the hated Nazis without bothering about a trial resounded around the world. Allied leaders such as Winston Churchill and Henry Morgenthau were among those calling for execution. Such cries haunted Jackson when he went to London to plan a trial, but in Hussein's case the reaction was otherwise: no major head of state called for anything but a decent trial for the former dictator. In Washington, no one was pressuring President Bush to seek anything but justice. All the commentators simply took it for granted that there would be a trial. Nuremberg made the difference. The world had changed because of what happened at the Palace of Justice sixty years earlier. Amid all his shouts of defiance, Hussein could thank Nuremberg for the fact that he was given a trial and, according to some experts at least, a reasonably fair one.[2] At his arraignment in July 2004, his first appearance in court, he questioned the legitimacy of the Iraq Special Tribunal set up to try him and his co-defendants. He called the court a "play aimed at Bush's chance of winning the U.S. presidential election."[3]

On October 19, 2005, the Iraqi authorities put Hussein and seven others on trial in Baghdad before a panel of five Iraqi judges in what was to be a series of trials against him. The prosecution charged the former dictator with ordering the killing of 148 men and boys from the Shi'ite village of Dujail in 1982, a relatively minor crime compared to the others on Hussein's hit list. Unlike every previous "war crimes" trial, the United Nations was not involved, the reason being that the Iraqi rules permitted imposition of the death penalty and the United Nations would have no part of trials where execution was a possible sentence.

Because of Hussein's notoriety, the Dujail case provided a tremendous opportunity to show Iraqis and the world that once-powerful dictators can be brought to justice in a fair trial conducted by their own people. But even before the case started, the proceedings were beset with cynicism and charges that the court was biased against Hussein. The United States, its advisers in the background, was certainly no impartial observer, being in the middle of a war against Hussein's supporters. The special tribunal administering the case was established by American officials using American money. The five judges on the case were all Iraqis trained by American experts.[4] Since the United States had a say in the appointment of the judges and presumably had some control over them, it was difficult to describe the court as an independent judiciary. In December 2004, Ramsey Clark, former Attorney General of the United States, highest law officer in the nation, went to Iraq to visit with Hussein's family. He promised to help as a member of the defense team. Clark came back convinced that Hussein would not receive a fair trial. "The United States," Clark said, "has already destroyed any hope of legitimacy, fairness or even decency by its treatment and isolation of the former president and its creation of the Iraq Special Tribunal to try him."[5]

Many of the Iraqi judges trained for the Hussein trials had previously handled only minor cases in lower-level courts, such as traffic matters. Higher-level judges were not selected because they had served in Hussein's system of justice and were considered corrupt.[6] Finding judges who could be impartial was a major problem. Most of the judges in the training program were antagonistic to Hussein and had difficulty giving him the benefit of the presumption of innocence.[7]

As the trial started, the judges' lack of experience in handling matters of such scope became apparent. At times they seemed unable to keep Hussein from controlling the court. This circumstance was unlike the Nuremberg court, where the judges had vast experience and did not need foreign experts to help them prepare for trial. "If the purpose of these trials," wrote William Langewiesche of the *Atlantic Monthly,* "is to promote courtroom justice as an alternative to the Arab tradition of vengeance, the best one can hope for is that the tribunal will be able to learn on the job."[8] One chief judge quit after government officials criticized his performance. A second judge was chosen to succeed him but he was denied the position because he was suspected of having ties to Hussein's Ba'ath Party. Security problems were extraordinary. Three defense lawyers were murdered and other defense lawyers and judges had to work under the constant threat of assassination or harm to their families. Several prosecution witnesses, fearing reprisal if they were identified, testified behind curtains to avoid being seen. Even their voices were digitized to avoid voice identification. Only the presiding judge dared show himself to the public. The other judges remained concealed and their names were not disclosed. During trial there were numerous harangues by Hussein before the court as well as walkouts and protests against the court's right to try him. *The New York Times* called the atmosphere in the courtroom "circuslike."[9]

On November 5, 2006, Saddam Hussein was found guilty of crimes against humanity and sentenced to death by hanging. His half brother and chief of intelligence, Barzan Ibrahim, and Awad Hamad al-Bandar, head of Hussein's former Revolutionary Court, received the same sentence.[10] When the verdict was announced and before the bailiff could restrain him, Hussein shouted to the judge: "You don't decide anything! You are servants of the occupiers and their lackeys! You are puppets!" The judge responded: "Take him out," and Hussein was forcibly led from the courtroom.[11]

There can be no question that the Dujail trial had serious legal defects which left experts doubting whether the trial lived up to Nuremberg's standards. Human Rights Watch, one of the world's leading human rights organizations, concluded that

> the level of legal and practical expertise of the key actors in the court— trial judges, administrators, prosecutors, and defense lawyers—is not sufficient to fairly and effectively try crimes of this magnitude.[12]

Amnesty International, another leading human rights organization, described the trial as "deeply flawed and unfair."[13] *The New York Times* said the trial was "too flawed to stand as Mr. Hussein's ultimate reckoning with the law."[14] The principal reasons for these unfavorable opinions were: (1) victors' justice (Iraqi judges selected by Hussein's enemies); (2) inexperienced judges; (3) removal of two presiding judges during trial for political reasons; (4) lack of security; (5) Hussein not being properly informed of the charges against him; (6) Hussein not being allowed to fully confront and examine all witnesses; (7) defense counsel being denied access to evidence; and (8) Hussein being executed within sixty days of his conviction, which was hardly sufficient time for appellate review.[15]

Certainly a carefully conducted, scrupulously fair trial it was not. And yet, despite the failure to meet standards of international justice, there remains much to be said of Hussein's first trial that is positive. That this hated man was given a trial at all under the perilous conditions of war-torn Baghdad was a triumph in itself. That he was tried in an open, transparent setting, the event broadcast on worldwide television—not a secret session but a genuine trial and with a team of lawyers including the former Attorney General of the United States to represent him—was still an advance for due process and the Nuremberg legacy. Hussein's trial, after all, was the first in history against a former head of state for crimes against humanity conducted in his own country by his own people.[16]

The Iraqi statute that governed the trial to a large extent adopted Nuremberg principles. The judges were required to presume Hussein innocent although they may have had difficulty understanding the concept. They should be commended, not criticized, for their courage in risking their lives under great danger. There was no sign that the former dictator was "railroaded." American lawyers have pointed out that there was substantial evidence to support the verdict and that the five Iraqi judges made a reasonable effort to conduct a fair trial.[17] This evidence included documents signed by Hussein ordering execution of many of his victims. Michael P. Scharf, professor at Case Western Reserve School of Law, was one of the American experts who advised the Iraqi tribunal during the trial. "Saddam was convicted on the strength of his own documents," Scharf said.[18]

"They could've easily allowed him to be arbitrarily executed," said Australian Prime Minister John Howard, "as has happened in so many other countries . . . but no, they were determined to demonstrate to the world that there was a new Iraq . . . this mass murderer was given due process."[19] The Australian prime minister may have had in mind the demise of another dictator. Near the end of World War II, the Italian fascist dictator Benito Mussolini was summarily executed by his political enemies, his body hung upside down in the public square for all to see and mock him. There was never a thought about a trial. But for Nuremberg, Hussein might have met the same fate.

Critics say the Hussein trial should have been moved to a safer place outside Iraq with non-Iraqi judges presiding. But the Iraqi government felt the people needed the trial at home, run by their own people, to help forge their own identity and build confidence in their own government. The new International Criminal Court at The Hague lacked jurisdiction to try the case because Hussein's crimes were committed before the court came into existence.

At Nuremberg the trial of the Nazi leaders eventually awakened the German people to the past and helped move Germany to a democratic government. So, too, the Hussein trial record may benefit Iraq and encourage its citizens toward democracy. Perhaps the Hussein trial should be judged by a different standard than that of international law. If the Iraqi people have learned from the evidence produced in the courtroom the true nature of their former leader's reign; if the oppressed people in the world have learned that dictators can be overthrown, brought to trial and put to death for their crimes, through a legal process, then the Hussein case will not have been in vain and the Nuremberg legacy will continue to grow.[20]

In August 2006 a second trial of Saddam Hussein began, charging him with genocide in the so-called "Anfal" case. This was a much bigger case than Dujail and much more relevant to the true character of Hussein's regime. The Dujail trial hardly began to reveal the horrors Hussein inflicted upon his people. The "Anfal" case involved a grisly campaign that Hussein waged against Iraqi Kurds in 1988. The charges alleged that Hussein sought to annihilate the entire Kurdish population in Iraq. On December 12, 2006, prosecutors showed graphic evidence of villagers dying from what prosecutors said was a chemical attack.[21] As the trial progressed the evidence exposed other examples of the former dictator's genocidal assault, such as use of deadly poison gas against thousands of helpless women and children. In the middle of this second trial, on December 26, 2006, the appeals court affirmed the death sentence in the Dujail case. The judge said the execution must occur within thirty days, but just four days later, on the morning of December 29, 2006, Hussein was hanged. All over the world his enemies and the families of his victims rejoiced.

As this book goes to press in 2007, debate goes on as to whether Hussein's execution was a mistake. On the one hand it is argued that by doing so, Hussein was allowed to escape his day of reckoning, that the world was deprived of the facts of his infamy,[22] and that the question of whether the U.S. invasion of Iraq was justified can now never be satisfactorily answered because crucial evidence such as Hussein's own testimony can no longer be revealed in a court of law.

In the first trial, Hussein freely admitted that he ordered the murder of 148 men and boys from Dujail and claimed in his defense that most of the victims were involved in an attempt to assassinate him.[23] Thus the argument is that he might have made further admissions, shedding new light on the campaign against the Kurds if the second trial had continued in his presence. In 1945 the American people wanted to know what Hitler did to justify drawing them into the bloodiest war in history. Nuremberg, with its mountain of evidence, provided the answer. In 2006 many Americans were asking a similar question about Hussein's reign. That is why the second trial of genocide was so important. On January 8, 2007, after Saddam Hussein had been dead for nine days, the Anfal trial reconvened with Hussein's six co-defendants still in the dock. Experts hoped they would be more likely to talk with the dictator out of the way. The first order of business was to dismiss all charges against Hussein, eliminating speculation that he might be tried *in absentia*.

Some say the execution was a good thing because it means that Hussein has finally been held accountable; that the hanging, botched as it was, brought relief to the hundreds of thousands of Iraqi Shi'ites and Kurds who suffered under Hussein's rule, and that it let other repressive leaders know what could happen to them if they commit similar acts; and that the decision was made by the Iraqis themselves and not by outsiders. In this regard, President Bush called the execution "an important milestone on Iraq's course to becoming a democracy that can govern, sustain and defend itself."[24] On Sunday, June 24, 2007, three chief aides to Saddam Hussein were found guilty of genocide war crimes and crimes against humanity by the Iraqi High Tribunal and sentenced to death by hanging for their roles in the slaughter of as many as 180,000 Kurds. The most notorious of these three was Ali Hassan al-Majeed, known as "Chemical Ali."

The debate on the timing of Hussein's execution will go on, but what is beyond question is the fact that it was Nuremberg precedent that forced Hussein's trial to occur in the first place.

PART THREE

THREATS TO THE LEGACY

CHAPTER TWENTY-ONE

WHAT HAPPENED TO DUE PROCESS?

ROBERT JACKSON'S PASSION FOR JUSTICE AT NUREMBERG ESTABLISHED America's reputation for fairness to persons accused of crime no matter how high or low their status, or how heinous the charge. When Jackson persuaded the Allies at the London pre-trial conference to adopt his version of due process for men despised as the worst criminals in history, he won for his country a deserved place as moral leader of the world. When he announced to a stunned audience in the Nuremberg courtroom that the Nazi defendants were presumed to be innocent and that that presumption of innocence had to be overcome by solid evidence, his opening statement by itself represented a giant step for humanity.

For more than half a century, from the last Nuremberg trial in 1949 to the 9/11 attacks of 2001, the United States continued to develop a legal system that was admired throughout the world. But after 9/11 that reputation began to suffer. America's image as a defender of international justice and human rights went into decline. Critics complained that the Bush administration's concerns for national security were going too far, eroding the nation's moral authority, denying the very freedoms that the war on terror was supposed to protect and thereby threatening the Nuremberg legacy, especially the legacy of fair trial.

Reports began to surface of systematic violations of the international law born at Nuremberg: prisoners being shipped off to Guantanamo Bay in Cuba without any serious attempt to find out who they were or what crime they were suspected of; the same prisoners being held for years without being charged under conditions that allegedly amounted to torture;[1] denial of the right of *habeas corpus,* of the right to challenge one's incarceration in an official court of law; and unfair trial procedures.[2] The two latter allegations—denial of the right of *habeas corpus* and denial of a fair trial—if true, are direct threats to the Nuremberg legacy.

Soon after 9/11, President Bush established military commissions to try the detainees in secret before military officers acting as judge and jury. But the prisoners were routinely barred from seeing evidence, confronting their accusers or having access to real legal representation.[3] The trouble with a secret court is that too often it can become a "kangaroo court" or a Kafkaesque proceeding.[4] Jeremy Bentham, the British philosopher, said publicity "is the very soul of justice. It keeps the judge, while trying, under trial."[5] Hence the public trial is often considered the best safeguard against abuse of judicial power. A major criticism of the military commissions was that they allowed for the proceedings to be closed to both the defendant and his counsel, who could then be excluded from ever learning what evidence was presented in their absence.[6]

When Jackson was planning the proceedings at Nuremberg, he realized the importance of opening the trial to the public and the press. He even helped design a courtroom to include a press gallery and a platform for the cameras, knowing that openness was the best disinfectant against abuse of due process. The doors to the Palace of Justice were usually open. Under the volatile circumstances of the current "war on terror" the Bush administration may have a legitimate argument that secrecy of trials of suspected terrorists is, in some cases, necessary to protect national security. But the need for secrecy does not excuse unfair trials. Complaints from defense attorneys or human rights activists that the military tribunals were not conducted fairly might be suspect because of the bias of the complainers or as part of their efforts to help the accused. However, in August 2005 *The New York Times* revealed that two military prosecutors—Captain John Carr and Major Robert Preston, both of the Air Force—had confidentially complained to their superiors that the military commissions were not fair to defendants, that the panel of officers hearing the evidence was "handpicked" to ensure convictions and that the trial system had been secretly arranged to deprive defendants of material that could prove their innocence.[7] There followed an investigation by the Pentagon's independent inspector general who found no evidence of unlawful behavior or ethical violations.[8] Because the trials are held in secret it was hard to know whom to believe, but if there is any truth at all to what Captain Carr and Major Preston said, it would mean that the Defense Department does not hold the Nuremberg legacy in high regard.

On May 4, 2006, *The New York Times* was moved to comment:

> So far only 10 of the 490 people still stashed away in Guantanamo have ever been charged with anything. The rest were hauled up before military proceedings that were a joke, if the available transcripts are any indication, to determine whether they should continue to be held without any rights or process under the phony label of "unlawful enemy combatant" that the Bush Administration concocted after 9/11 for just this purpose.[9]

The administration has also apparently ignored the Nuremberg precedent of trial conducted in a timely manner. In 1945 Jackson and the other Allied prosecutors wasted little time bringing the captured Nazi defendants to justice. The war ended in May and by the fall the trial was underway. Jackson saw to it that the Nazis received a speedy trial, open to the world, with reasonably competent counsel and no secret sessions. Defendants had the right to be present at all times. No one languished in jail for years wondering what the charges were against them or when or how they would be tried.

In two landmark decisions, *Rasul* v. *Bush*[10] and *Hamdan,* cited earlier, the U.S. Supreme Court rebuked the administration for denying the detainees their right to due process. In *Hamdi,* Supreme Court Justice Sandra Day O'Connor went so far as to warn the administration that "a state of war is not a blank check for the President when it comes to the rights of the Nation's citizens."[11] The rulings appeared be a victory for the Nuremberg legacy but the victory did not last long.

First of all, the *Hamdan* ruling in no way changed the administration's authority to hold the detainees captive at Guantanamo indefinitely so long as it does not put them on trial.[12] Second, and much more important, in September 2006, Congress passed the Military Commissions Act, which denied 430 Guantanamo detainees and other enemy combatants the right to file a *habeas corpus* petition. If allowed to stand, this means that the men detained at Guantanamo can be held there indefinitely without ever having a federal judge decide the legality of their imprisonment.[13] The act also redesigns the military commissions along guidelines set by the Supreme Court, which will supposedly conform to the Constitution. The president signed the act into law in October 2006. The act not only effectively wiped out many of the human rights gains that had been made by the Supreme Court in the *Hamdi, Rasul* and *Hamdan* cases, but it abolished the writ of *habeas corpus* for many innocent persons who have never even been accused of a crime.

Habeas corpus, an established doctrine of English Common Law going back to the Middle Ages, is the right of a person in custody to petition the court and question the legality of his incarceration. It was recognized by the framers of the American Constitution, who further declared that the right could only be suspended under very narrow circumstances.[14] In fact the last time *habeas corpus* was suspended before 2006 was in 1871 when President Ulysses S. Grant sent federal troops to South Carolina to prevent the Ku Klux Klan from attacking black citizens who had just been freed from slavery.[15]

As to the new Military Commissions Act, Senator Patrick Leahy, Chairman of the Senate Judiciary Committee, said, "This undercuts everything the nation stands for. . . . [Are] our people so terrified that we must do what no bomb or attack could ever do by taking away the very freedoms that define America?"[16] As this book went to press in 2007 the question of whether the new military commissions trials at Guantanamo would honor the spirit of Nuremberg was still undecided. In June 2007, the government's new system of trying Guantanamo detainees ran into trouble. Military judges dismissed war crimes charges against two Guantanamo detainees for failure to follow required legal procedures. Senator Arlen Specter, the senior Republican on the judiciary committee, said that the decisions could prompt Congress to reevaluate the legal rights of detainees.[17]

These trials have been called the first war crimes trials conducted by the United States since Nuremberg[18] although the charges are not technically war crimes as the term was used at Nuremberg. An appeal by the detainees is pending before the United States Supreme Court, claiming that the new system is just as unfair as the previous one, which was declared unconstitutional. On March 26, 2007, David Hicks, who was charged with providing material support to terrorists, was the first detainee to face a judge under the Military Commissions Act passed by Congress in 2006.[19] Hicks faced a life term in prison and had been held virtually incommunicado without a hearing for five years at the Guantanamo detention center.[20] He pled guilty to one count before the military commissions court at Guantanamo, and his plea meant there would be no trial on the issue of his guilt and thus the fairness of the new trial procedure was left in question. On March 30, 2007, an eight-member panel of military officers imposed a sentence of nine more months in custody. Hicks' military defense lawyer, U.S. Marine Major Michael Mori, criticized the military commissions as unfair and reportedly called them kangaroo courts.[21] Meanwhile, the Military Commissions Act and the fairness of the trials conducted by the military commissions are almost certain to come up before the Supreme Court. Surely the ghosts of Nuremberg will be watching.

In 2004 threats to the Nuremberg legacy emerged in still another form, causing many Americans to feel ashamed and further damaging America's reputation as a protector of human rights. It hardly seems possible that in the first decade of the new century this great American nation found itself on the brink of making torture legal. Before 9/11 no one could imagine that someday our high officials would consider torture as an unofficial policy of the U.S. government.[22]

Nuremberg inspired the law that made torture an international crime. The Nuremberg judges sent Nazi officials, SS men in particular, to their deaths for acts of torture. The evidence both in the main trial and in the trials that followed showed that in territories occupied by the Nazis so-called "third degree interrogations" were often used to try to obtain information about the Allied forces.[23]

From the Nuremberg precedent came the United Nations' 1948 Universal Declaration of Human Rights which declared in the simplest of terms: No one shall be subjected to torture or to cruel, inhuman or degrading treatment or punishment.[24] There were no exceptions. All human beings were protected, wherever and whoever they were, even terrorists and enemy combatants, suspected or convicted. Torture was unlawful under any circumstances. In 1949 the Geneva Conventions adopted the same rule, as did the United Nations Convention Against Torture in 1984.[25]

In April 2004 American newspapers and television shocked the public with photographs taken from the Abu Ghraib prison outside Baghdad showing Iraqi prisoners being mistreated and humiliated by U.S. soldiers. Later investigations alleged a system of torture practiced by U.S. personnel in Guantanamo, Afghanistan and Iraq.[26] Secretary of Defense Donald Rumsfeld, since retired, said that only a small number of U.S. military were involved and denied any policy in his department authorizing torture.[27]

Soon after the Abu Ghraib scandal broke, a document prepared by the Justice Department was leaked to the press. Later known as the "Torture Memo," the document authorized the Central Intelligence Agency to inflict pain and suffering on detainees during interrogations. The document advised that the president could supersede laws prohibiting torture under the doctrine of "necessity."[28]

In the fall of 2005 an ABC news report revealed that interrogators for the Central Intelligence Agency, using officially approved tactics, were forcing suspected terrorists to stand handcuffed, feet shackled to the floor, for more than forty hours; others were made to stand naked in fifty-degree temperatures while being doused with cold water; and still others were subjected to a procedure called "water boarding" in which the prisoner was bound to an inclined board, feet raised higher than the head, and then cellophane was wrapped over his face and water poured over him causing a fear of drowning.[29]

In November 2005, the administration's support for torture came out in the open when Vice President Cheney lobbied senators to allow torture as U.S. policy. Specifically, Cheney appealed to the senators to authorize exceptions for the CIA in the proposed ban on torture.[30] His attempt failed, and instead Congress overwhelmingly passed an amendment proposed by Senator John McCain outlawing torture. The president then issued a "signing statement," which implied that as Commander-in-Chief he will follow the ban on torture as he sees fit.[31] In effect, the White House told Congress that it had no intention of complying with laws restricting their power to torture detainees.[32]

Despite the ban by Congress, torture apparently continued at Guantanamo in 2006. In February 2006, the United Nations Human Rights Commission called for the United States to shut down the camp at Guantanamo. The commission declared that some of the practices at the detention center "must be assessed as amounting to torture."[33]

Albert J. Mora was no casual observer of the scene at Guantanamo Bay. He was general counsel of the United States Navy—a position equivalent to a four-star general—before his departure from that office in January 2006. For years Mora was deeply involved in investigating charges of abuse against suspected terrorists at the infamous detention camp. He could hardly be said to have any bias against the Bush administration, having served in both the first and second Bush administrations as a political appointee. But Mora pleaded with his superiors to stop what he believed to be cruelty and torture of the detainees and warned the administration that the new legal theory granting the president the right to authorize abuse was dangerous and illegal.[34]

In a notable story, *The New Yorker* magazine reported in February 2006 that Mora's efforts "to halt what he saw as a disastrous and unlawful policy of authorizing cruelty toward terror suspects" were largely undermined by a small contingent of administration lawyers working closely with Vice President Cheney.[35] Referring to the administration lawyers and their determination that the Geneva Conventions did not apply, Mora wondered "if they were even familiar with the Nuremberg trials."[36]

In the spring of 2007, as this book went to press, many Americans feared that the Bush administration was dismantling the rule of law in America. The administration was accused of systematically denying the right to counsel, the right to evidence and the right to a fair trial—or any trial for that matter—to prisoners who may have committed no crime at all.[37] Even the conservative press was complaining. Said *The San Diego Union Tribune:*

> The word needs to get out that the current detainee policy is unacceptable and harmful, not just to those being detained but the country as a whole. Americans are better people than this, and it's time we started acting like it.[38]

After World War II, Nuremberg convinced most of the world that the United States was guardian of the highest ideals of justice. American men and women were willing to fight and die for those ideals. But the use of torture, the denial of *habeas corpus* and the denial of due process is not the legacy that Nuremberg promised. America must take back that legacy and save it from being lost in the name of national security.

CHAPTER TWENTY-TWO

SABOTAGE OF THE
INTERNATIONAL CRIMINAL COURT

SABOTAGE. THE WORD SOUNDS HARSH. BUT IT IS NOT UNFAIR TO USE the term in describing the Bush administration's policy toward the International Criminal Court (ICC). Other terms like "opposed" or "resistant" would be milder but hardly accurate. Sabotage is the right description.

How disappointed Robert Jackson would be if he knew that his own country not only refuses to participate in the ICC but threatens other countries with sanctions unless they do the same. Jackson did what no other Supreme Court justice had ever done before when he took leave from the court to do what he could not do on the bench. He feared civilization could not survive a third world war so he took the job as chief prosecutor of the Nuremberg trial because he saw Nuremberg as a way to deter war. Jackson knew that the case against the major Nazi war criminals was only the beginning of a long march to international justice. A permanent court would be the natural next step after Nuremberg.

Henry T. King, Jr., who worked closely with Jackson as a prosecutor at Nuremberg, also attended the United Nations conference at Rome on the creation of the ICC in June 1998. "It is indeed a matter of supreme irony," wrote King,

> that the United States of America, which led the way in the Nuremberg proceedings through Jackson's leadership, has turned its back on Jackson by renouncing, and making every effort to sabotage, the introduction of the International Criminal Court into today's world.[1]

In 2000 President Clinton signed the Rome Statute that created the new court. Two years later Clinton's successor, President Bush, let it be known that his administration would not respect Clinton's signature. In May 2002 the Under Secretary of State John R. Bolton sent a letter to Kofi Annan, U.N. Secretary-General, announcing that the United States did not consider itself bound by the Rome Statute.[2] The United States then "unsigned" Clinton's signature, an unprecedented event in the history of diplomacy. Bolton outlined the nature of the administration's policy on the new court. He listed three things the United States would *not* do with regard to the International Criminal Court: no financial support; no help to make the court function; and no working with other nations to improve the court. "This policy," Bolton said, "will maximize the chances that the court will not come into existence."[3] This was unabashed opposition and a betrayal of the Nuremberg legacy. Bolton was later appointed U.S. ambassador to the United Nations.

Further sabotage came when the United States suspended military aid to 35 countries that supported the court, when they refused to pledge to give American citizens immunity before the ICC.[4] Congress passed another law in 2004 that requires that economic aid be suspended to nations refusing to sign "agreements" to exempt Americans from prosecution.[5]

When the delegates at the Rome conference were discussing the statute, the United States took the position that it would only approve the statute on the condition that no American would be prosecuted without prior consent by the Bush administration. That sounds to foreigners like the kind of arrogance that only fuels more anti-American sentiment. "Obviously," wrote Henry King, "had other nations taken this position, there would indeed have been no court. I believe the U.S. approach was designed to kill the court even before its birth."[6]

A basic precedent set at Nuremberg was that no one is above the law. The Bush administration makes a mockery of that precedent when it insists that Americans abroad are above the law. Put simply, the administration's policy is: Prosecute anyone you like, but not Americans.

In 2006, as mentioned earlier, the ICC was up and running despite the absence of the most powerful country in the world. The court's fiery prosecutor, Luis Moreno-Ocampo, is naturally disappointed by the lack of American support but he is undeterred. He sees the court as a real chance to advance civilization, to finally realize Jackson's vision, and as the only way to deter war criminals.

Many Americans wonder why their country has taken such a strong position against the ICC. Foreigners wonder also, judging by their questions every time I have lectured in Europe. Even conceding that there may be legitimate reasons for not participating, they wonder with good reason why the United States must go to such extreme measures to coerce other nations not to join. Surely the American people want to see the perpetrators of genocide and crimes against humanity prosecuted and punished, and they want to have a say in that process. American men and women have fought and died to stop Hitler and Saddam Hussein and their ilk. It seems inconsistent for America to oppose a court that brings such persons to justice and exposes their agendas.

The main reason for America's objection is the fear that anti-American nations will use the court to prosecute American service people and officials in their countries on trumped up charges, just to embarrass the United States. In other words, Americans abroad would be unjustly turned over to the court by parties who are politically motivated.

Specifically, one of the stated reasons for the United States' refusal to join the ICC is that the court lacks sufficient checks on the prosecutor.[7] There was a fear that "unchecked power in the hands of the prosecutor" could lead to prosecutions based on political motives.[8] Another reason for opposition to the ICC is that the Rome treaty that created the court only covers countries that join while non-members are beyond the court's jurisdiction; and furthermore, that it would be unconstitutional to submit U.S. citizens to judges and trial procedures not supervised by Americans.

Many experts find such arguments unpersuasive and say there is no need for the United States to fear involvement in the ICC. The court's statute contains checks and balances designed to ensure justice. The court has promised to deal only with top leaders and it will only try cases that a national court is unwilling or unable to investigate. The eighteen judges are elected by the member states.

If the ICC prosecutor intends to investigate a case, he or she must notify the country involved. The prosecutor must defer any action if that country says it will handle the matter and shows its investigation is

not a sham. As far as the claim that the court lacks the due process protections of the U.S. Constitution, the ICC requires Miranda-type
warnings before police can take a statement from a defendant, and the
right to a speedy and public trial, competent defense attorneys, recipro-
cal discovery of evidence, confrontation of witnesses and protection
against double jeopardy. The court does not provide for jury trials, but
neither did Nuremberg nor any of the other ad hoc tribunals sponsored
by the United Nations such as those for Yugoslavia, Rwanda and Sierra
Leone.

Judge Patricia M. Wald has served on the International Criminal
Tribunal for the Former Yugoslavia, and was chief judge of the United
States Court of Appeals for the District of Columbia Circuit. As to why
she supports the ICC, Judge Wald said:

> The ICC represents a critical step forward in the century-long journey
> toward holding accountable individuals who have engaged in wide-
> spread wartime and peacetime atrocities against civilians. There is sim-
> ply no other game in town, and abandonment of the court effectively
> abandons the journey toward international norms of responsibility at a
> time when globalization in other domains—communications, technol-
> ogy, trade, even civil law—forges ahead at an accelerating pace. Unless
> the international community of nations drops all pretense of holding
> war criminals accountable, there is no alternative to the ICC.[9]

Critics of the administration's position say that one reason for the
opposition to the ICC is the fear that high American officials might actually violate international law and then be legitimately prosecuted. But
how much stronger, how much more influential, the ICC would be if it
had United States' support! If the court fails because it lacks U.S. support, the consequences could be serious for human rights and world
peace. Totalitarian dictators who have innocent victims killed and tortured, maimed and raped, would go unpunished. The message of
Nuremberg that Robert Jackson wanted sent out to tyrants across the
world will fall flat, and the atrocities will go on. *The San Francisco
Chronicle* had this to say:

> This country needs the world's nations to support its efforts to prevent
> terrorist attacks. The ICC was designed to provide a moral compass by

which the world can judge war crimes, and crimes against humanity. As the world's only superpower, the United States should be supporting, not sabotaging, the creation of an international institution that can help stamp the newly emerging global culture with the rule of law. We should be offering moral leadership, not violating our own democratic principles. Every country deserves equal protection before the law and no nation should be above the law.[10]

The United States led the way in the creation and implementation of the Nuremberg trials. As a soldier in Europe at the time of the 1945 pre-trial conference in London, I remember feeling proud of my country for insisting that the great trial would be run on the principle that no one is above the law. Yet today, with its opposition and sabotage of the ICC, the Bush administration sends a message that insults the Nuremberg legacy—a message that says the rule of law is only for other people.

CONCLUSION

IN 1945 ROBERT JACKSON CAME TO NUREMBERG WITH NOBLE GOALS. He saw his role as far more than the prosecution of twenty-two Nazi war criminals. He wanted to find a better way to control both aggression and revenge. Specifically, he wanted to deter war and the atrocities of war. Critics say he failed, that the hope of Nuremberg left nothing but "historic ash."[1] Wars continue. Atrocities still shock the world. Too often little is done to halt the carnage until it is too late.

The violence in Darfur is the most recent example. As in Rwanda, the world looks elsewhere while women and children are slain in Darfur by the fighting between rebels and government forces.[2] Nuremberg made the waging of aggressive war "the supreme crime," and at the time many historians believed this to be the trial's greatest achievement. But since Nuremberg no one has been prosecuted on such a charge and the crime remains undefined.

We shall never know, however, how many national leaders have been deterred from initiating military conquest and cruel abuse of innocent civilians by the threat of a Nuremberg-type prosecution. History teaches that critical judgment of a controversial event should be reserved until a substantial period of time has passed. In the case of Nuremberg, over sixty years have gone by since Jackson made his opening statement. The time is right to step back and examine the trial's deeds and flaws and whether its initial reputation as a beacon of justice has stood up over the years.

Nuremberg had many defects, the worst of these being victors' justice and the possible application of *ex post facto* law. But such shortcomings are outweighed by the trial's legacy, a great leap forward in the evolution of a civilized world.

The major points of this legacy can be summarized as follows:

- A new standard of justice and fair trial. The Nuremberg judgment not only served as precedent for other trials of war criminals but also influenced domestic trials.
- The birth of the international human rights movement. Many experts say that Nuremberg's most important legacy was to recognize crimes against humanity.[3]
- Individual accountability and the rule of law applied to heads of state. This remarkable change in international law meant the end of sovereignty as a shield for leaders who commit war crimes or crimes against humanity.
- A written authoritative record that showed how low a highly civilized nation could sink under ruthless dictatorship. This was a lesson that has influenced over sixty years of peace and democracy in Germany.
- The principle that waging aggressive war and conspiracy to wage aggressive war are crimes.[4]
- The principle that obedience to superior orders is not a defense for war crimes and human rights violations, but may be considered only in mitigation of punishment.
- The dramatic change in the legal relationship between governments and the governed and how they perceive each other.
- Prevention of martyrdom for Nazi leaders, a status which would have been accorded them had they been summarily executed.
- The concept of an international trial, with judges and lawyers from different nations overcoming obstacles of language, custom and procedure.
- The principle of universal jurisdiction. This outgrowth of Nuremberg means that some crimes are so grave that no matter where a crime is committed, any country that captures the perpetrator may subject the individual to a trial and to punishment on behalf of all nations.
- Vindication of the United States' intervention in the war against Nazi Germany by exposing the Holocaust and Hitler's plans of aggression.
- The effect of the trial record in making Americans aware that they could no longer be an isolationist nation, that they had become

responsible for protecting western democracy. This is true despite the current administration's opposition to the International Criminal Court.

- The effect of the trial record in raising America's awareness of the consequences of racial prejudice and lessening discrimination against blacks and Jews in America.
- The influence of the Nuremberg judgment on the United States Supreme Court, particularly in cases involving treatment of suspected terrorists.
- The establishment of the Nuremberg Code, which set the guidelines for medical research involving human beings and which evolved into the medical doctrine of informed consent.
- The trials' influence in causing changes in the rules of war and the treatment of prisoners.
- The Nuremberg trials of Nazi industrialists laid the groundwork for current lawsuits against business firms accused of exploitation, abuses and even crimes against humanity in foreign lands.

Nuremberg also saw the emergence of a new American hero in the person of Robert Jackson. On the one hand, the trial exposed his frailties, his indiscretions (especially his inept cross-examination of Hermann Goering), unethical contacts with a judge and lack of interest in administration. But these flaws paled beside his performance as a crusader for justice. More than anyone else Jackson made the trial happen and established its reputation as remarkably fair and effective, despite the charged circumstances under which it was held.[5] Years later Judge Biddle, in a calmer, cooler tone than the impetuous letter to his wife quoted earlier, commented:

> The trial was the result of Mr. Jackson's patience and perseverance and unflagging determination that these men should be given a fair trial by an impartial international tribunal.[6]

On his return from Nuremberg, Jackson should have been honored with national acclaim. Instead he resumed his seat on the Supreme Court without fanfare. In 1954, five years after the last of the Nuremberg trials, Jackson was driving to work from his home in McLean,

Virginia, when he suddenly became ill. He died later that day. One of his last acts on the court was to affirm the end of racial segregation in American public schools via *Brown* v. *Board of Education.*

On January 24, 2005, the United Nations held a special session of the General Assembly to mark the sixtieth anniversary of the liberation of the Nazi concentration camps. A few days later heads of state, survivors and a few liberators from the Soviet Red Army gathered at Auschwitz-Birkenau for a ceremony commemorating the freeing of thousands of inmates from the notorious death camp. Jewish organizations expressed concern that because most survivors and liberators were in their eighties or nineties there will soon no longer be any living memory of the Holocaust. The presidents of Russia, Poland, and Israel and U.S. Vice-President Dick Cheney spoke of the need to keep awareness of the Holocaust alive after the last survivors have died.[7]

They may have forgotten that the principal and most reliable source of our knowledge of the Holocaust will never die—the record established at Nuremberg and the evidence specifically collected and gathered there, a record that will withstand the test of history.[8] Nuremberg is the single event that more than any other guarantees that those atrocities will not be forgotten. "Nuremberg remains," writes Gary Jonathan Bass of Princeton, "legalism's greatest moment of glory."[9]

Perhaps the ideals of justice set at Nuremberg were too high to expect future generations and their governments to uphold them. Soon after the attack of 9/11, Nuremberg's light began to flicker. With its treatment of suspected terrorists held at Guantanamo Bay, the Bush administration chose to defy Jackson's most cherished principle: Justice for all. It did so on the ground that when it comes to fighting terrorism, anything goes. The government took the position that it can do anything it chooses to anyone determined to be an "enemy combatant." It can hold detainees incommunicado indefinitely—unable to challenge their detention, unable to see the evidence against them or even know the charges. If there must be a trial, then it will be a secret proceeding lacking the elements of due process. Nuremberg was ignored.

When the Supreme Court ruled in 2004 that even terrorist suspects had a right to challenge their detention in a U.S. court,[10] and when the court declared later in 2006 that secret military commissions were un-fair,[11] these rulings meant that the Nuremberg legacy of fair trial for every accused human being was still alive.

Our leaders in government would do well to sit back and remind themselves how efforts for justice and human rights have evolved over the years. The high points would include the Magna Carta, the inven-tion of the writ of *habeas corpus,* the Constitution and Bill of Rights, the Geneva Conventions, and the Universal Declaration of Human Rights, to name a few.

Now we might consider adding another historic moment to the list, a moment that almost never happened: *the decision in London to have a fair trial at Nuremberg.* That was a splendid victory for Robert Jackson, an even greater victory for humanity.

ACKNOWLEDGMENTS

MANY PEOPLE MADE THIS BOOK POSSIBLE. FOREMOST I AM INDEBTED to my wife, Jill, who typed every one of several drafts, rewrote unwieldy paragraphs and made innumerable editorial suggestions. Bernard "Bud" Liebes, friend and former colleague on *The Stars and Stripes* during the Nuremberg trials, edited the manuscript, made substantial improvements and researched the National Archives and old *Stripes* stories at the Library of Congress. William J. Aceves, professor of international law at the California Western School of Law in San Diego; Marianna Lee, former editor at the Harcourt Brace Publishing Company; Lindsey Burcham, my student research assistant; and Joan McNamara, deputy city attorney in San Diego, all reviewed the entire manuscript and offered helpful criticisms, pro and con. Ms. Burcham's extensive research deserves special mention.

My sister Rose Treat risked her health at age 97 to make a flight from her home on Martha's Vineyard to San Diego for the purpose of helping me edit the manuscript. My other sister, Laura Lohman, provided much encouragement and advice.

My editor at Palgrave Macmillan, Alessandra Bastagli, was of remarkable assistance in guiding me through the manuscript, line by line, to its final draft. Jill Marsal, my agent at the Sandra Dijkstra Literary Agency, went far beyond the usual duties of an agent in carefully editing the manuscript and offering suggestions for its improvement.

Professor Jonathan A. Bush of Columbia Law School, one of the nation's foremost authorities on Nuremberg, sent me valuable materials from his research collection. Eugene C. Gerhart, who wrote the first biography of Justice Robert H. Jackson after interviewing Jackson over a seven-year period, granted me interviews and enriched the story from his notes. Four former prosecutors from Jackson's staff at Nuremberg—Drexel A. Sprecher, Whitney R. Harris, Henry T. King, Jr. and Roger Barrett—all gave enlightening interviews.

Holocaust survivors Lou Dunst and Mendel Flaster provided heartrending personal accounts of victimization at the Auschwitz and Mauthausen concentration camps.

Law professors Michael Scharf and Herbert Bowman, both of whom were involved in training Iraqi judges, added to the section on the trial of Saddam Hussein. Professor Bowman also contributed his expertise on the East Timor section. Moritz Fuchs, now a retired priest, was Jackson's bodyguard and driver as a young soldier at Nuremberg, and kindly shared his observations.

I am especially grateful to my friend Ursula von Haxthausen of Darmstadt, Germany, who arranged my tour of German universities, organized my lecture schedule in Germany and provided translations. Ms. von Haxthausen spent countless hours on my behalf to ensure the success of this project. Also of great help in Germany were Professor Florian Jessberger of the Humboldt Law School in east Berlin, Judge Juergen Maruhn of the Frankfurt Appellate Court, Professor Joachim Rueckert of the Frankfurt University School of Law, Oisin Morris of Halle, Sabrina Roy of Jena, Alexander Rettig of Leipzig and Dr. Schimon Stazewski of B'nai B'rith in Frankfurt.

In Washington, D.C., Dr. Jonathan Levin, friend and colleague in *The Stars and Stripes* newsroom, located personal correspondence between Judge Francis Biddle and Biddle's wife. At Syracuse University, Tom Franta located other Biddle correspondence stored there. Alan Dreyfus was the lead *Stripes* correspondent at the main Nuremberg trial when I was a cub reporter and he refreshed my memory as to many incidents. Chris Landers, a graduate journalism student, investigated sources in the Washington, D.C. area.

I had support and assistance from many other good friends, including: Alan Douglas, Nelson Brav, Stephen Perrello (now deceased and dearly missed), Tom Adler, Jack Cosgrove, Mary Lynn Price, Albert Phillips, Jeffery Larrimore, Professor Marjorie Cohn, Lou Boyle, Ehren

Brav, Faye Girsh, Nicole Bayer, Cornelia Lundell, Lena Petrie, Katharina Petrie, Victoria Lieb, and Tuck and Evalyn Stadler.

My former literary agent Vicky Bijur reviewed the manuscript and inspired me with her comments. Tyler Giannini, associate clinical director of the Human Rights program at Harvard Law School, and Richard Herz of EarthRights International, shared their expertise on the impact of Nuremberg precedent on lawsuits alleging human rights violations by major business firms.

I am especially indebted to Harvard law students Yukyan Lam and Jacob Kopas for enriching the manuscript with their research on complex questions of Nuremberg law. Three human rights attorneys, Terry Collingsworth, Michael Hausfeld and Paul Hoffman, took time from their crowded schedules to grant interviews.

At the Columbia Law School library, archivist Christopher Laico opened various files for my perusal. Judge William Dressler, president of the National Judicial College in Reno, Nevada, organized the joint judges' conference in Germany and invited me to speak there, an event that started me on the road to this book.

I would be amiss if I failed to mention the counsel of the Honorable William B. Enright, U.S. District Court judge in San Diego, and his sprightly club of San Diego judges and lawyers, mostly retired, all of whom contributed their wisdom to critical editorial decisions.

I am grateful also to the California Western Law School and its library staff, especially Barbara Gleinan, Kim Sterner, Bobbi Weaver and Karen Reilly; and also to legal research attorney Monica Barry.

Finally, my daughter Laurel and my son Zachary gave me continuous encouragement and always answered my calls for help whenever I needed them.

FURTHER READINGS

THE MOST MEMORABLE PART OF THE NUREMBERG TRIALS WAS Robert H. Jackson's opening statement before the International Military Tribunal on November 21, 1945 (*The Nürnberg Case*, N.Y.: Knopf, 1947). The speech is still hailed as a masterpiece, both for its literary merit as well as its historical importance.

A later book, Telford Taylor's *The Anatomy of the Nuremberg Trials* (N.Y.: Knopf, 1992) is highly recommended. As Jackson's chief deputy and eventually chief counsel of the twelve other trials in Nuremberg, Taylor was a key participant in all proceedings from 1945 to 1949.

Another excellent eyewitness account is Whitney R. Harris' *Tyranny on Trial: Evidence at Nuremberg* (Dallas: Southern Methodist University Press, 1954). Three outstanding histories are: *Nuremberg, Infamy on Trial*, by Joseph E. Persico (N.Y.: Penguin, 1995); *Justice at Nuremberg*, by Robert E. Conot (N.Y.: Carroll & Graf, 1983); and *The Nuremberg Trial*, by Ann and John Tusa (first published by Macmillan, London, 1983, and later by BBC London, 1995). Bradley F. Smith's *Reaching Judgment at Nuremberg* (London: Andre Deutsch, 1977) contains a good description of the judges' deliberations.

Among documents of particular relevance are: The Charter of the International Military Tribunal (1945), The Geneva Convention (No. III) Relative to the Treatment of Prisoners of War (1949), and the Universal Declaration of Human Rights (1948), all published in *Human Rights, Documentary Supplement* by Louis Henkin, Gerald L. Neuman, Diane F. Orentlicher and David Leebron (N.Y.: Foundation Press, 2001); and The Nuremberg Code found in *The Nazi Doctors and the Nuremberg Code*, edited by George J. Annas and Michael A. Grodin (N.Y.: Oxford University Press, 1992).

NOTES

INTRODUCTION

1. See Jackson's Opening Statement to the International Military Tribunal in the Palace of Justice at Nuremberg, November 21, 1945 [hereafter cited as "Jackson's Opening Statement"], found in *Trial of the Major War Criminals before the International Military Tribunal, Nuremberg,* vol. 2 (Buffalo, N.Y.: William S. Hein & Co, 1995), pp. 98–155; hereafter cited as "IMT Trial Transcript."
2. From Jackson's Opening Statement; see also Jackson's *The Nürnberg Case* (N.Y.: Knopf, 1947), p. 30.
3. Terry Collingsworth, "Recent International Labor Rights Fund Cases to Enforce Human Rights Under the ATCA," *International Civil Liberties Report 2002* (1/31/2003), p. 176; see also Richard Herz, *Text of Remarks: Corporate Alien Tort Liability and the Legacy of Nuremberg,* 10 Gonz. J. Int'l L. (2006), available at http://www.gonzagajil.org/.
4. Joseph E. Persico, *Nuremberg, Infamy on Trial* (N.Y.: Penguin, 1994), p. ix.
5. Robert E. Conot, *Justice at Nuremberg* (N.Y.: Carroll & Graf, 1984), p. 521.
6. Justice Sandra Day O'Connor, retired justice of the United States Supreme Court; majority opinion in *Yaser Esam Hamdi v. Donald H. Rumsfeld* 542 U.S. 507, 536 (2004).
7. "The Death of Gitmo," *The New York Times,* June 12, 2006, p. A20.

CHAPTER ONE

1. *The History of the 71ˢᵗ Infantry Division,* prepared by Division public relations staff (Augsburg, Bavaria, Germany: E. Kieser KG, Druckerei und Verlag, 1946), p. 71.
2. Stephen E. Ambrose, *Citizen Soldiers,* (N.Y.: Simon & Schuster, 1997), p. 454.
3. *History of the 71ˢᵗ Infantry Division,* p. 91.

CHAPTER TWO

1. Bradley F. Smith, *The Road to Nuremberg,* (N.Y.: Basic Books, 1981), p. 47; see also Persico, pp. xi, 8, 437.
2. Ibid., pp. 12–47.

3. Bradley F. Smith, *Reaching Judgment at Nuremberg* (London: Andre Deutsch, 1977), p. 23.
4. Smith, *Road to Nuremberg*, p. 45.
5. Joseph E. Persico, *Nuremberg, Infamy on Trial* (N.Y.: Penguin, 1994), p. 17.
6. Smith, *Road to Nuremberg*, p. 53.
7. Ibid., pp. 42–55.
8. Ibid., p. 195.
9. Eugene C. Gerhart, *America's Advocate: Robert H. Jackson* (N.Y.: Bobbs-Merrill, 1958), pp. 315–17.
10. Ibid., p. 317.
11. Ibid., p. 310.
12. Ann Tusa and John Tusa, *The Nuremberg Trial* (London: BBC Books, 1995), p. 78.
13. Gerhart, p. 328.
14. Quoted in Tusa and Tusa, p. 78.
15. Telford Taylor, *The Anatomy of the Nuremberg Trials* (N.Y.: Knopf, 1993), p. 66.
16. Quoted in Gerhart, p. 446.
17. Jonathan A. Bush, "The Supreme . . . Crime and its Origins: The Lost Legislative History of the Crime of Aggressive War," *Columbia Law Review* 102 (Dec. 2002): 2324.
18. Taylor, *Anatomy*, p. 64
19. Ibid., p. 36.
20. Tusa and Tusa, p. 103.
21. Smith, *Reaching Judgment*, p. 51.
22. Michael P. Scharf, *Balkan Justice* (Durham, N.C.: Carolina Academic Press, 1997), p. 13.
23. Jonathan A. Bush, "Lex Americana: Constitutional Due Process and the Nuremberg Defendants," 45 *St. Louis Univ. Law Journal* (Spring 2001): 536.
24. *Charter of the International Military Tribunal* (hereafter cited as "London Charter"), Article 26, *Anatomy*, p. 645.
25. Louis Henkin, Gerald L. Neuman, Diane F. Orentlicher, and David W. Leebron, *Human Rights: Documentary Supplement* (N.Y.: Foundation Press, 2001).

CHAPTER THREE

1. Ann Tusa and John Tusa, *The Nuremberg Trial* (London: BBC Books, 1995), p. 140.
2. Robert E. Conot, *Justice at Nuremberg* (N.Y.: Carroll & Graf, 1984), p. 91.
3. Ibid., pp. 59–60.
4. Tusa and Tusa, pp. 109–10.
5. Joseph E. Persico, *Nuremberg, Infamy on Trial* (N.Y.: Penguin, 1994), pp. 54–55.
6. Telford Taylor, *The Anatomy of the Nuremberg Trials* (N.Y.: Knopf, 1993), p. 90.
7. Robert Jackson, *The Nürnberg Case* (N.Y.: Knopf, 1947), p. 9.
8. See William Manchester, *The Arms of Krupp* (Boston: Little, Brown, 1968), p. 630.
9. Ibid.
10. Ibid.
11. Taylor, *Anatomy*, p. 91.

12. Manchester, p. 630.
13. Conot, p. 76.
14. Taylor, *Anatomy*, p. 90.
15. Bradley F. Smith, *Reaching Judgment at Nuremberg* (London: Andre Deutsch, 1977), pp. 68–70.
16. Ibid., p. 78.
17. Quoted in Manchester, p. 632.
18. Manchester, p. 632.
19. Ibid.
20. Persico, p. 110.
21. Smith, *Reaching Judgment*, p. 79.
22. Ibid.; see also Persico, pp. 110–11.
23. Tusa and Tusa, p. 133.
24. Ibid.
25. Ken Zumwalt, *The Stars and Stripes* (Austin, Tx.: Easkin Press, 1989), p. 108.
26. Tusa and Tusa, pp. 41, 334.
27. "Province leader."

CHAPTER FOUR

1. See Jackson's Opening Statement to the International Military Tribunal in the Palace of Justice at Nuremberg, November 21, 1945, found in *Trial of the Major War Criminals before the International Military Tribunal, Nuremberg*, vol. 2 (Buffalo, N.Y.: William S. Hein & Co, 1995), pp. 98–155.
2. Ibid.
3. Ibid.
4. *The Philadelphia Inquirer*, November 22, 1945.
5. *Christian Science Monitor*, November 20, 1945, p. 9.
6. Telford Taylor, *The Anatomy of the Nuremberg Trials* (N.Y.: Knopf, 1993), p. 167.
7. From Jackson's opening statement (here, second day of trial, 11/21/1945), vol. 2, IMT Trial Transcript.
8. From Jackson's opening statement.
9. Daniel Jonah Goldhagen, *Hitler's Willing Executioners: Ordinary Germans and the Holocaust* (N.Y.: Knopf, 1996), pp. 375–454.
10. Taylor, *Anatomy*, p. 148.
11. Ann Tusa and John Tusa, *The Nuremberg Trial* (London: BBC Books, 1995), pp. 99, 100.
12. Eugene C. Gerhart, *America's Advocate: Robert H. Jackson* (N.Y.: Bobbs-Merrill, 1958), p. 359; Tusa and Tusa, p. 101.
13. Robert E. Conot, *Justice at Nuremberg* (N.Y.: Carroll & Graf, 1984), p. 19.
14. H. R. Trevor-Roper, "The Lasting Effects of the Nuremberg Trial," *New York Times Magazine*, Oct. 20, 1946.
15. Ibid.

CHAPTER FIVE

1. Quoted in Telford Taylor, *The Anatomy of the Nuremberg Trials* (N.Y.: Knopf, 1993), p. 64.
2. London Charter, Articles 16, 24; see also Taylor, *Anatomy*, p. 64.

3. Report of Robert H. Jackson, U.S. Representative to the International Conference on Military Trials, London, 1945 (Washington, D.C.: Dept. of State Publication 3080, GPO, 1949), p. 48.

4. Bradley F. Smith, *Reaching Judgment at Nuremberg* (London: Andre Deutsch, 1977), pp. 114–42.

5. Taylor, *Anatomy,* p. 630.

6. Jonathan A. Bush, "Lex Americana: Constitutional Due Process and the Nuremberg Defendants," 45 *St. Louis Univ. Law Journal* (Spring 2001): 528.

7. Taylor, *Anatomy,* pp. 174–75.

8. Ibid.

9. Ibid.; see also John Mendelsohn, *Trial by Document: The Use of Seized Documents in the United States Proceedings at Nürnberg* (N.Y.: Garland Publishing, 1988), pp. 109–11.

10. See, for example, California Penal Code §1054; see also 18 U.S.C. §3500 (2000), the so-called "Jenks Act"; *Brady* v. *Maryland,* 373 U.S. 83 (1963); and Federal Criminal Rule 16, see also California Constitution, Art. 1, §30(c) compelling discovery; and *In Re Littlefield* (1993) 5 Cal. 4th 122, listing the purpose of the discovery rules.

11. Quoted in Joe J. Heydecker and Johannes Leeb, *The Nuremberg Trial,* ed. and trans. R. A. Downie (Cleveland: World Publishing Co., 1962), pp. 337–38; see also Joseph E. Persico, *Nuremberg, Infamy on Trial* (N.Y.: Penguin, 1994), p. 318.

12. Author's interview of Whitney R. Harris, August 4, 2006.

13. Leon Goldensohn, *Nuremberg Interviews* (N.Y.: Knopf, 2004), p. 295.

14. Harris interview; see also Whitney R. Harris, *Tyranny on Trial: The Evidence at Nuremberg* (Dallas: Southern Methodist University Press, 1954), p. 355.

15. Ann Tusa and John Tusa, *The Nuremberg Trial* (London: BBC Books, 1995), p. 156.

16. Eugene C. Gerhart, *America's Advocate: Robert H. Jackson* (N.Y.: Bobbs-Merrill, 1958), p. 437.

17. Quoted in Taylor, *Anatomy,* p. 626.

18. Taylor, *Anatomy,* pp. 16–17.

19. Frederick J. P. Veale, *Advance to Barbarism,* (N.Y.: Nelson, 1953), p. 164; see also Scharf, p. 11.

20. Taylor, *Anatomy,* p. 626.

21. *Temple Law Quarterly* (1946), p. 170; see also Gerhart, p. 441.

22. Smith, *Reaching Judgment,* p. 76.

23. Stephen Breyer, "Crimes Against Humanity: Nuremberg 1996," *New York University Law Review,* vol. 71, no. 5, Nov. 1996, p. 1161.

24. Taylor, *Anatomy,* pp. 634–35.

25. Smith, *Reaching Judgment,* p. 301; Tusa and Tusa, p. 491.

26. Quoted in Taylor, *Anatomy,* p. 600.

27. Taylor, *Anatomy,* p. 600.

28. Persico, p. 35.

29. Article 47, German Military Code, quoted by Jackson at the International Military Tribunal, November 21, 1945, as noted in Tusa and Tusa, pp. 87–88.

30. IMT Trial Transcript, vol. 2.

31. *Manual for Courts-Martial United States,* (2000) Part IV, 14, Article 90.c(2)(a)(i). Available online at: www.jag.navy.mil/documents/mcm2000.pdf.

32. London Charter, Article 8.

33. Tusa and Tusa, p. 132.
34. Ibid.
35. Taylor, *Anatomy,* p. 630.
36. Donald Bloxham, *Genocide on Trial: War Crimes Trials and the Formation of Holocaust History and Memory* (N.Y.: Oxford University Press, 2001), p. 161; see also William J. Bosch, *Judgment on Nuremberg: American Attitudes toward the Major German War-Crimes Trials* (Chapel Hill, N.C.: University of North Carolina Press, 1970), pp. 83, 178.
37. *Mitchell* v. *Harmony* 54 U.S. (13 How.) 115, 137 (1851).
38. See Telford Taylor, *Nuremberg and Vietnam: An American Tragedy* (Chicago: Quadrangle Books, 1970), pp. 45–46.
39. Scott Horton, "A Nuremberg Lesson," *The Los Angeles Times,* Jan. 20, 2005, p. B13.
40. Latin, "No one shall be tried for any act which was not forbidden by law at the time when it was committed."
41. U.S. Constitution, Art. I, sec. 9(3).
42. Robert E. Conot, *Justice at Nuremberg* (N.Y.: Carroll & Graf, 1984), p. 23.
43. Gerhart, p.446
44. Quoted in Taylor, *Anatomy,* p. 20.
45. Persico, p. 33.
46. Michael Biddiss, "Victors' Justice," *History Today,* vol. 45 May 1995, p. 40.
47. Quoted in John F. Kennedy, *Profiles in Courage* (N.Y.: Perennial Classics, 2000), p. 200.
48. Ibid.
49. Ibid., p. 198.
50. U.S. Army Pamphlet 27–10, p. 239; see also Donald Wells, *War Crimes and Laws of War* (Lanham, Md.: University Press of America, 1984).
51. Quoted in Yehuda Melzer, *Concepts of Just War* (Leyden, Netherlands: A.W. Sitjhoff, 1975) pp. 28–29.
52. Persico, pp. 33–34; see also Tusa and Tusa, p. 81.
53. From Jackson's opening statement.
54. Persico, p. 138.
55. IMT Trial Transcript, vol. 1.
56. Ibid.; see also David Luban, "The Legacies of Nuremberg," vol. 54 *Social Research,* no. 4 (1987), p. 797.
57. Francis Biddle, *In Brief Authority* (Garden City, N.Y,: Doubleday, 1962), pp. 480–81.
58. Taylor, *Anatomy,* p. 635.
59. Telford Taylor, "An Approach to the Prosecution of Axis Criminality" (June 1945) reprinted in Bradley F. Smith, *The American Road to Nuremberg: The Documentary Record* (Stanford, Ca.: Hoover Institution Press, c.1982), pp. 209–12.
60. Taylor, *Anatomy,* p. 629.
61. Judith Shklar, *Legalism,* rev. ed. (Cambridge, Mass: Harvard University Press, 1964), 2004, pp. 153–55.
62. Max Frankel, "The War and the Law," *New York Times Magazine,* May 7, 1995.
63. Quoted in Harris, p. 115.
64. Luban, p. 805.
65. Steven Fogelson, "Note: The Nuremberg Legacy: An Unfulfilled Promise," 63 *Southern California Law Review* 833 (March 1990), p. 844; see also Michael R.

Marrus, "The Nuremberg Trial: Fifty Years Later," 55 *American Scholar,* Fall 1997, no. 4, p. 563.

66. Shklar, pp, 153–55.
67. Luban, p. 805.
68. Michael Walzer, *Just and Unjust Wars: A Moral Argument with Historical Illustrations,* 2nd ed. (N.Y.: Basic Books, 1992), p. 250.
69. London Charter, Article 6(b).
70. Persico, p. 35.
71. Luban, p. 810.
72. Quoted in Conot, p. 68; State Department files, East-West Prosecution, Box 3697, letter from Jackson to President Truman dated Oct. 12, 1945.
73. Luban, pp. 810–12.
74. London Charter, Article 18.
75. Persico, p. 339.
76. Quoted in Persico, p. 338
77. Quoted in Conot, p. 496.
78. Biddle, p. 454.
79. See Bush, "Lex Americana," p. 536.
80. Biddiss, p. 44.
81. Taylor, *Anatomy,* pp. 192–93, 307.
82. Biddiss, p. 44.
83. Airey Neave, *Nuremberg: A Personal Record of the Trial of the Major Nazi War Criminals in 1945–6* (London: Hodder and Stoughton, 1978), pp. 270–71.

CHAPTER SIX

1. Janet Flanner, *The New Yorker,* March 30, 1946.
2. Airey Neave, *Nuremberg: A Personal Record of the Trial of the Major Nazi War Criminals in 1945–6* (London: Hodder and Stoughton, 1978), p. 67.
3. See Neave, p. 257.
4. Ibid.
5. Quoted Joseph E. Persico, *Nuremberg, Infamy on Trial* (N.Y.: Penguin, 1994), p. 270. On Goering's performance on the witness stand, see also H. Montgomery Hyde, *Norman Birkett: The Life of Lord Birkett of Ulverston* (London: Hamish Hamilton Ltd, 1964), p. 510.
6. Robert E. Conot, *Justice at Nuremberg* (N.Y.: Carroll & Graf, 1984), p. 336.
7. Oral History [of Robert Jackson] 1429 *et seq.,* Butler Library, Columbia University, New York.
8. *Trial of the Major War Criminals before the International Military Tribunal, Nuremberg,* vol. 2 (Buffalo, N.Y.: William S. Hein & Co, 1995), vol. 9.
9. *Classics of the Courtroom,* vol. VII (Minnetonka, Minn.: Professional Education Group, c1988), pp. 40–41; highlights from the direct and cross-examinations of Hermann Goering.
10. IMT Trial Transcript, vol. 9.
11. London Charter, Article 19.
12. Jackson oral history, pp. 1432–33.
13. See Ann Tusa and John Tusa, *The Nuremberg Trial* (London: BBC Books, 1995), p. 280; see also Telford Taylor, *The Anatomy of the Nuremberg Trials* (N.Y.: Knopf, 1993), pp. 338–39.

14. Persico, p. 278.
15. IMT Trial Transcript, vol. 9.
16. Ibid.
17. Ibid.
18. Ibid.
19. Tusa and Tusa, p. 287.
20. Hyde, *Norman Birkett,* p. 511.
21. Letter from Hon. Francis Biddle, Chief United States Judge, International Military Tribunal, to Katherine Biddle, March 19, 1946. On file with the Syracuse University Special Collections Research Center: IMT Collection, Box 19, Transcript Folder; Syracuse, N.Y. Here and elsewhere, correspondence from Francis Biddle to his wife Katherine is reproduced by permission of the Special Collections Research Center, Syracuse University Library.
22. Taylor, "The Nuremberg Trials," 55 *Columbia Law Review* 507 (1955).
23. IMT Trial Transcript, vol. 9.
24. William Shakespeare, *Richard III,* I.2.
25. IMT Trial Transcript, vol. 9.
26. *The New Yorker,* September 7, 1946, p. 44.

CHAPTER SEVEN

1. Francis Biddle, *In Brief Authority* (Garden City, N.Y.: Doubleday, 1962), p. 410.
2. Joseph E. Persico, *Nuremberg, Infamy on Trial* (N.Y.: Penguin, 1994), p. 279.
3. Biddle, pp. 410–11.
4. Eugene C. Gerhart, *America's Advocate: Robert H. Jackson* (N.Y.: Bobbs-Merrill, 1958), p. 397.
5. Letter from Biddle to Katherine Biddle, quoted in Telford Taylor, *The Anatomy of the Nuremberg Trials* (N.Y.: Knopf, 1993), p. 359; also in Biddle's papers, Syracuse University Collection, Box 3, vol. II, p. 226.
6. See Gerhart, pp. 455–68.
7. Canon 3 of Professional Ethics (est. 1908), American Bar Association; see also David M. Rothman, *California Judicial Conduct Handbook,* 2nd ed. (St. Paul, MN: West Publishing, 1999), pp. 122–23.
8. Author's interview with Whitney Harris, February 11, 2005.
9. Personal interviews with Roger Barrett, Drexel Sprecher, Henry T. King, Jr. and Whitney R. Harris, all members of Jackson's staff, conducted during 2000–2004.
10. Interview with Roger Barrett, December 13, 2003.
11. See Rothman, California Code of Judicial Ethics, Canon 3B(7), pp. 121–24.
12. Biddle, p. 411.
13. Gerhart, pp. 148, 164–65, 181.
14. Ibid., p. 198.
15. Biddle, p. 411.
16. *Ex Parte Quirin,* 317 U.S. (1942).
17. Quoted in Ann Tusa and John Tusa, *The Nuremberg Trial* (London: BBC Books, 1995), p. 290; Herbert Wechsler was an advisor to Biddle at Nuremberg, and later established an outstanding reputation as a professor at Columbia Law School.
18. Biddle, pp. 364–65.
19. Ibid., p. 372.
20. Taylor, *Anatomy,* p. 95.

21. Persico, p. 62.
22. Ibid., p. 76.
23. Ibid., pp. x, 76, 102.
24. Bradley F. Smith, *Reaching Judgment at Nuremberg* (London: Andre Deutsch, 1977), p. 77; see also Taylor, *Anatomy,* pp. 133, 134.
25. Gerhart, pp. 360–61.
26. Interview with Drexel Sprecher, February 3, 2005.
27. Tusa and Tusa, p. 208.
28. London Charter, Article 28.
29. Gerhart, pp. 374–75.
30. Persico, pp. 279–80.

CHAPTER EIGHT

1. See generally Bradley F. Smith, *Reaching Judgment at Nuremberg* (London: Andre Deutsch, 1977).
2. Francis Biddle, *In Brief Authority* (Garden City, N.Y,: Doubleday, 1962), p. 466.
3. *Trial of the Major War Criminals before the International Military Tribunal, Nuremberg* (Buffalo, N.Y.: William S. Hein & Co, 1995), vol. 22.
4. Ann Tusa and John Tusa, *The Nuremberg Trial* (London: BBC Books, 1995), p. 441.
5. Biddle, p. 466.
6. Ibid., pp. 467–68.
7. Ibid., p. 470.
8. Tusa and Tusa, p. 451.
9. See Robert E. Conot, *Justice at Nuremberg* (N.Y.: Carroll & Graf, 1984), pp. 481–507, for discussion of verdicts and executions.
10. Joseph E. Persico, *Nuremberg, Infamy on Trial* (N.Y.: Penguin, 1994), pp. 430–31; see also *The New York Times,* Oct. 18, 1946.
11. Persico, p. 441.
12. Telford Taylor, *The Anatomy of the Nuremberg Trials* (N.Y.: Knopf, 1993), pp. 618–24.
13. Ibid., p. 624.
14. Bob Pool, "Former GI Claims Role in Goering's Death," *Los Angeles Times,* Feb. 7, 2005, p. A1.

CHAPTER NINE

1. *Official Gazette of the Control Council for Germany,* No. 3, January 31, 1945 (Berlin: Allied Secretariat), p. 50.
2. Telford Taylor, "Nuremberg Trials: War Crimes and International Law," *International Conciliation* (monthly publication by Carnegie Endowment for International Peace, N.Y.), April 1949, No. 450, p. 254.
3. Ibid., p. 273.
4. Ibid., p. 279.
5. From Telford Taylor's opening statement, documented in *Trials of War Criminals before the Nuremberg Military Tribunals under Control Council Law* No. 10 (Washington, D.C.: GPO, 1949–1953), hereafter cited as "Law No. 10 transcript."
6. See Vivien Spitz, *Doctors from Hell,* (Boulder, Colo.: Sentient Publications, 2005).

7. Telford Taylor, *The Anatomy of the Nuremberg Trials* (N.Y.: Knopf, 1993), p. 171.
8. Taylor, "Nuremberg Trials," p. 282.
9. Gerald L. Posner and John Ware, *Mengele: The Complete Story* (New York: Dell, 1987).
10. See *United States* v. *Josef Alstoetter et al.,* Law No. 10 transcript, Vol. 3, p. 36.
11. Ibid.
12. Taylor, "Nuremberg Trials," p. 320.
13. Ibid., p. 297.
14. Ibid., p. 298.
15. Ibid., p. 301; see also Law No. 10 transcript (re *Ohlendorf*), pp. 6653–54.
16. Law No. 10 transcript (re *Ohlendorf*), p. 6648.
17. Ibid., p. 6769.
18. Taylor, "Nuremberg Trials," p. 295.
19. Ibid., p. 640.
20. Ibid., p. 308.
21. Ibid.
22. *United States* v. *Krupp,* Law No. 10 transcript, pp. 13396–97.
23. Author's interview with Mendel Flaster, January 31, 2005.
24. Whitney R. Harris, *Tyranny on Trial: The Evidence at Nuremberg* (Dallas: Southern Methodist University Press, 1954), p. 549.
25. Law No. 10 transcript (*United States·v. Wilhelm Lust et al.*), pp. 10498, 1051.
26. See Taylor, "Nuremberg Trials," p. 325.
27. Law No. 10 transcript (re *List*), p. 10446.
28. See *Department of the Army Field Manual 27–10,* 1976, "The Law of Land Warfare," Chapter 1, Sec 1.11.b(1)(b). Available online at: www.globalsecurity.org/military/library/policy/army/fm/27–10/Ch1.htm.
29. Law No. 10 transcript (*United States v. Wilhelm List et al.*), pp. 10441–442.
30. 542 U.S. 507 (2004); see also *Rasul* v. *Bush* 542 U.S. 466 (2004).
31. Robert E. Conot, *Justice at Nuremberg* (N.Y.: Carroll & Graf, 1984), pp. 317–18.
32. Taylor, *Anatomy,* p. 279.
33. Conot, pp. 317–18.
34. Taylor, *Anatomy,* pp. 279–80.
35. Department of State Bulletin, XV (October 27, 1946), p. 776; see also Harris, pp. 561–62.

CHAPTER TEN

1. Bradley F. Smith, *The Road to Nuremberg,* (N.Y.: Basic Books, 1981), p. 234.
2. Ibid.
3. Michael Mandel, *How America Gets Away With Murder* (Ann Arbor, Mich.: Pluto Press, 2004) p. 94.
4. Article 28 of the London Charter stated: "In addition to any punishment imposed by it, the Tribunal shall have the right to deprive the convicted person of any stolen property and order its delivery to the Control Council for Germany."
5. Statute of the Yugoslavia tribunal, paragraph 7 of the preamble; see Scharf, p. 245.
6. Articles 68, 75, 79 of the International Criminal Court Statute.
7. ICC statute, Articles 68, 75, 79.
8. ICC statute, Article 75.1.

9. See Salvatore Zappalà, *Human Rights in International Criminal Proceedings* (N.Y.: Oxford University Press, 2003), pp. 24–25.
10. Initially the program was called the Board of Central Crime Victims Program. The name was later changed to the Victim Compensation and Governmental Claims Board.
11. Author's interview with Lou Dunst, July 13, 2006.
12. "Holocaust Aid Offer Draws Hundreds in L.A.," *San Diego Union-Tribune* (Associated Press), July 6, 2006, p. A4.

CHAPTER ELEVEN

1. Minear, Richard H., *Victors' Justice: The Tokyo War Crimes Trial* (Princeton, N.J.: Princeton University Press, 1971), p. 5.
2. Ibid., p. 3.
3. Ibid., p. 20; see Solis Horwitz, "The Tokyo Trial," *International Conciliation,* 465: 480 (November 1950).
4. Ibid., p. 20.
5. Ibid., p. 19.
6. *Charter of the International Military Tribunal for the Far East,* April 26, 1946, Sec. II; hereafter cited as "Tokyo Charter;" see also London Charter, Sec. II. (The Charter can be found in the Appendix of *Victors' Justice* by Richard H. Minear.)
7. Tokyo Charter, Sec. II, Art. 6; see also London Charter, Sec. II, Art. 8.
8. Tokyo Charter, Sec. IV, Art. 13(a).
9. Douglas MacArthur, *Reminiscences* (N.Y.: McGraw-Hill, 1964), pp. 287–88.
10. Sir William Webb, "Separate Opinion to the Judgment of the International Military Tribunal for the Far East," as quoted in Minear, p. 162.
11. Tim Maga, *Judgment at Tokyo: The Japanese War Crimes Trials* (Lexington, Ky.: University Press of Kentucky, 2001), p. 133.
12. Minear, pp. 4, 172–73.
13. Quoted in Minear, p. 63.
14. Minear, p. 54.
15. Ibid., p. 64.
16. 338 U.S. Reports 197 (June 27, 1949).
17. Ibid., p. 215.
18. Arnold C. Brackman, *The Other Nuremberg: The Untold Story of the Tokyo War Crimes Trials* (N.Y.: William Morrow, 1987), p. 225.
19. Brackman, p. 225.
20. Minear, p. 115; also Geoffrey Robertson, *Crimes Against Humanity: The Struggle for Global Justice,* rev. ed. (N.Y.: New Press, 2002), p. 238.
21. Minear, p. 180.

CHAPTER TWELVE

1. Geoffrey Robertson, *Crimes Against Humanity: The Struggle for Global Justice,* rev. ed. (N.Y.: New Press, 2002), p. 235; see also David Luban, "The Legacies of Nuremberg," vol. 54 *Social Research,* no. 4 (1987), p. 787.
2. The Magna Carta. Available online at: www.archives.gov/exhibits/featured_documents/index.html.
3. Louis Henkin, Gerald L. Neuman, Diane F. Orentlicher, and David W. Leebron, *Human Rights* (N.Y.: Foundation Press, 1999), p. vii.

4. Theodore Roosevelt, "On Human Rights in Foreign Policy, State of the Union Message 1904," republished in Walter Laquer and Barry Rubin, eds., *The Human Rights Reader* (N.Y.: Penguin, 1978), quoted in Robertson, p. 15.
5. Robertson, p. 35.
6. This convention was not ratified by the United States until 1988.
7. Full texts of all declarations and conventions are found in Louis Henkin et al., *Human Rights: Documentary Supplement*, 41ff, 426ff.
8. *Salim Ahmed Hamdan v. Donald H. Rumsfeld* 126 S.Ct. 2749 (2006).
9. Henkin et al., p. 306.
10. Michael P. Scharf, *Balkan Justice* (Durham, N.C.: Carolina Academic Press, 1997), p. xiii.
11. Quoted in Robertson, p. 37.
12. Robertson, p. 229.
13. Telford Taylor, *Nuremberg and Vietnam: An American Tragedy* (Chicago: Quadrangle Books, 1970), pp. 12–13.
14. See Smith, *Reaching Judgment*, p. xv.
15. See John Hagan and Scott Greer, "Making War Criminal," *Criminology*, 40: 2 (2002), p. 231.
16. Bradley F. Smith, *Reaching Judgment at Nuremberg* (London: Andre Deutsch, 1977), p. 640.
17. Luban, pp. 729–829.
18. Scharf, p. xi.
19. Jonathan Kandell, "Augusto Pinochet, 91, Dictator Who Ruled by Terror in Chile, Dies," *The New York Times,* December 11, 2006, p. A1. See also "Augusto Pinochet Dies," MSNBC News Service, December 11, 2006; (available online: www.msnbc. msn.com).
20. Robertson, p. 399.
21. Robertson, p. 421.
22. London Charter, Article 7.
23. Speech by Professor Henry T. King, Jr., delivered June 13, 2003, at the Chautauqua Institution, Chautauqua, New York. King was a Nuremberg prosecutor.
24. London Conference transcript, p. 297, as quoted in Minear, p. 43.
25. Ibid.
26. Nsongurua J. Udombana, "Pay Back Time in Sudan? Darfur in the International Court," 13 *Tulsa Journal of Comparative and International Law* 1, 38 (Fall 2005).
27. Francis Biddle, *In Brief Authority* (Garden City, N.Y.: Doubleday, 1962), pp. 482–83.

CHAPTER THIRTEEN

1. Universal Declaration of Human Rights (United Nations).
2. *Brinegar* v. *United States,* 338 U.S. 160 (1949).
3. Ibid.
4. Shklar, p. 219.
5. Dennis J. Hutchinson, "Justice Jackson and the Nuremberg Trials," vol. 1, *Journal of Supreme Court History* (Washington, D.C.: Supreme Court Historical Society, 1996), p. 105 at 114.
6. *Almeida-Sanchez* v. *United States* 43 U.S. 266 at pp. 273–274 (1973); *California* v. *Acevedo* 500 U.S. 565 at p. 586 (1990); *United States* v. *Leon et al.* 468 U.S. 897 (1984) at p. 972.

7. William H. Rehnquist, *All the Law But One: Civil Liberties in Wartime* (N.Y.: Knopf, 1998), p. 195.

8. *Brown* v. *Board of Education of Topeka* 347 U.S. 493 (1954).

9. Richard Kluger, *Simple Justice* (N.Y.: Knopf, 1976), p. 690; see also Robert E. Conot, *Justice at Nuremberg* (N.Y.: Carroll & Graf, 1984), p. 520.

10. As quoted in Michael J. Klarman, *The Supreme Court and the Struggle for Racial Equality* (N.Y.: Oxford University Press, 2004), p. 304. The letter is from the Fairman file, Box 12, of Jackson's papers at the Library of Congress.

11. Alan M. Dershowitz, *Chutzpah* (Boston: Little, Brown, 1991), pp. 116, 130.

12. Ibid., p. 116.

13. Jonathan D. Sarna, e-mail letter to the author, February 28, 2006.

14. Author's interview with Professor Sheehan, February 10, 2006.

15. Ellen Ash Peters, "Symposium: Law, War and Human Rights: International Courts and the Legacy of Nuremberg," 12 *Connecticut Journal of International Law* 219 (Spring 1997).

CHAPTER FOURTEEN

1. Thomas Darnstadt, "The Tribunal of Death," *Der Spiegel,* Oct. 16, 2006, pp. 66–86, and Oct. 23, 2006, pp. 170–72.

2. Judith Shklar, *Legalism,* rev. ed. (Cambridge, Mass: Harvard University Press, 1964), 2004, p. 193.

3. J. D. Montgomery, *Forced to be Free* (Chicago: University of Chicago Press, 1957), pp. 59–67, 127.

4. Sybille Bedford, *The Faces of Justice* (N.Y.: Simon & Schuster, 1961), pp.83–153; also Shklar, p.169.

5. Gary Jonathan Bass, *Stay the Hand of Vengeance* (Princeton, N.J.: Princeton University Press, 2000), p. 288.

6. See Gerhard Werle and Florian Jessberger, "International Criminal Justice Is Coming Home: The New German Code of Crimes Against International Law," *Criminal Law Forum* 13 (2002), pp. 191–223.

7. Deborah Lipstadt, *Denying the Holocaust: The Growing Assault on Truth and Memory* (N.Y.: Plume, pp. 8, 181.

8. D. D. Guttenplan, *Holocaust on Trial* (N.Y.: Norton, 2001), p. 2.

9. Trial transcript: *David John Cadwel Irving v. Penguin Books, Ltd. and Deborah Lipstadt,* 1996–1–1113. High Court of Justice, Queen's Bench Division (April 11, 2000, London).

10. Deborah E. Lipstadt, *History on Trial: My Day in Court With David Irving* (N.Y.: Ecco, c2005).

11. Lipstadt, *History on Trial,* pp. 7, 8, 231; also trial transcript, *Irving* v. *Penguin Books.*

12. Letter to the author from Deborah E. Lipstadt, April 29, 2005.

13. Nasser Karimi, "Under 'pretext of . . . freedom' Iran gathers Holocaust deniers," *San Diego Union-Tribune,* December 12, 2006, p. A11.

CHAPTER FIFTEEN

1. George J. Annas and Michael A. Grodin, *The Nazi Doctors and the Nuremberg Code* (N.Y.: Oxford University Press, 1992), p. 2; see also M. Cheriff Bassiouni, Thomas G. Baffes and John T. Evard, "An Appraisal of Human Experimentation

in International Law and Practice: The Need for International Regulation of Human Experimentation," *Journal of Criminal Law and Criminology* 72 (Winter 1981), pp. 1597–1666.

2. Annas and Grodin, *Nazi Doctors,* p. 153.
3. *Geneva Conventions,* Article 12 of the First and Second Conventions; Article 13 of the Third Convention, and Article 14 of the Fourth Convention.
4. See Albert Deutsch, "A Note on Medical Ethics," as quoted in *Doctors of Infamy: The Story of the Nazi Medical Crimes,* by Alexander Milscherich and Fred Mielke, trans. Heinz Norden (N.Y.: H. Schuman, 1949).
5. Annas and Grodin, *Nazi Doctors,* p. 153.
6. Federal Drug Amendments Act, 1962.
7. Code of Federal Regulations 46, 306(a)(A)-(D), 1983.
8. University of Virginia Health Sciences Center, Student Tutorial (2002). Available online at: www.med-ed.virginia.edu/courses/rad/consent/home2.html.
9. George J. Annas, *American Bioethics: Crossing Human Rights and Health Law Boundaries* (N.Y.: Oxford University Press, 2005).
10. *United States* v. *Stanley* 438 U.S. 669 at p. 687 (1986).
11. Neil A. Lewis, "Interrogators Cite Doctors' Aid at Guantanamo, Ethics Questions Raised," *The New York Times,* June 24, 2005, p. A1.
12. Lewis, "Interrogators."

CHAPTER SIXTEEN

1. Michael P. Scharf, *Balkan Justice* (Durham, N.C.: Carolina Academic Press, 1997), p. 89.
2. Geoffrey Robertson, *Crimes Against Humanity: The Struggle for Global Justice,* rev. ed. (N.Y.: New Press, 2002), p. 344.
3. Frank C. Carlucci, "The War We Haven't Finished," *The New York Times,* Feb. 22, 2005, p. A19.
4. The Yugoslav Tribunal is not to be confused, as it often is, with the new International Criminal Court (ICC), which did not come into existence until nine years later in 2002. The ICC is a permanent court and also operates at The Hague.
5. Joseph Lelyveld, "The Defendant Slobodan Milosevic's trial, and the debate surrounding international courts," *The New Yorker,* May 27, 2002, p. 82.
6. Scharf, p. 63.
7. Ibid., p. 71.
8. Quoted in Scharf, p. 54.
9. Scharf, p. xi.
10. William H. Home, "The Real Trial of the Century," *American Law,* September 1995, p. 8.
11. Quoted in Scharf, p. 214.
12. Scharf, p. 214; also "Tadic, Case Information Sheet." Available online at: www.un.org/icty/glance/tadic.htm.
13. Scharf, p. 220.
14. Lelyveld, "Milosevic's Trial," p. 82.
15. Marlise Simons, "The Milosevic Lessons: Faster and More Efficient Trials," *The New York Times,* April 2, 2006, p. 4.
16. Quoted in *The New York Times,* "The Death of Milosevic," March 14, 2006, p. A30.

17. "The Hague UN Tribunal Issues Last Indictment," *The New York Times*, March 16, 2005, p. A6.

18. "Taking Genocide to Court," *The New York Times*, March 5, 2007; see also Ruth Wedgewood, "Slobodan Milosevic's Last Waltz," *The New York Times*, March 12, 2007.

19. "Rwanda: Accountability for War Crimes and Genocide," United States Institute of Peace, January 1995. Available online at www.usip.org/pubs/specialreports/ early/rwanda1.html.

20. Quoted in Scharf, pp. 226–27.

21. John Darton, "Revisiting Rwanda's Horrors with a Former National Security Adviser," *The New York Times*, December 20, 2004, p. 81.

22. Quoted in Robertson, p. 78.

23. Article 2, Statute of the International Criminal Tribunal for Rwanda.

24. International Criminal Tribunal for Rwanda (1998), Amnesty International Library, p. 2. Available online at: http://web.amnesty.org.

25. "Ex-Rwanda Official Gets Life in Prison," *The San Diego Union-Tribune* (Associated Press), April 29, 2005, p. A15.

26. "Rwandan gets 25-year term in Tutsi genocide," *The San Diego Union-Tribune* (Associated Press), December 14, 2005, p. A24.

27. "Rwanda: Broadcaster Sentenced in Genocide," *The New York Times* (Reuters), June 3, 2006, p. A7.

28. "Rwanda: Mayor Gets 15 Years for Role in '94 Genocide," *The New York Times* (Associated Press), April 14, 2006, p. A10.

29. "International Criminal Tribunal for Rwanda," *Jurist* (online), University of Pittsburtgh School of Law, December 2006.

30. "ICTR on the Right Track Three Years Before the End of its Mandate (President)," Hirondelle News Agency, *Global Policy Forum*, October 29, 2005. Available online at: www.globalpolicy.org/intljustice/tribunals/rwanda/2005/1029 interview.htm.

31. Andrew Meldrum, "War Crimes Trials Open in Freetown," *The Guardian*, June 4, 2004.

32. Kofi Annan, UN Secretary-General, "Report of the Secretary-General on the establishment of a Special Court for Sierra Leone," October 4, 2000.

33. Ibid.

34. Ed Royce, "Bring Charles Taylor to Justice," *The New York Times*, May 5, 2005, p. A27.

35. Somini Sengupta, "Sierra Leone War Crimes Trial Opens Without Chief Suspect," *The New York Times*, June 4, 2004.

36. Ibid.

37. Robertson, pp. 469–70.

38. Sengupta; see also Kofi Annan, "Report of the Secretary-General."

39. "Sierra Leone: War Court Opens Junta Trial," *The New York Times*, March 8, 2005, p. A6.

40. Lydia Polgreen, "Liberian Seized to Stand Trial on War Crimes," *The New York Times*, March 30, 2006.

41. Marlise Simons, "Former Liberian President in The Hague for Trial," *The New York Times*, June 21, 2006, p. A6.

42. "Justice, Finally: Liberia's Taylor faces War Crimes Charges," *San Diego Union-Tribune*, April 7, 2006, p. B8.

43. Seth Mydans, "Indonesians to Avoid Trials for Crimes in East Timor," *The New York Times,* May 15, 2005, p. 12.
44. Robertson, p. 462.
45. Kofi Annan, "Two Concepts of Sovereignty," *The Economist,* Sept. 18, 1999, p. 49.
46. Herbert D. Bowman, "Letting the Big Fish Get Away: The UN Justice Effort in East Timor," 18 *Emory International Law Review* 371, 380 (Fall 2004).
47. Ibid.
48. Ibid., p. 380.
49. Ibid.
50. On Transitional Rules of Criminal Procedure (East Timor), as amended Sept. 14, 2001, sec. 6: "Rights of the Suspect and Accused" (United Nations). Available online at: www.un.org/peace/etimor/untaetR/2001–25.pdf#search.
51. Bowman.
52. "Ad-Hoc Court for East Timor," *Global Policy Forum* (2006). Available online at: www.globalpolicy.org/intljustice/etimorindx.htm.
53. "Justice Denied for East Timor," Human Rights Watch, *Global Policy Forum* (December 2002). Available online at: www.globalpolicy.org/intljustice/tribunals/timor/2002/1202deny.htm.
54. Seth Mydans, "Indonesians to Avoid Trials for Crimes in East Timor," *The New York Times,* May 15, 2005, p. 12.
55. Ibid.
56. Ibid.
57. Jill Jollife, "Justice at a Crossroads in East Timor," *Asia Times,* February 24, 2005. Available online at: www.globalpolicy.org/intjustice/tribunals/timor/2005/0224 crossroads.htm.
58. Ibid.
59. "Justice for Victims Still Elusive," (on-line newsletter) Judicial System Monitoring Programme (JSMP), Dili, East Timor, May 24, 2005. Available online at: www.jsmp.minihub.org/Press%20Release/2005/May/050524%20End%20SPSC.pdf.
60. Jollife.
61. Bowman.
62. Elizabeth Becker, "New Links in Khmer Rouge Chain of Death," *The New York Times,* July 16, 2001.
63. Robertson, p. 298.
64. "The Killing Fields," *The New York Times,* July 6, 2006, p. A22.
65. "Ta Mok, Khmer Rouge Head Facing Genocide Trial, Dies," *The New York Times* (Associated Press), July 21, 2006, p. A19.
66. Seth Mydans, "Former Cambodian Leaders to Face Trial," *The New York Times,* Jan. 23, 2006, p. A6.
67. The Law on the Establishment of Extraordinary Chambers in the Courts of Cambodia for the Prosecution of Crimes Committed During the Period of Democratic Kampuchea; published online by Derechos Human Rights: www.derechos.org/human-rights/seasia/dec/krlaw.html.
68. Mydans, "Lawmakers in Cambodia," p. 2.
69. Mydans, "Skulls Haunt Cambodia, Demanding Belated Justice," *The New York Times,* March 20, 2005, p. 6.
70. Alex Hinton, "Seeking Justice for the Killing Fields," *San Diego Union-Tribune,* June 4, 2006, p. G4.

71. Mydans, "27 Years after the Atrocities, Khmer Rouge Inquiry Begins," *San Diego Union-Tribune,* August 6, 2006, p. A19.

72. Mydans, "Rules Dispute Imperils Khmer Rouge Trial," *The New York Times,* January 26, 2007, p. A3.

CHAPTER SEVENTEEN

1. Elisabeth Rubin, "If Not Peace, Then Justice," *New York Times Magazine,* April 2, 2006, p. 44.

2. Henry T. King, Jr., "Tribute: Robert Jackson's Transcendent Influence Over Today's World," 68 *Albany Law Review* 23 (2004).

3. King, "Tribute," p. 24.

4. Nsongurua J. Udombana, "Pay Back Time in Sudan? Darfur in the International Court." 13 *Tulsa Journal of Comparative and International Law* 1, 38 (Fall 2005), p. 38.

5. Markus Wagner, "The ICC and its Jurisdiction—Myths, Misperceptions and Realities," from *Max Planck Yearbook of United Nations Law,* vol. 7 (Boston: Brill, 2003).

6. Rubin, p. 46.

7. "Questions and Answers about the ICC," Human Rights Watch. Available online at: http://hrw.org/campaigns/icc/qna.htm.

8. "Questions and Answers," as above.

9. Rubin, p. 43.

10. "The Hague: Congo Warlord to Face Global Justice," *The New York Times,* January 30, 2007, p. A4.

11. Joel Brinkley, "State Department Sending Deputy to Sudan to Push for End of Violence in Darfur," *The New York Times,* April 8, 2005, p. A12.

12. Rubin, p. 46.

13. Ibid.

14. Marlise Simons, "Sudan Poses First Big Trial for World Criminal Court," *The New York Times,* April 29, 2005, p. A10.

15. Brinkley, p. A12.

16. Warren Hoge, "International War Crimes Prosecutor Gets List of 51 Sudan Suspects," *The New York Times,* April 6, 2005, p. A6.

17. George Gedda, "U.S. Remains Opposed to International Criminal Court," *San Diego Union-Tribune,* April 2, 2005, p. A6.

18. "Sudan: U.N. Court Rejected," *The New York Times,* April 2, 2005, p. A2.

19. "Court Gets Sudan War Crimes Case," *San Diego Union-Tribune,* April 6, 2005, p. A6.

20. Alfred de Montesquieu, "Violence in Darfur Said to Be Near Worst Ever," *The San Diego Union-Tribune* (Associated Press), November 19, 2006. p. A3.

21. Marlise Simons, "2 Face Trials at The Hague Over Atrocities in Darfur," *The New York Times,* February 28, 2007, p. A3.

22. "Sudan: Trial of Darfur Suspect Delayed," *The New York Times,* March 8, 2007, p. A9.

23. "Talking Darfur to Death," *The New York Times,* March 31, 2007, p. A26.

CHAPTER EIGHTEEN

1. William Manchester, *The Arms of Krupp* (Boston: Little, Brown, 1968).

2. See, e.g., *United States* v. *Karl Krauch*, 8 Trials of War Criminals Before the Nuremberg Military Tribunals Under Control Council Law No. 10 (1952). There, the Tribunal found that although "Krauch was neither a moving party (nor) an important participant in the initial enslavement of workers . . . in view of what he clearly must have known about the procurement of forced labor and the part he voluntarily played in its distribution and allocation . . . he was a willing participant in the crime of enslavement." p. 1189.

3. 630 F.2d 876 (2nd Cir. 1980).

4. Alien Tort Statute 28 U.S.C. §1350 (1789).

5. ATS.

6. *Filartiga*, 630F.2d at 884.

7. Jenna Greene, "Obscure Alien Tort Claims Act Resurfaces with Alarm," *Legal Intelligencer*, vol. 29, No. 17, July 24, 2003.

8. *Doe v. Unocal Corp.*, Third Amended Complaint. Available online at: www.ccr-ny.org/v2/legal/corporate_accountability/docs/Third_Amended_Complaint.pdf.

9. Ibid., 8–9.

10. *Doe*, 963 F.Supp. 880 (C.D. Cal. 1997); opinion vacated by stipulation.

11. *Doe I v. Unocal Corp.*, 110 F.Supp.2d 1294 (C.D. Cal. 2000); opinion vacated by stipulation.

12. *Doe I* at 1306.

13. *Doe I* at 1306–07. Quotations removed.

14. *Doe I* at 1307. Quotations removed.

15. *Doe I* v. *Unocal Corp.*, 395 F.3d 932 (9th Cir. 2002), rehearing granted *en banc*, 395 F.3d 98 (9th Cir. 2003), dismissed by parties' stipulation, 403 F.3rd 708 (9th Cir. 2005).

16. *Doe 1*, 395 F.3d 932, p. 948, footnote 22.

17. *Doe 1*, 395 F.3d 932, p. 954.

18. *Doe 1*, 395 F.3d 932.

19. Ibid.

20. *In re Agent Orange* (E.D.N.Y. 2005) 373 F.Supp. 2d7, 83.

21. Interview with Paul Hoffman on December 2, 2006, Cambridge, Mass.

22. Phone interview with Terry Collingsworth on November 30, 2006; *Text of Remarks: Corporate Alien Tort Liability and the Legacy of Nuremberg*, Rick Herz, 10 Gonz. J. Int'l L. 76, 101 (2006–2007).

23. *Sosa v. Alvarez-Machain*, Brief for the United States as Respondent Supporting Petitioner, 2004 WL 182581, Jan. 23, 2004.

24. *Sosa* v. *Alvarez-Machain*, 542 U.S. 692 (2004).

25. *Sosa* v. *Alvarez-Machain* 124 S.Ct. 2769, 2764 (2004); see also Beth Stephens, "*Sosa* v. *Alvarez-Machain*: The Door is Still Ajar for Human Rights Litigation in U.S. Courts," 70 *Brooklyn Law Review* 533, 538, 562 (2004); see also Igor Fuks, "*Sosa* v. *Alvarez-Machain* and the Future of ATCA Litigation," 106 *Columbia Law Review* 112 (2006).

26. *Sosa* v. *Alvarez-Machain*; see also Beth Stephens; and Igor Fuks.

27. Jenna Greene, "Suits that Claim Overseas Abuse are Putting U.S. Executives on Alert and Their Lawyers on Call," *Legal Times*, July 21, 2003.

28. Phone interview with Terry Collingsworth on November 30, 2006.

29. Terry Collingsworth, phone interview, December 4, 2006; see also "Total to Pay Burmese Compensation," BBC News, Nov. 2, 2005. Available online at: http://news.bbc.co.uk/1/hi/business/4482536.stm.

30. Veronica Bessmer, "The Legal Character of Private Codes of Conduct: More Than Just A Pseudo-Formal Gloss on Corporate Responsibility," 2 *Hastings Bus. L.J.* 279, 284 (2006).

CHAPTER NINETEEN

1. Bob Herbert, "The Law Gets a Toehold," *The New York Times,* July 13, 2006, p. A23.
2. Article 3(d), Geneva Convention No. III Relative to the Treatment of Prisoners of War, concluded at Geneva August 12, 1949, signed by the United States August 12, 1949, ratified by the United States, July 14, 1955; see also Louis Henkin, Gerald L. Neuman, Diane F. Orentlicher, and David W. Leebron, *Human Rights: Documentary Supplement* (N.Y.: Foundation Press, 2001), p. 736.
3. "A Victory for the Rule of Law," *The New York Times,* June 30, 2006, p. A22.
4. "Due Process," *The New York Times,* May 4, 2006, p. A30.
5. "Degrading America's Image," *The New York Times,* June 6, 2006, p. A22.
6. *Hamdi* v. *Rumsfeld,* 542 U.S. (2004).
7. *Hamdi* v. *Rumsfeld,* p. 2640, quoting decision of Nuremberg Military Tribunal, reprinted in 4 *American Journal of International Law,* 172, 229 (1947).
8. *Hamdan* v. *Rumsfeld,* p. 2749.
9. "Justices, 5–3, Broadly Reject Bush Plan to Try Detainees," *The New York Times,* June 30, 2006, pp. A1, A18.
10. *Hamdan* v. *Rumsfeld,* p. 2759.
11. *Hamdan* v. *Rumsfeld,* p. 2761.
12. *Hamdan* v. *Rumsfeld,* p. 2785.
13. *Hamdan* v. *Rumsfeld,* pp. 2784, 2785.
14. On February 20, 2007, a divided federal appeals court upheld the constitutionality of the Military Commissions Act. Boumediene, *Detainee* v. *Bush,* U.S. Court of Appeals, Washington, D.C., No. 05–5062, February 20, 2007.

CHAPTER TWENTY

1. "The Saddam Hussein Trials," *The New York Times,* April 10, 2006, p. A24.
2. Julia Preston, "Hussein's Trial was Flawed but Reasonably Fair, and Verdict Justified, Legal Experts Say," *The New York Times,* November 6, 2006, p. A8.
3. "Saddam defiant in court," Al-Jazeera, July 2, 2004. Available online at: http://english.aljazeera.net/English/archive/archive?ArchiveId=4886.
4. Michael P. Scharf, "Saddam Hussein on Trial," Court TV News, December 6, 2006. Available online at: www.courttv.com/talk/chat_transcripts/2005/1206 hussein-scharf.html.
5. Ramsey Clark, "Why I'm Willing to Defend Hussein," *The Los Angeles Times,* January 4, 2005, p. 139.
6. "Low-Level Judges Picked to Handle Hussein Trial" (Associated Press), *San Diego Union-Tribune,* November 30, 2004, p. A25.
7. Author's interviews on December 28, 2004, with Prof. Herbert Bowman, assigned by the U.S. Department of State to prepare Iraqi judges for trial.
8. William Langewiesche, "The Accuser," *Atlantic Monthly,* March 2005, p. 54.
9. "Iraq's Trials," *The New York Times,* September 21, 2006, p. A30.
10. John F. Burns and Kirk Semple, "Hussein is Sentenced to Death by Hanging," *The New York Times,* November 6, 2006, p. 1.

11. Ibid., p. A8.
12. "Judging Dujail: The First Trial before the Iraqi High Tribunal," *Human Rights Watch.* Available online at: http://hrw.org/reports/2006/iraq1106/2.htm.
13. Hassan M. Fattah, "Europeans Oppose Death for Hussein," *The New York Times,* November 7, 2006, p. A6.
14. "Saddam Hussein Trials," p. A24.
15. See William J. Aceves, "History's Judgment of Saddam's Trial," *The San Diego Union-Tribune,* January 1, 2007, p. B7; see also "The Rush to Hang Saddam Hussein," *The New York Times,* December 29, 2006, p. A24.
16. Geyer, Georgie Anne, "Final Judgment of Saddam Hussein," *The San Diego Union-Tribune,* November 7, 2006, p. B6.
17. Preston, p. A8.
18. Quoted in Julia Preston, "Hussein's Trial."
19. "Saddam trial 'heroic'," says Howard. *TheAge.com,* November 6, 2006. Available online at: www.theage.com.au/news/world/saddam-trial-heroic-says-howard/2006/11/06/1162661578964.html.
20. See Anne Applebaum, "Nurembergs results offer guidance for Saddam's trial," *The San Diego Union-Tribune,* October 23, 2005, p. G4.
21. Mark Santora, "Hussein's Trial Sees Videotapes of Chemical Attacks on Kurds," *The New York Times,* December 20, 2006, p. A14.
22. Najmaldin Karim, "Justice, But No Reckoning," *The New York Times,* December 30, 2006, p. A23.
23. "One Less Tyrant," *The San Diego Union-Tribune,* December 30, 2006, p. B8.
24. Santora, p. 1.

CHAPTER TWENTY-ONE

1. "Due Process," *The New York Times,* May 4, 2006, p. A30.
2. "The Military Commissions Act of 2006—Turning bad policy into bad law," Amnesty International, September 29, 2006. Available online at: http://web.amnesty.org/library/index/ENGAMR511542006.
3. "The President and the Courts," *The New York Times,* March 20, 2006, p. A22.
4. See Franz Kafka, *The Trial,* in which the defendant is never told what his crime is.
5. Geoffrey Robertson, *Crimes Against Humanity: The Struggle for Global Justice,* rev. ed. (N.Y.: New Press, 2002), p. 121.
6. *Hamdan* v. *Rumsfeld,* p. 2755.
7. Neil A. Lewis, "2 Prosecutors Faulted Trials for Detainees," *The New York Times,* August 1, 2005; see also "Guantanamo Maze: Even Prosecutors Dispute Fairness of Tribunals," *San Diego Union-Tribune,* August 5, 2005, p. B8.
8. "Guantanamo Maze," p. B8.
9. "Due Process," p. A30.
10. *Rasul* v *Bush,* 544 U.S. 466 (2004) held that U.S. courts have authority to decide whether foreign nationals (non-U.S. citizens) detained at Guantanamo were rightfully imprisoned.
11. *Hamdi* v. *Rumsfeld,* p. 534.
12. *Hamdan* v. *Rumsfeld,* p. 2798.
13. See Marjorie Cohn, "Why Boumediene Was Wrongly Decided," CDBA-CDLC (Criminal Defense Newsletter), March 2007, p. 4.
14. U.S. Constitution, Article 1, Section 9.

15. Jeffrey Toobin, "Killing Habeas Corpus," *The New Yorker,* December 4, 2006.
16. Nat Henthoff, "Congress Bows to Bush." Available online at: www.villagevoice.com/news/0641,henthoff,74664,6.html.
17. William Glaberson, "Military Judges Dismiss Charges for 2 Detainees," *The New York Times,* June 5, 2007, p. A1.
18. William Glaberson, "Result of Military Trial Is Familiar to Civilians," *The New York Times,* March 28, 2007, p. A15.
19. Glaberson, "Result of Military Trial," p. A15.
20. Glaberson, "Australian to Serve Nine Months in Terrorism Case," *The New York Times,* March 31, 2007, p. A10.
21. Glaberson, "Detainee's Lawyers Seek Removal of Chief Prosecutor," *The New York Times,* March 26, 2007, p. A12.
22. Hendrik Herzberg, "Terror and Torture," *The New Yorker,* March 24, 2003, p. 29.
23. Whitney R. Harris, *Tyranny on Trial: The Evidence at Nuremberg* (Dallas: Southern Methodist University Press, 1954), p. 437.
24. Article 5, Universal Declaration of Human Rights (United Nations).
25. Ratified by the United States, October 2, 1994.
26. Alfred W. McCoy, *A Question of Torture: CIA Interrogation, From the Cold War to the War on Terror* (N.Y.: Metropolitan Books, 2006), p. 1.
27. Ibid.
28. Jane Mayer, "The Memo: How an Internal Effort to Ban the Abuse and Torture of Detainees Was Thwarted," *The New Yorker,* February 27, 2006, p. 36.
29. Paul Krugman, "King of Pain," *The New York Times,* September 18, 2006, p. A29.
30. "Cheney Pushes Senators for Exemption to Torture Ban," *USA Today* (Associated Press), Nov. 5, 2005, p. 1; also Michael Ratner, "U.S. Must Stop Outsourcing Torture," *San Diego Union-Tribune,* April 13, 2005, p. B11.
31. Robert Pear, "Legal Group says Bush Undermines Law by Ignoring Select Parts of Bills," *The New York Times,* July 24, 2006. Available online at: www.nytimes.com/2006/07/24/washington/24prexy.html.
32. "Time for Clarity" (editorial), *San Diego Union-Tribune,* July 25, 2006, p. B6; see also "Read the Fine Print" (editorial), *The New York Times,* July 25, 2006, p. A22.
33. Quoted in Mayer, "The Memo," p. 41.
34. Ibid., p. 32.
35. Ibid., p. 33.
36. Ibid., p. 41.
37. "A Libby Verdict," *The New York Times,* March 7, 2007, p. A22.
38. "We Can Do Better: Current Detainee Policy Harms the Nation," *The San Diego Union-Tribune,* January 27, 2007, p. B6.

CHAPTER TWENTY-TWO

1. Henry T. King, Jr., "Tribute: Robert Jackson's Transcendent Influence Over Today's World," 68 *Albany Law Review* 23 (2004), p. 23.
2. Elisabeth Rubin, "If Not Peace, Then Justice," *New York Times Magazine,* April 2, 2006, p. 44.
3. Ibid.
4. Elizabeth Becker, "U.S. Suspends Aid to 35 Countries over New International Court," *The New York Times,* July 2, 2003, p. A1.

5. "International Court, Pressure for U.S. Exemptions Risks Relations," *The San Diego Union-Tribune,* March 27, 2006, p. B6.

6. King, "Tribute," p. 24.

7. See "American Foreign Policy and the International Criminal Court," Marc Grossman, Under Secretary for Political Affairs. Remarks to the Center for Strategic and International Studies, Washington, D.C., May 6, 2002.

8. *Presbyterian Church of Sudan v. Talisman Energy, Inc.* 374 F.Supp. 2d 331, 339–340 (S.D.N.Y. 2005).

9. Patricia M. Wald, "Remarks on the International Criminal Court," delivered to the Washington, D.C. Bar International Law Section Annual Luncheon, May 28, 2003.

10. "U.S. Sabotages World Court," *San Francisco Chronicle,* August 21, 2002, p. A20.

CONCLUSION

1. Joseph E. Persico, *Nuremberg, Infamy on Trial* (N.Y.: Penguin, 1994).

2. Lydia Polgreen, "Civilians Bear Brunt of the Continuing Violence in Darfur," *The New York Times,* January 24, 2005, p. A3.

3. Gary Jonathan Bass, *Stay the Hand of Vengeance* (Princeton, N.J.: Princeton University Press, 2000), p. 205.

4. See Henry T. King, Jr., "The Judgments and Legacy of Nuremberg," 22 *Yale Journal of International Law* 213 (1997); see also Whitney R. Harris, *Tyranny on Trial: The Evidence at Nuremberg* (Dallas: Southern Methodist University Press, 1954), pp. 555–58.

5. See Steven R. Ratner and Jason S. Abrams, *Accountability for Human Rights Atrocities in International Law: Beyond the Nuremberg Legacy* (N.Y.: Oxford University Press, 2001), p. 190.

6. Quoted in Eugene C. Gerhart, *America's Advocate: Robert H. Jackson* (N.Y.: Bobbs-Merrill, 1958), pp. 447–54.

7. Craig S. Smith, "Liberators and Survivors Recall the Auschwitz That Was," *The New York Times,* Jan. 28, 2005, p. A6.

8. Harris, p. vii.

9. Bass, p. 203.

10. *Hamdi v. Rumsfeld.*

11. *Hamdan v. Rumsfeld.*

INDEX

Amended
3/17